For all of [our] times with family and friends at NTA. We've been thru the good, bad and ugly. W. James Host taught all of us and gave us business skills and life skills. Happy to share his book.

Dottie and Jim
Macellan

Sept 2020

Changing the Game

Changing the Game

My Career in Collegiate Sports Marketing

Jim Host with Eric A. Moyen

UNIVERSITY PRESS OF KENTUCKY

Scholarly publisher for the Commonwealth,
serving Bellarmine University, Berea College, Centre
College of Kentucky, Eastern Kentucky University,
The Filson Historical Society, Georgetown College,
Kentucky Historical Society, Kentucky State University,
Morehead State University, Murray State University,
Northern Kentucky University, Transylvania University,
University of Kentucky, University of Louisville,
and Western Kentucky University.
All rights reserved.

Editorial and Sales Offices: The University Press of Kentucky
663 South Limestone Street, Lexington, Kentucky 40508-4008
www.kentuckypress.com

All photos are from the author's collection.

Cataloging-in-Publication data available from the Library of Congress

ISBN 978-0-8131-7955-1 (hardcover)
ISBN 978-0-8131-7957-5 (pdf)
ISBN 978-0-8131-7956-8 (epub)

This book is printed on acid-free paper meeting
the requirements of the American National Standard
for Permanence in Paper for Printed Library Materials.

Manufactured in the United States of America.

Member of the Association of University Presses

Contents

Photos follow page 112

Preface

Eric Moyen

In the spring of 2017 the executive director of the Kentucky Humanities Council, Bill Goodman, approached me with the idea of writing a book about Jim Host for the University Press of Kentucky. My own scholarly interest in higher education and athletics made the project intriguing. I knew Jim remained active with various athletic and civic initiatives in Kentucky, and a few years earlier, he had been kind enough to meet with me when I was researching the history of college athletics. So Jim and I met again, and we agreed to partner in writing his memoir.

Like many others, I knew who Jim Host was, but I knew few details of his career. One simple Google search changed that. I scrolled through a *Sports Business Journal* article written in 2010, when Host was being inducted into the first-ever class of "Champions of Sports Business"—an honor for pioneers and innovators in the industry bestowed by the *Sports Business Journal,* which is considered the bible of the sports marketing world. Author Michael Smith stated that Host had "essentially founded college sports marketing." As Smith's article outlined Host's career, other quotes about Jim appeared. The late SEC commissioner Mike Slive stated, "He's a pioneer and a founder in an area that has grown to become an important part of conferences, institutions, and the NCAA. . . . He took a bright idea and turned it into an industry." Clyde Lear, then CEO of Learfield Communications (now Learfield IMG College), acknowledged, "I did not see the future like Host did. . . . He forced me into a business that we didn't envision. I owe a lot to him for that." Smith stated, "Host forever changed the relationship between sports and business in the conservative world of university presidents and athletic directors." He added, "It was common for them to turn to Host whenever they had to make a business decision, whether it was hiring a coach or negotiating a new media deal. No one was more connected, no one was more indispensable." The article ended with a quote from ESPN vice president Rob Temple, who noted, "He really was the Daniel Boone of college sports." The journal then listed thirty-five individuals who had worked with or for Jim Host and gone on to become executives in the industry. Sports marketing executive Pat Battle declared, "When the book on collegiate sports marketing is written, the first chapter will simply be entitled 'Jim Host.'"[1]

With this one article, I gained a glimpse into Host's reputation in the world of college sports marketing. My next goal was researching exactly how and why he had made such an indelible imprint on his profession. Jim provided me with boxes of articles, letters, personal notes, photos, and corporate publications so that I could delve into his professional life. Most important, he gave me access to transcripts from his dozens of hours of interviews with Dr. Terry Birdwhistell for the University of Kentucky's Nunn Center for Oral History. I also read numerous secondary sources on the history of college sports to gain a better understanding of the context in which Host had worked.

From that point forward, Jim and I spent hundreds of hours together (either in person or on the phone) discussing his career. It soon became apparent that a successful career in college sports marketing had not always been his dream, and he took a somewhat winding road to become an industry leader. This memoir traces that personal history and then transitions into a chronicle of Host's professional life.

Host grew up in Ashland, Kentucky, and dreamed of playing professional baseball. When he accepted one of the first two baseball scholarships at the University of Kentucky (UK) in 1955, he became the first member of his family to attend college. During his four years on campus, he focused on pitching and sports broadcasting. At the conclusion of his senior year in 1959, he signed with the Chicago White Sox and played in the team's minor league system. Host spent the next few years broadcasting UK games, working for Procter & Gamble, and growing an insurance, real estate, and home construction business. In 1967, at age twenty-nine, he accepted a position as commissioner of public information in Kentucky governor Louie Nunn's administration. After an unsuccessful campaign for lieutenant governor in 1971, Host returned to Lexington and used the $107 left in his bank account to start a business in an office above Ray's Barbershop: Jim Host & Associates, which later became Host Communications Incorporated (HCI).

From these humble beginnings, Host managed to win the radio rights for UK athletics in 1974. That first year, Kentucky made it to the championship game of the National Collegiate Athletic Association (NCAA) tournament. Before the final game, Host convinced tournament organizer Tom Jernstedt to consider a deal that would allow HCI to broadcast NCAA tournament games. A short time later, NCAA executive director Walter Byers accepted Host's offer of $30,000 to establish and operate the NCAA Radio Network to carry the tournament. Host's company also published the programs for all the tournament games. Host's most important innovation came when he convinced Byers to let him sign corporate sponsorships for the men's (and eventually women's) NCAA tournament. The involvement of corporate sponsors fundamentally altered the future of NCAA athletics.

As an entrepreneur, Host saw an untapped "affinity" market in college athletics and built a premier sports marking company based on that vision. HCI began to work with conferences such as the SWC and the SEC. At the same time, Host expanded his sports marketing partnerships with individual universities. Over the years, HCI organized and operated the media and marketing rights to nearly thirty "big-time" university athletic programs. The company's portfolio included contracts with UK, Texas, Alabama, Louisiana State, Auburn, Mississippi State, South Carolina, Florida State, Notre Dame, Michigan, Purdue, Virginia, Tennessee, Georgia, and many more. Host's primary innovation was the idea of "bundled rights" for corporate sponsors— that is, he had companies sign exclusive deals to become the "official partners" of universities, which included a full spectrum of marketing through radio, print programs, and television. This dramatically increased athletic revenue at the universities that hired Host's company. At its zenith, HCI had more than thirty offices around the country and employed in excess of 500 individuals.[2]

Host had opportunities to work with Major League Baseball and the National Football League, but he rebuffed their overtures because he had made a commitment to Walter Byers to focus on intercollegiate athletics. As Host tells it, this was not a difficult decision. His own baseball scholarship had changed his life for the better. Because he remained focused on college sports, he made an indelible imprint on the industry. Before Host retired from the sports marketing business, he brokered a billion-dollar sponsorship deal with Coca-Cola and the NCAA. This was a different world from the one in which he had paid $30,000 for the radio rights to the NCAA tournament. This memoir explains that evolution.

While Host's work in intercollegiate athletics brought him national acclaim in the sports world, his professional life included many other endeavors. Far less public but no less important to HCI, Host had a three-decade relationship with the National Tour Association (NTA), an organization that he managed to grow considerably. In addition, Host literally changed the landscape of athletics for the commonwealth of Kentucky. His efforts led to the construction of Rupp Arena, the Kentucky Horse Park, and the KFC Yum! Center in Louisville. He also helped bring the World Equestrian Games to Kentucky in 2010.

In the pages that follow, Host shares his fascinating interactions with politicians and corporate leaders, as well as university presidents, athletic directors, and coaches. Some of these entertaining dialogues lend themselves to the cliché, "You can't make this stuff up!" Taken as a whole, however, these stories are more than mere anecdotes. They illuminate parts of a complex story about the growth of business and commercialism in college athletics. When possible, this memoir connects Host's personal story to the larger world of college sports marketing.

Although written from a first-person perspective in a conversational tone, Host's memoir constitutes a valuable addition to the scholarship of the history of higher education and athletics. It reveals a piece of history that might otherwise be difficult for academics to trace: a business insider's interactions with university executives that cannot be found in board minutes or archives. By definition, a memoir is written from the individual's personal perspective. However, Host's story also provides a source for historians and other scholars, allowing them to draw their own conclusions about the growth of college sports marking and its relationship with higher education.

Jim Host's involvement in the business side of intercollegiate athletics from the 1970s into the twenty-first century helped generate substantial revenue for individual universities, athletic conferences, and the NCAA. This has only increased during the last two decades with the expansion of television contracts, conference networks, and digitally delivered content. It has become an even more important topic as the NCAA grapples with its own interpretation of amateurism, as well as the pressure to allow student athletes to share in the wealth generated by "big-time" programs. Host's memoir provides valuable insight into how the current landscape developed and why these topics have become such serious issues.

A few words regarding the limits of Host's memoir are in order. Until the epilogue, he does not address issues related to student athletes. This is not an attempt to avoid controversial topics but a natural outgrowth of the fact that Host and his company were strictly prohibited from dealing with college athletes on any level. The conversation about student athletes in the epilogue sheds light on a current issue rather than a historical one. In addition, Jim decided to focus on the professional, rather than personal, aspects of his life. Personal stories from his youth are included, however, to provide context regarding his worldview and how it impacted his business practices. Finally, the many conversational quotes in the book are from recent personal interviews with Host, and as such, they reflect his memory of conversations that took place decades earlier.

Jim Host enjoys an interesting level of celebrity. In certain circles, such as college sports marketing and Kentucky politics, he is well known by many. At the same time, many individuals who have been impacted by his career are not familiar with his name. I hope this memoir provides a platform to better understand Jim Host and the role he played in changing the game.

1

Growing Roots

With more than eight decades of a remarkable life behind me, I owe much to so many selfless individuals and extraordinary circumstances. To understand me—or anyone, for that matter—my origins must be considered. This includes "place," but it involves far more than just location. Heredity, culture, community, and upbringing all play major roles. Every individual decides how to respond to these influences, good and bad. Hard work, luck, the kindness of others, and, I believe, a higher power figure in the story of every successful person. I am certainly no exception.

While I love my old Kentucky home, I spent my first years outside of the Bluegrass State. I lived in many small Appalachian Mountain towns filled with hardworking blue-collar families of modest means. I learned about the importance of family and community in my childhood, but I always yearned to do more, to do better. I had big dreams, what some would call the American dream; it was the kind of yearning that filled the minds of so many of my contemporaries who were born during FDR's New Deal and raised in the seemingly boundless optimism of postwar America.

I entered this world on November 23, 1937, in Kane, Pennsylvania, the eldest child of Beatrice "Bea" Hattie Jones Host and Wilford "Will" Joseph Host and the first-born grandchild on both sides of the family. My mother was the third of fifteen children, twelve of whom were girls. Her parents, Lloyd and Ella, lived in neighboring Sheffield, Pennsylvania. I was much closer to Mother's side of the family, since Dad's family lived in Michigan. My parents' families could not have been more different. Mother and Dad each brought their unique childhood experiences and influences into their marriage and family.

My mother's huge family hailed from eastern Pennsylvania, where my grandfather opened the first Chevrolet dealership in that part of the state. I deeply admired and emulated my maternal grandfather. He worked hard and planned ahead, always considering new ideas. I saw him as a strategist. Today he would be called an entrepreneur.

Never lacking for work with fifteen children, my grandmother somehow found time to make me feel special. For instance, when I visited their modest home during my childhood, she would take me to the attic, where she saved stacks of newspapers with the sports sections intact. I spent hours up there clipping out pictures of my favorite baseball players. My maternal grandparents were devout Methodists, which influenced Mother's faith. Most important, their house was always filled with laughter and love. Even as a young child, I felt the closeness of family in their home, and I loved being a part of it.

Unlike my maternal grandparents, my father's family showed little emotion or affection. A devout blue-collar Catholic family with German roots, they settled in Comstock Park, Michigan, where my dad grew up. We spent most of Dad's vacation every year visiting his parents, Art and Wilhelmina, in Michigan. We would leave on a Friday after work and drive through the night. Dad hoped we would sleep, but we usually spent the night taking turns getting carsick. We always showed up exhausted but ready for adventure.

During my time there, I watched my grandfather rise early for work at a dairy plant every morning. He worked long hours, and upon arriving home, he immediately washed his hands, sat down in his chair, and started drinking beer. He was an absolute stoic, a tough guy. I cannot remember him smiling— ever! He viewed emotion as weakness. During one of our visits, he walked into the house and seemed visibly upset. I said, "Granddaddy, what's wrong?" Remaining silent, he washed his hands at the sink. I walked over and saw blood, but he replied, "Nothing." Then my dad realized that Granddaddy had cut off his finger. He exclaimed, "I gotta take you to the hospital!" My grandfather initially refused but eventually went, and the doctors removed the top half of his finger. Through it all, he never showed any emotion.

I enjoyed spending time with my father's family, but the stern atmosphere was much different from that at my other grandparents' home in Pennsylvania. Only later would I learn that Dad's parents, especially his mother, never

2

approved of his marrying a non-Catholic or raising us as Methodists. Even if this tension had not existed, my dad's family was just much more reserved than my mother's.

Growing up, many of these traits found their way into my own developing personality and worldview. My parents graduated from high school but never attended college, even though my mother would have loved that opportunity. In the Host tradition, my father took a blue-collar job with U.S. Leather, working in a tannery; this brought him to Pennsylvania, where he met my mother. They married at a relatively young age, and I was the oldest of three boys. Mother gave birth to my brother Jon when I was two, and my youngest brother Jay came along eighteen months after Jon.

When I was four, my dad received a promotion and moved the family about sixty miles north to Salamanca, New York. Controlled by the Seneca Nation, this town on the Allegheny River had a unique policy that required non–Native Americans to rent property from the Seneca Nation. We had fantastic neighbors, some of whom remained longtime family friends.

Starting school in Salamanca, I developed an affinity for math, as numbers came easily to me. I kept statistics (albeit rudimentary) about almost everything within my limited purview. Dad taught me how to keep score in bowling, so I scored his games and learned how to figure the bowling averages of everyone in Dad's league. I took on a paper route while in elementary school, which we called "passing papers." I stuffed the newspapers into my bike's basket and delivered them daily. I kept close tabs on all my accounts and saved most of the money I made. With my earnings, I opened a savings account at a local bank and joined a Christmas Club, depositing a small amount each week to save up to buy gifts during the holidays. When I did spend money, it was usually on movies. I rode my bike downtown to see friends on Saturdays and to watch Roy Rogers or other movie stars in westerns.

Our time in Salamanca coincided with World War II. As a young boy, I could not appreciate the impact of world events on small communities like Salamanca. People talked about the war regularly, but I do not remember many specifics. I do recall listening to radio reports about the Normandy invasion and people celebrating downtown when the war ended. At my age, I had no memory of a time without war, and I recall a real sense of pride and optimism when the United States won.

Although unrelated to the war, my first experience with death came in Salamanca. After we moved to New York, my mother's mother struggled with stomach problems. She had been seriously ill for weeks when my parents received word that she had passed away at only fifty-eight years old. My family assumed she had died from some sort of stomach cancer. As a young boy, my sadness came not only from losing my grandmother but also from watching my mother grieve. My grandfather also suffered. He had always been friendly and smiling, but losing his wife permanently changed him, as a certain sadness overtook him. My grandmother's passing taught me an unwelcome but valuable lesson about the temporal nature of life and the importance of relationships.

I also developed a lifetime love of baseball in Salamanca. There were no organized leagues, so the neighborhood kids would recruit one another and play sandlot baseball. I enjoyed every minute of it. The feeling was euphoric. I loved watching the sport too. I will never forget Dad taking me to see the minor league Olean Dodgers play an exhibition game against their major league team, the Brooklyn Dodgers. I watched Gil Hodges at first base and Pee Wee Reese at shortstop. Just as important, 1947 was Jackie Robinson's first year in the league. At the time, I did not understand the significance of Robinson breaking the color barrier and its social and political implications. In fact, I have no memory of even thinking about Jackie Robinson being a black man, but I did see a large section of African Americans watching the game. Little did I know how significant that event was for all people, but for the black community in particular. I was simply smitten with being at the ballpark, watching the game.

After six years in New York, Dad was promoted to assistant superintendent at a tannery in Iron Gate, Virginia. I was ten when we moved into a duplex in Iron Gate owned by U.S. Leather, probably because housing was in short supply after the war. My parents, my two brothers, and I shared a single bedroom. As the oldest, I got the top bunk, while my brothers were relegated to a mattress below. The duplex had only one bathroom, with a door on either side, that we shared with our neighbors. I cannot imagine how my mother managed to live in that space. My dad had supposedly moved up in the company, but our lifestyle definitely had not changed for the better. Even at ten years of age, I knew that our situation was far from ideal.

We lived in Iron Gate for less than a year, but a few memories from that time have stayed with me. Dad bought a cow in Virginia, which we named Moo Moo. Of course, he had bought it to feed the family, and I was with him when he walked out to the field, aimed his gun, and shot poor Moo Moo right between the eyes. Then he took the cow to the butcher. I was mortified. I know that my aversion to guns stems from witnessing that event.

When I was not in school or doing chores, I was playing baseball. I would find rocks to set up as bases and recruit my friends to join me. I played any position—even catcher—if it meant we could have a game. I even skipped meals if the neighborhood kids were willing to keep playing. Dad, who also loved the game, took me to see the Roanoke Red Sox when we were in Virginia. I remember watching Jim Suchecki pitch that night, and I decided then and there that I was going to pitch in the big leagues.

After nine months in Iron Gate, Dad became superintendent of a tannery in Paw Paw, West Virginia. My junior high school did not have a baseball team, so I settled for basketball. I was taller than most of my classmates, but I was slow. I also followed professional baseball. One day, Grandpa Jones took me to see the Washington Senators play the Boston Red Sox. We arrived at the Old Griffith Stadium in time to watch batting practice, and I was starstruck watching Bobby Doerr, Vern Stephens, and Johnny Pesky. Ted Williams, however, was unlike any player I had ever seen. During batting practice, he hit pitch after pitch off the giant wall in right field. The sights and smells of that stadium—popcorn, hotdogs, and peanuts—were magical.

Grandpa Jones passed away unexpectedly not long afterward, apparently from a heart attack or an aneurysm. However, I believe he died from a broken heart. He outlived my grandmother by three years, but he never recovered from her death. The joy he had when I was young had left him. I had lost two of the most important individuals in my life before finishing junior high school.

After witnessing that major league game, I started collecting every baseball card I could find. I also clipped newspaper and magazine photos and articles about my favorite players, organized them, and kept the players' stats. While in Paw Paw, I had a little transistor radio tucked under my pillow at night so I could listen to Rosie Rosewell and Bob Prince call Pittsburgh games. Their vivid descriptions of the stadium and the players made the action come alive. I looked forward to every game. Dad also took me to hear the Philadelphia A's Hall of Fame pitcher Lefty Grove speak at the local Lions Club. He autographed a photo I had of him, which I still have. Virtually every experience with baseball made me love the sport more.

I enjoyed other sports and recreational activities as well, including swimming, until one small incident impacted my feelings about water. One day, at a swimming hole in West Virginia with friends, I dove into the water and split my head open on some shallow rocks. It knocked me out briefly, and when I recovered, I noticed blood coming from the gash on my head. Although the injury was not serious, I was fortunate that I didn't end up paralyzed, and from that day forward, water terrified me. This fear eventually kept me from becoming an Eagle Scout, and in my required college swimming class, I was scared to swim any length in the pool. I knew it was irrational, but that fear stayed with me.

Not long after we moved to West Virginia, Dad lost his job. Shoes were converting from leather soles to rubber ones, and Dad's job was a casualty of this transition. I helped Mother in the garden, where she grew all kinds of vegetables, along with watermelons and cantaloupes. She canned as many fruits and vegetables as possible. I joined 4-H that year and grew an award-winning watermelon. During the summer I also worked in a nearby apple orchard. We got paid based on the amount of apples we picked, and I was determined to pick more than anyone else, which I did! Mother's garden helped the family through that rough patch while Dad searched for work. Looking back, I am amazed that my parents were able to ensure that their sons never went without.

Dad also managed to send me to a YMCA camp in Bradford, Pennsylvania. I subsidized part of the cost by serving as a camp counselor. The camp program offered numerous activities, but I focused on baseball. I benefited from some good coaching and learned new aspects of the game. Paul Owens, future general manager of the Philadelphia Phillies, actually scouted me. He lived in Bradford and had heard about me. I thought it was only a matter of time until I reached the big leagues.

Dad eventually found work as an assistant superintendent at A. C. Lawrence Leather in Ashland, Kentucky. I entered the eighth grade when we moved to Kentucky. Excited that my dad had found another job, I had no idea that this would be our family's last move and that Kentucky would become "home." Ashland, a rough-and-tumble blue-collar town with around 30,000 residents, seemed huge to me. Steel and oil were the primary industries, and the factories and plants billowed smoke, creating serious smog for such a small place. The tannery where Dad worked, like all the others, emitted the most god-awful smell. I will never forget the odor of burnt animal hair. The whole treatment process was noxious, but it paid the bills. I never wanted to earn a living in a tannery.

My parents purchased a three-bedroom, one-bathroom house just outside of town on Elm Street. Modest even by 1950s standards, it was the nicest place we had ever lived. I enjoyed finally having my own bedroom, and my brothers shared a room. A nearby field next to the Old Putnam Stadium (along with Central Park downtown) provided a place to play sandlot baseball. Those games produced some of the fondest memories of my childhood. I also picked up another paper route to earn a little extra cash. Most important to me, my school was large enough to have a baseball team!

I delivered papers early in the morning, returned home to bathe, and then hitched a ride to the high school, located downtown on Central Avenue. Even when I was old enough to drive, Dad wouldn't let me near his car, so I usually thumbed a ride or occasionally rode my bike to school. After spending the day in classes, I headed out to practice whatever sport I could.

While playing on the baseball team, I decided to participate in basketball as well. In my sophomore year (1952) I tried out for Coach George Conley, the father of future University of Kentucky (UK) great and sportscaster Larry Conley. He coached both baseball and basketball, but he loved basketball. Ashland High School was loaded with talent. I thought I could make the team, but I was far too slow. Conley knew I was a much better baseball player, so he cut me from the basketball team but asked me to be its manager. I decided to be the best manager possible. I also spent time in spring football camp. I could throw the football farther than anyone, but I could not scramble at all. My speed, or lack thereof, made it clear that I should focus on baseball.

I spent my afternoons over the next few years learning from Coach Conley. Without question, he was the biggest influence in my life during high school. One of the toughest, meanest coaches ever, he motivated through fear. Not wanting to experience his wrath, his players usually did exactly what he told them. Later in life, whenever anyone asked me, "Wasn't Harry Lancaster tough?" I just laughed and said, "He was nothing compared to George Conley!" Today, most of his tactics would be forbidden, but he taught me what it means to work hard, and I learned that wholehearted effort produces results.

Coach Conley experienced a couple of heartbreaking losses in the Kentucky state basketball tournament. My sophomore year, we had one of the most talented high school teams in the state's history. Ten players from that roster played college basketball. We breezed through the regular season with only two losses, and then we beat a Lafayette team that included Doug Shively, Vernon Hatton, and "Big" Bill Florence. After making it to the state tournament at Memorial Coliseum, we thought we were destined to win the championship. Dewayne McIntosh from Paducah Tilghman High School crushed those dreams when he hit a last-second shot to win the game by a single point. Coach Conley went ballistic in the locker room. I had seen him upset many times, but this seemed like the worst outburst he could possibly muster. I was wrong.

The next year, Conley did a masterful job with a less talented team. We advanced to the semifinal game of the state tournament, and with less than a minute left in the game, we held a three-point lead on Newport Catholic. Coach Conley called a time-out and told the players, "We've got the ball. We're ahead by three points. Hold the ball. I don't care if you are open. Do NOT shoot it! Hold it!" Back on the court, a wide-open Bill Gray drove to the basket, shot, and missed. Newport Catholic rebounded and took it down the court for a quick score. They stole the ball on the ensuing play, scored another basket, and won the game. Coach Conley walked into the locker room and threw his clipboard at the wall, smashing it to pieces. He then punched the side of a toilet stall. Everyone was dead silent. He turned to us and said, "All you sons of bitches, I have coached my last game. There is no justification that you didn't just listen to me." He quit right then and did not show up for the consolation game later that night. The loss was so devastating that I cannot recall anything that happened later that evening. I'm not even sure if we won or lost the consolation game. Sure enough, George Conley had coached his last game. He served four years as a state senator and then became a college basketball referee. Despite the short time I spent with him, Coach Conley had a lasting influence on me.

Even though I focused on sports, I actually looked forward to going to school. I was comfortable being alone but also enjoyed the company of my classmates. Public speaking came easy to me, and I developed good relation-ships with my teachers. I enjoyed most of my classes, but history and English were my favorite subjects. I also found what I call "concrete" math fascinat-ing—the basics through algebra. Now "abstract" math, like geometry and physics, that was a different story.

I wanted to make a little extra cash to supplement the earnings from my paper route, so I took a night job at the YMCA, often working until midnight. At the time, the Y rented rooms, primarily for men coming off the railroad in Ashland. For about a dollar a night, the Y provided a small bedroom and a communal bathroom. I made sixty cents an hour and managed to complete my homework in between checking people in and selling snacks in the lobby.

I worked a lot with Bob Barney, who later succeeded Dave Thomas as the CEO of Wendy's. Norris "Bo" McMillan (UK quarterback in the 1930s) and Ernie Chattin managed the Y and looked out for us boys. For example, either Ernie or Bo would come down to Central Park and furnish bats and balls so that the kids in Ashland could play baseball.

During those days, the Catholic kids attended school at Holy Family, and the black kids attended Booker T. Washington School. When we played baseball, however, Ernie and Bo never separated us. They treated everyone the same, regardless of their race or religion. We played *together* all day, taking a break only to get a bologna sandwich or an RC Cola. At the time, I was totally unaware of the important lessons being taught to me, but I would try to implement them for the rest of my life.

School, sports, and work consumed all my time. Terrified that I would wreck his car, Dad was unwilling to teach me how to drive. This dashed any hopes of dating or having a social life, so I rarely went out with girls. Finally, during my senior year, Mother decided to sneak me out of the house and teach me how to drive in empty parking lots near our home.

My classmates elected me president of both the junior and senior classes. I also served as president of the Key Club. I never campaigned for such positions. I was too focused on my schoolwork, jobs, and sports to think much about leadership, but apparently, others thought I possessed the necessary skills. Once elected, I tried my best to make changes for the better.

Both my personality and my upbringing made me a rule follower. I never got into trouble because I did not want to disappoint my parents or myself. I did not drink or smoke or curse because I had been told not to. However, I never wanted to be a "holier-than-thou" friend. When kids would invite me to go across the river to West Virginia or Ohio to drink or party, I always said something like, "Naw, you go on. I've got homework." So I had straitlaced friends as well as some who were a bit more rowdy.

Between school and work, I was rarely home during my last two years of high school. Dad and Mother rarely knew what I was doing or trying to accomplish. They focused on making ends meet, and I focused on making it to the big leagues.

Attending church remained our one family activity outside the home. Mother made us wear our Sunday best to the First United Methodist Church. The faith instilled in me during those years stuck, and the social aspects of a church community grew more important. I sang in the church choir and participated in Methodist Youth Fellowship activities. I seriously considered becoming a minister, since I stayed out of trouble and was a good public speaker. However, I decided to chase my dream of becoming a major league pitcher.

I worked incessantly to improve my pitching. I played on a Junior Legion team coached by Marvin Hall the summer between my freshman and sophomore years. Mr. Hall noticed that I had some talent and took it upon himself to make me a better pitcher. Over the next couple of years, he spent hundreds of hours with me, working on my form, delivery, and accuracy. My younger brothers often succumbed to my continual pleading to let me pitch to them, even though they complained that my fastballs hurt their hands. By my junior and senior years, I was winning a lot of games, thanks to Marvin Hall and my brothers.

At school or on the field, I was outgoing and willing to speak up around my peers. At home, though, I kept quiet because my parents did not seem interested in my extracurricular activities. I'm not sure they even knew that I was president of my junior and senior classes. I can remember my parents coming to only one or two of my high school baseball games. They never asked me much about it, so I didn't volunteer any information. During my junior year, I pitched a no-hitter, came home, finished my homework, and went to bed. The next day my exploits were headlined in the local newspaper. Dad said, "Why didn't you tell me about it?" I responded, "You didn't ask. It's no big deal." That was standard operating procedure at home.

During high school I listened to radio broadcasts of major league baseball for countless hours. I tuned in at the YMCA or listened until I fell asleep at home. From Ashland, I could pick up the Pittsburgh Pirates, the Cincinnati Reds, and even the St. Louis Cardinals. Back then, Harry Caray was the voice of the Cardinals, and I loved listening to him. I also started tuning in to UK football and basketball broadcasts. In those years, multiple broadcasters called UK games. Ashland's radio station carried J. B. Faulconer with the Ashland Oil Network, but Claude Sullivan was my favorite. I became a fan of the Wildcats, and these great radio announcers planted a seed that would grow in the future.

As I studied the game of baseball as both a fan and a pitcher, I learned the importance of statistics and strategy. I loved that baseball was such a cerebral game. Even in high school, I kept stats on the teams I pitched against, and I took notes on the different batters I faced—whether they could hit my curveball or chased high fastballs. I looked for a batter's weakness to exploit.

I also loved that the game was both a true team sport *and* an individual sport. Players had various roles, but the nature of the game made baseball like a one-on-one chess match, especially for pitchers.

George Conley's decision to quit coaching created new opportunities for me on the baseball team. Assistant football coach Bob Sang started to coach baseball, but he knew little about the game. He would say, "Jim, tell me what to do." So, during my junior and senior years, I pitched, coached third base, and helped out the head coach as well. We had a good team, and I loved every minute of it. I became the team's ace pitcher. Marvin Hall continued to work with me at Central Park for no other reason than to help me utilize my talents to the best of my ability.

One postseason, I had already pitched two games in the regional tournament. Coach Sang knew I was not supposed to pitch, but he asked if I could go an inning or two. I said I could go two or three. I came in and held Wheelwright High School scoreless. My best friend, Jon Zachem, hit a home run for us with two outs in the bottom of the seventh inning, so we advanced to the state tournament in Louisville. In the tournament I pitched against Central City High School. Their star player, Corky Withrow, hit a double off me, and we lost 3–2. That was a tough pill to swallow.

I had pitched well enough in my senior year to get a scholarship offer from Eastern Kentucky University (EKU)—a half scholarship for baseball and another half scholarship to serve as manager of the basketball team. I had previously been manager for the Kentucky All-Star Basketball Team. Paul McBrayer of EKU, who had coached the team, knew that Turkey Hughes, the baseball coach and athletic director, wanted me at EKU. Since the university could not offer me a full-ride scholarship for baseball, they created the manager's scholarship. With no other options, I accepted the offer.

That same year I attracted some attention from pro scouts. Major League Baseball had not yet introduced the draft. Instead, teams sent scouts all over the country looking for talented high school seniors. Detroit Tigers scout Wayne Blackburn offered me $25,000 to sign with the team—a lot of money at the time. I was torn about what to do, but Dad made the decision easy. He said, "You're not gonna sign. I have to sign for you, and you're going to college." Still only seventeen, I needed his permission. It was difficult to hear, but it was some of the best advice my father ever offered. Nobody in my family had attended college, and my dad wanted to make his dream for me a reality. So I made plans to attend EKU that fall.

The summer after high school graduation, I pitched for Yates Coal out of Ashland in a semiprofessional league. Our team advanced to the state finals in Paintsville, where I pitched against Steve Hamilton, who became a major league baseball player, athletic director at Morehead State, and a good friend of mine. After we won the game, Harry Lancaster found me and introduced himself as UK's assistant basketball coach and head baseball coach. He offered me one of UK's first two full scholarships to play baseball. I was ecstatic and immediately knew that I wanted to attend UK. However, I let Coach Lancaster know that I had already told Turkey Hughes I would play at EKU. Lancaster responded, "He won't mind you going to UK, I'll call and let him know." Coach Hughes, who had been a star athlete at UK in the 1920s, called me and said he understood why I wanted to attend UK. I learned later that Ernie Chattin and Bo McMillan from the YMCA had called Lancaster and asked him to come see me play. I have often wondered how different my life would have been if they hadn't convinced Lancaster to watch me pitch. So, in the summer of 1955 I prepared to become a student and a baseball player at UK.

By the time I left for college, my life's experiences had made an indelible impact on who I was and what I would become. Obviously, my parents were key in this development. Dad's dutiful work ethic influenced me greatly. He left for the tannery at 6:00 a.m. and came home between 5:00 and 6:00 p.m. every weekday. He tried his best to wash the smell of the tannery off his skin, and Mother did everything she could to get the stench out of his clothes. Each night after supper, Dad sat down with a slide rule and worked on the tannery's finances and operations. He also recorded every single penny he earned, saved, gave, or spent. Extremely disciplined and very stern, he rarely displayed emotion. He was quick to take a razor strap to our butts if my brothers or I stepped out of line. He rarely joked or laughed, but I never heard him fight or yell (much) either. He picked up these traits from his family, but I also think his temperament was a product of living through the Great Depression.

Mother, in contrast, was brilliant and a real firebrand. She excelled at everything she undertook, except personal relationships. She did not suffer fools lightly and let them know it. Although she was a wonderful woman, diplomacy was not her gift. A tough taskmaster, she possessed an incredible eye for detail. I was a first-born perfectionist already, and Mother only exacerbated this trait of mine. If I washed the dishes, she would find a speck of dirt. If I cleaned the house, she would find something unsatisfactory. Between Dad's discipline and Mother's demanding personality, I developed a real fear of failure. It motivated me, and I am thankful for that. If someone set a goal for me, I did not want to simply meet it; I wanted to crush it. At the same time, though, I never learned how to relax around my parents.

My relationship with Mother and Dad revolved around the home. A man of few words, Dad's questions were usually straight to the point: "Did you get all your homework done?" Mother was far more outspoken. With eleven sisters and three brothers, she had to be. But Mother did less questioning and much more sharing of her opinions, even when unsolicited. She could find fault with anything or anyone, and this often meant telling the neighbors what she thought of them. As a kid, I accepted the role of the family diplomat, apologizing for Mother's comments and trying to make amends with the neighbors.

We moved three times before settling in Kentucky. I hated saying goodbye to friends, but moving taught me that there are good people everywhere. I learned to be at ease in unfamiliar situations and grew comfortable meeting new people, but I did not mind being alone. My brothers shared a bedroom and were much closer to each other. I became a bit of a loner, but I was not lonely; I was simply okay being in my own company. I read up on baseball and spent a lot of time practicing my pitching in front of a mirror. Occasionally my dad would take me to a Reds game, where I studied pitchers' form and technique. When we got home, I worked on my windup and delivery.

Having already learned a number of life lessons, I left for Lexington in the fall of 1955. I appreciated the challenges my parents had faced raising a family without the benefit of a college education or financial resources. Mother and Dad taught me strict discipline, which Coach Conley reinforced. From Ernie Chattin, Bo McMillan, and Marvin Hall I learned to give back and to help those who asked for it. These men cared about people and gave of their time and resources, and I hoped to emulate them.

I also learned that if I was going to accomplish anything, it would take hard work. Whether it was at school, at work, or in sports, I learned not to expect anything to be handed to me. Everything needed to be earned. I also learned the importance of faith and family. For better or worse, I knew that I would not be content with the kind of life I had lived as a child. My self-sacrificing parents had provided me with a good childhood, but I knew I wanted more—and not necessarily more money. I just knew that I wanted to take a different path from the one my parents had chosen. I believed that playing baseball at UK could be my path to success.

2

Chasing Dreams

My parents drove me to Lexington for the fall semester at the University of Kentucky in 1955. Cognizant of being the first person on either side of my family to go to college, I felt nervous but possessed confidence in my ability to make the most of the opportunity. More than anything, anticipation dominated my heart and mind. I knew UK offered a bridge to a different life, but success or failure was in my hands.

My mom and dad, however, displayed more skepticism. Dropping their oldest child off at school, without any higher education experience themselves, created some fear of the unknown. After they helped me move into the dorm, I wanted them to leave. I was ready to start a new chapter of my life. That feeling may have been mutual. They shed no tears as they left. Instead, they basically said, "Work hard and do well," and headed back to Ashland.

Donovan Hall housed the nonfootball athletes on campus. The football players lived in separate housing. When my parents left, I immediately went about meeting my new neighbors. My roommate Joe Dawson and I hit it off well, and I developed a close friendship with track athlete Dave Frantz. I already knew Lincoln Collinsworth (father of NBC's Cris Collinsworth) because I had been the manager of his all-star basketball team. My first encounters with Coach Adolph Rupp's players Bob Burrow, Jerry Calvert, and Ray Mills stunned me. They were huge! I distinctly remember walking into the bathroom where Bob was shaving. He just towered over me. I had gone from being the "big man on campus" at my high school to feeling like a scrawny little kid.

UK was much larger and more complex than I expected. I had been on the UK campus before, when Dad had taken me to a couple of sporting events there. In October 1953 we watched "Bear" Bryant's team defeat Mississippi State, which was ranked at the time. In December of that year we also watched Rupp's basketball team beat LaSalle to win the UK Invitational Tournament. We simply watched the games and then drove home, so I developed no understanding of the school itself. When I began to realize the scope of the university as a freshman, I was genuinely amazed.

On the social side, I had the good fortune of meeting a few guys who belonged to the Delta Tau Delta fraternity. They stopped by my room one evening and asked me to "rush" the fraternity. I had no idea what rushing entailed or whom it involved. Basketball player Dick Howe told me, "Just put on a suit." I donned the only suit I owned, an off-gray flannel, and completed the outfit with a purple shirt and a flowery tie. I can only imagine what I looked like.

I rode with Dick to the fraternity house. When we pulled up to that southern mansion with the huge columns out front, I was dumbfounded. The scene inside overwhelmed me. Everyone was dressed to the nines in high-dollar suits. Nobody teased me, but I definitely felt out of my element. These college undergraduates possessed a social capital I did not understand, but there was something about it that intrigued me. They exuded confidence and seemed destined to do great things. They lived a life I never knew, and I wanted to be a part of it.

Delta Tau Delta invited me to join, even though I had no legacy or social connections. I did not even have the money to pay the dues, but someone in the fraternity offered me an anonymous scholarship. It provided a totally different environment outside of athletics, and I developed some lifelong friendships during my time as a Delt. Jim Hampton became the editor of the *Miami Herald*; Lee Eaton and Tommy Gentry both became leaders in the horse industry. Later in life I served on the national foundation board of Delta Tau Delta. The organization had helped me accomplish my own goals, and I wanted to see other young college students afforded the same opportunity.

My college dreams involved playing professional baseball and connecting myself with sports in any way I could. When I discovered UK's radio arts program, I visited its offices on the top floor of McVey Hall. I first met Professor Cam Halyard, who introduced me to Professor Stu Hallock and a young professor named Len Press. These three individuals constituted the entire radio arts department. I asked them what I classes I needed to take to study sports broadcasting, and they told me to sign up for every class I could find in speech, English, and journalism. I needed to learn how to speak, write, and communicate professionally. So I did as they said. After my freshman year, Len Press took over the radio arts program. He became an invaluable mentor to me during my time at UK and beyond.

I fell into an (unpaid) dream job my first semester. I started hanging out with Ernie Coyle, a senior and the play-by-play voice for the student radio station (WBKY). He asked me to be his color analyst on air. I jumped at the chance and started assisting Ernie at football and basketball games my freshman year.

Back in the 1950s, freshman athletes did not play varsity sports. The NCAA wanted first-year athletes to focus on their studies and acclimate to college. I was itching to play for the varsity team, but I now understand the wisdom of this policy, which protected new students from some of the pressures of "big-time" athletics. Freshmen were allowed to practice and play a few games against local teams, but we could not travel.

Our baseball coach, Harry Lancaster, also served as Rupp's assistant basketball coach, so the baseball team rarely saw Coach Lancaster until basketball season was over. Harry had Abe Shannon, an interesting character from Georgetown, Kentucky, serve as a volunteer coach. Abe monitored our conditioning during basketball season. Bad weather kept us inside most days during the winter, so we ran sprints in Memorial Coliseum's hallways or in tobacco warehouses. Guys on the team got terrible shin splints from all the running on those concrete floors without any modern sneakers. Our freshman team played a few junior varsity games against local high school clubs and other freshman teams from the small colleges around Lexington.

By the end of my freshman year, I had taken advantage of all UK had to offer. I declared a major and found an academic home in the radio arts program. I loved playing baseball and looked forward to joining the varsity team my sophomore year. I found friends and a social circle in the Delta Tau Delta fraternity and served as a sportscaster for the student-run radio station. With everything going so smoothly, I decided to stay in Lexington that first summer. I lived in the Delt house and took a job as an ironworker's apprentice on the Cooperstown project near campus.

I spent that summer welding with a construction crew. It didn't pay much, but it was the best money I had ever made. A couple evenings a week,

I played semipro baseball for what had previously been an all-black team at Hustlers Park in Lexington. I joined the team with a few other white guys, including Bill Marksbury, who had a distinguished career studying aging and Alzheimer's disease at UK, as well as Bobby Flynn, whose son Doug played major league baseball. I pitched as often as they let me. Unaware of the social significance of joining an African American team in the summer of 1956, I am glad that integration of that team never became an issue. It certainly wasn't something I spent any time thinking about. My parents had taught me to treat everyone with respect, and my experience playing baseball with a diverse group of guys in Ashland made playing with African Americans seem totally normal to me. On Sundays I pitched for West Liberty in the semipro Bluegrass League. I enjoyed playing baseball that summer and earning a little extra cash.

As I entered my sophomore year at UK, everyone on the baseball team believed we had a competitive club, but we were sorely mistaken. In one game against Florida at the beginning of the season, it was still spitting snow in Lexington and we suffered an embarrassing 22–0 loss. However, my most humiliating personal experience as a sophomore came when I was pitching a game against the University of Louisville. We had a 1–0 lead going into the top of the ninth. I walked one guy, and the next batter up was hitting in the eighth spot. With two strikes on him, I got cute and threw him a changeup that I left a little high. He hit a high pop fly that managed to hit the top of the left-field fence and bounce over for a home run. We did not score in the bottom of the inning, and I lost a one-hitter by a score of 2–1.

After the game, Coach Lancaster said a few words to the team before dismissing everyone to the locker room. Then Coach said, "Host, stay out here." We walked out to the left-field line, and he told me to start running sprints to center field and back. Every time I slowed down, he said, "I didn't tell you to stop." Once darkness fell, he followed me to the outfield, grabbed me by my shirt, threw me up against the fence, got right in my face, and said, "You don't have any guts! You have absolutely no courage. I'm taking you off meals for a week, and I hope you quit!" Then he just walked off. I followed him back to the locker room, contemplating what he had said. I could quit, but then I would have to face my parents. Telling them I had lost my scholarship seemed worse than trying to figure out how to find food to eat for the next week.

Sure enough, my name was no longer on the list of athletes who could eat for free at the student union. So I asked different players to grab some extra sides or extra meat for me. I decided to be the first one to show up at practice and the last one to leave. I never worked so hard, sprinting whenever the coach told me (or the team) to do something. After that week, I went back to the student union, and my name had been returned to the list. I kept up that work ethic, and Coach Lancaster never said another negative word about my effort for the next three years.

Today, Lancaster's methods would not be allowed, but he focused my attention. I decided to learn from my mistakes and to try my best at every practice and with every pitch. As I improved as a player, Lancaster had me serve as the first-base coach when I was not pitching. Harry did his work on me one time, and that was enough to teach me how to stay on his good side. Apparently, it stuck. When Lancaster wrote his book *Adolph Rupp as I Knew Him,* which my company published, he wrote a note to me that said: "To the young man I coached who made me the proudest." Looking back, I learned a great deal about life and work from his gruff coaching style. These were priceless life lessons.

On the academic side, I did pretty well in my communications courses. Some of my general education classes were a different story. My less-than-stellar grades were a product of my focus on broadcasting and the time I invested to improve as a baseball player. Communications professor Len Press and a new professor named Elizabeth Taylor both became influential personalities in my life. They offered invaluable academic and personal advice, and Professor Taylor became my mom away from home.

After radio announcer Ernie Coyle graduated, I assumed all the duties of both play-by-play and color as a sophomore. This provided excellent on-the-job training, and I loved the work. The student station, WBKY, did not cover away games, but the games in Lexington allowed me to make some valuable connections that would serve me well in the years ahead. I met Charlie Thornton from Tulane and Elmore "Scoop" Hudgins from Vanderbilt. I remember shaking hands with Harry Caray when he came to town with Saint Louis University. I also met Eddie Einhorn from Northwestern, who became a TV sports legend by starting TVS and airing college basketball games, which vastly increased interest in the game.[1]

My broadcasts on WBKY gained some local attention and created another important opportunity. Claude Sullivan announced UK games on WVLK for the Standard Oil Network. He asked if I would cover high school games on WVLK when he was on the road with the Wildcats. Of course, I said yes.

So at nineteen years of age I was announcing home games on the university's radio station and traveling around central Kentucky broadcasting high school football and basketball games.

Kentucky's athletic director Bernie Shively had made it clear to all scholarship athletes that receiving pay for work during the school year violated NCAA rules. We could work during holiday breaks, as long as we were not employed by a booster. So I asked WVLK, which had offered me $10 a game, to hold my earnings and pay me only in December and over summer breaks. The station agreed. This may have violated the spirit of NCAA regulations, but it adhered to the letter of the law. In addition, scholarship athletes were given a $15 "laundry allowance." Once a month, all the scholarship athletes lined up and took turns with Shively. He would talk to us individually as he peeled off dollar bills. He would ask, "Are you keeping up with your studies?" Then he would say, "Use this money wisely." I rarely used the "laundry" money to wash clothes, but it was a godsend.

I found other ways to make some cash while in school. When I had free time, I often bowled at Wildcat Lanes across from Memorial Coliseum or at Congress Lanes downtown. One day Jimmy Bradley (who wrote a bowling column for the newspaper) asked me to join a semipro team sponsored by Budweiser. The Bud team paid me to bowl, and I enjoyed the challenge. Things went well until someone at the university found out about it. Harry Lancaster called me into his office and said, "Just what in the hell are you doing bowling for money?!" I responded, "Why wouldn't I? I need it!" He raised his voice even louder and said, "That's against NCAA policy, and you have to quit!" So I quit the Budweiser team and looked for other ways to survive financially.

I had become friends with a number of UK basketball players. They trusted me, so when UK had home games, I would stand outside (before going to the press table to broadcast the games) and sell the extra tickets the players had been allotted. I always brought back all the money from these ticket sales. In return, they paid me a commission. I also benefited from a policy that gave scholarship athletes free movie passes, and various merchants downtown occasionally gave scholarship athletes clothes—all activities the NCAA would crack down on during the ensuing decades.

This extra money really helped a student like me make it through college, but I still needed to work summers to make ends meet. After my sophomore year, I moved back home for the summer and took a job with Ashland Oil. They would tie a harness around me and drop me down into massive oil drums, where I welded pieces of scaffolding on the inside to keep them structurally sound. On weeknights I played baseball for a team in the semipro Huntington Industrial League, and on Sundays I played for a team sponsored by Yates-Packard. They paid me $25 for each game I pitched. Needless to say, I was on the mound as much as possible.

During my junior year, I took more classes in my major and found them engaging. Though I was by no means a scholar, I did satisfactory work in my classes, with one exception: Spanish. I needed four semesters of a foreign language to meet the BA degree requirements. Fellow students had warned me to avoid one particular professor: Dr. Alberta Server. Rumor had it that she didn't like athletes in her class. I thought I could win her over with my interpersonal skills, so I signed up for her class. I tried everything in my power to woo her, but it was impossible. The more I tried to impress her, the worse things got. Then my competitive nature kicked in and I thought, "I'm going to show her I can pass this." Well, I did not pass, and at the end of my senior year, I still lacked one Spanish class. I should have listened to my friends, but I bore the blame. I was horrendous at foreign languages. I just couldn't seem to memorize the vocabulary, the verb conjugations, or anything else for that matter.

Despite my studies and sports, I found a little time to socialize. I never owned a car, so whenever I asked a girl out, it had to be a double date. We usually went to the movies and out to eat. The fraternity also kept us busy with social activities. Some of the best times I had with friends occurred at the Paddock, a little bar and grill just off campus. I would meet up with Brit Kirwan, D. G. Fitzmaurice, and Don "Horse" Schmidt, and we would drink beer and play sports trivia. I lost touch with Don, but D. G. went on to be a sportswriter. Brit become a mathematics professor, president of the University of Maryland, president of Ohio State, and then chancellor of the University of Maryland system. Our games were always good-natured but quite competitive.

I continued broadcasting for WBKY and WVLK and developed a close relationship with Claude Sullivan. Claude was the most professional broadcaster I had ever known, and he was an even better person. He tirelessly researched statistics and trivia in preparation for games. He taught me how to analyze my broadcasts by cutting taped recordings with a razor blade and splicing the tape back together to review specific calls from a game. He took the time to listen to my broadcasts and coach me on ways to improve my play-by-play and color. This training was invaluable, and I considered him one of my closest friends and mentors. He was under no obligation to help me, but he was generous and kind enough to support an aspiring young broadcaster.

On the baseball diamond, I was a solid college-level pitcher during my first two seasons. However, I was not making the progress necessary to play professionally. I spent as much time as possible trying to improve every aspect of my game. That paid off in my junior year, but before the season was over, I dislocated my shoulder sliding head-first into third base. A doctor at Good Samaritan Hospital popped it back into place, introducing me to the most excruciating pain I had ever experienced. That injury ended my junior year of baseball.

I spent the next summer in Ashland again. I accepted a job doing blasting work for a construction crew widening Route 23 through eastern Kentucky. It was a crazy job, but it paid well. I would rappel down the side of a mountain with a jackhammer-type tool, drill into the rock, stick dynamite into the hole, and ascend to the top, at which point someone would blast the rock. Then I would go back down and do the same thing again. As usual, I played semipro baseball in the evenings or on the weekends.

With the close of my junior year, it was "do or die" with regard to my major league dreams. I worked as hard as I knew how, and it paid off. My win-loss record my senior year was 5–5, but that was because the team didn't have much offense. I posted a 1.52 earned run average (ERA). It was the first year we had a competitive team, and we made a run at the conference championship but eventually lost out to Georgia Tech. Although our team fell short, I got the individual shot I so desperately wanted.[2]

UK's volunteer assistant coach Abe Shannon also scouted for the Chicago White Sox. After my senior season, he sent me to the old Comiskey Park in Chicago for a workout. Al Lopez managed the team, and that was the year the Sox made it to the World Series. When I showed up, they put me in a White Sox uniform, which was like a dream, and asked me to pitch in the bullpen. During my workout, Lopez walked over, watched me for a few minutes, and then had a few words with pitching coach Ray Berres. Berres followed me into the locker room and said that Jack Sheehan would be offering me a contract with the White Sox's rookie league farm team. When I met with Sheehan, I didn't even read the contract. I just signed it and headed back to Kentucky.

When I got back to Lexington, I learned that Jerry Sharp and Doug Shively had also made the Class D minor league team. Jerry had an old two-door Plymouth, so we loaded it up with all our suitcases and then drove eighteen hours straight through to Holdrege, Nebraska. We arrived at around 3:00 a.m., and the only hotel in town was locked up for the night, so we decided to sleep in the car. The worst storm I ever witnessed came through that night, and hail the size of softballs shattered the Plymouth's back window.

We showed up the next day tired but eager to show our stuff. To our shock, the White Sox had signed seventy-one players for eighteen spots, and the next two weeks would determine who made the final roster. The coaches broke us up into our positions and put us through workouts. Then they divided us into teams and we played each other. I pitched well in Nebraska. I knew that my friend Doug could knock fastballs out of the park but couldn't hit a curveball, so I struck him out multiple times. After a couple of weeks, they provided bus tickets home for fifty-three guys. Doug was one of the casualties, and he never really forgave me for striking him out. Although we were sad for Doug, Jerry and I were both relieved that we had made the team.

Pitching in the D league for Holdrege wasn't glamorous, but it was a dream come true for me. I earned $375 a month, along with a $3 meal stipend when we were on the road. I tried to save my meal money and usually spent it with my teammates at a diner near the baseball field. Finally, I was focused solely on baseball. I quickly learned that I could no longer expect to strike out batters through force. I pitched fastballs at over 90 miles per hour, which had worked well in college, but even minor league batters could hit my best heat. So I spent most of my days working on my changeup, curveball, screwball, and slider. I also spent more time studying our opponents' hitters when I was not on the mound. Keeping stats on batters provided an advantage because Class D teams had not yet started doing so.

My time in Holdrege allowed me to practice with some of the best players in baseball. Our team alone had half a dozen guys who ended up playing in the majors, but Fred Talbot and Al Weis were the best. Every night I faced batters who would succeed at the highest level. My most notable win while playing for Holdrege came against another young pitcher on the McCook Braves named Phil Niekro. We both entered the game in relief during regulation play and pitched into the fifteenth inning, when Al Weis managed to steal home and we won the game. I loved every minute of the journey, despite the modest wages and long trips through Nebraska and South Dakota.

Halfway through the season, I was promoted to the B league team (which would now be AA) for the White Sox farm team in Lincoln, Nebraska. One step closer to my dream, I faced even tougher competition. One particularly rewarding experience came when I faced Corky Withrow, whose hit off me in high school had ended our run at the state title. This time, I struck him out with curveballs. Nobody else cared, but it provided me with a little satisfying revenge.

One of my friends on the team in Lincoln, Joel Horlen, was a rising star. We all called him a "bonus boy" because he had received a $100,000 bonus for signing with the White Sox. Even so, Joel was thinking about quitting the team. I was pitching much better than Joel at the time, but the coaching staff spent most of their time working to develop his talent. Of course, the White Sox were simply trying to make good on their investment. However, I knew my numbers needed to stay better than Joel's to get the attention of the organization. By the closing week of the season, I had lost only one game for Lincoln. My coaches were telling me I had the stuff to get promoted to the next level. It appeared that my dreams were going to come true.

With less than one week remaining in the minor league season, I started against a team in Cedar Rapids. I had it going on all cylinders that night. Everything was working. Then, in the eighth inning, I wound up for a pitch and felt something go wrong with my shoulder. The pitch sailed over the catcher's head and into the backstop netting. My manager Ira Hutchison came out to the mound and asked, "What happened to you?" I responded, "I don't know," and he pulled me from the game. By the end of the ninth inning, I couldn't lift my arm.

The team sent me to a doctor, who said I had injured my deltoid strap and then shot my shoulder full of cortisone. He told me I could return to the mound after resting my arm during the off-season. A week later, the season was over, and I headed back to Kentucky. Future major league centerfielder Mike Hershberger drove me to Cincinnati. When we said good-bye, I wondered if I would ever play professional baseball again.

I decided to return to Lexington rather than Ashland. I held out hope for a miracle, but deep down, I knew that my major league dreams had died with that wild pitch. Wrestling with this reality, I thought Lexington would provide better opportunities for work. Those first months were tough emotionally as I planned a new course for my life.

When I returned to Kentucky in September 1959, it was the first time since early childhood that I was no longer a student. I still had not earned my degree because I lacked one semester of Spanish, which I eventually earned in 1961 through a correspondence course. I did not have a diploma in 1959, but I had certainly received an education that broadened my view of the world and expanded my opportunities.

Looking back, my time at UK served me well as I grew into a responsible adult. I worked hard at my classes because if I didn't, my professors would have been quick to give me grades reflecting that. UK provided me with incredible practical experience working at the student-run radio station. My professors in the radio arts program were tough but caring. They made it their mission to help me succeed academically and personally. Sports also taught me valuable life lessons that stayed with me well beyond my time on the pitching mound. My social circles helped me mature in terms of dealing with people. In sum, after four years in college, I had gained academic preparation, philosophical knowledge, practical training, and social networking—all of which provided a foundation I could utilize beyond athletics.

3

In Search of a New Dream

Returning to Lexington with a torn shoulder and a shattered dream, I needed to fill the vacuum. I called my mentor Claude Sullivan and asked if he knew of any available radio jobs. He immediately helped me secure a position at a Frankfort radio station as a DJ and play-by-play announcer for high school football games.

I rented a room in Frankfort and tried to settle into a work routine. About two months later, I answered my office phone and heard, "Host, this is Kincaid. Be in my office tomorrow at eleven o'clock." I said, "Excuse me, what was that?" The response: "This is Garvice Kincaid," and he hung up the phone. I turned to my colleague Ken Hart and said, "A guy named Garvice Kincaid told me to meet him at 11:00 a.m. tomorrow." Ken exclaimed, "He owns this station!" Kincaid actually owned several radio stations, but he had to list each one under a loyal employee's name to get around FCC regulations. Ken offered this simple advice: "Dress up and be on time."

The next morning, I drove my hand-me-down Chevy, given to me by my youngest brother, to the old Central Bank building in Lexington. When I entered Kincaid's office at eleven sharp, he sat behind a massive desk. His pants were held up to his chest by suspenders, and a napkin was draped from his shirt collar. He held a massive bowl of chocolate ice cream covered in chocolate syrup. Behind him, a series of red telephones lined the wall as if he had direct lines to the White House and the Soviet Union. Looking back on the scene now, it sounds silly, but at the time, it certainly intimidated me!

Kincaid looked up at me said, "Host, I've listened to your broadcasts, and Claude Sullivan tells me you're really good. Do you know what Kentucky Central is?" I responded, "I don't have any idea." He jumped in and said, "It's an insurance company I just bought. To promote it, I've started the Kentucky Central Network." Kincaid informed me that Walter "Dee" Huddleston (who managed a radio station in Elizabethtown and would eventually become a US senator) did play-by-play for UK games on the Kentucky Central Network. His color commentator had shown up drunk for a football game the previous weekend, so Kincaid fired him. He said, "I want you to work with Dee the rest of the year doing color for the network. In addition, you'll work at WVLK here in Lexington and report to Ted Grizzard."

Although I had no choice in the matter, I was happy to move back to Lexington and call UK games again. After renting a room in town, I headed to the station to learn more about my responsibilities. In addition to my sports broadcasting duties, I joined WVLK's sales team and worked as the evening DJ. Claude Sullivan was the program manager, and the afternoon DJ was future US congressman Hal Rogers. Each afternoon Rogers concluded his show with, "And now, for the Host of hosts!" I was back on the air spinning hits!

WVLK played a top-forty format, so I played the same songs each night. I disliked Elvis Presley, so I removed his songs from the rotation for a couple nights. On the third evening, Claude Sullivan called and asked, "Did you just skip Elvis Presley?" I responded, "Yes, sir." He said, "The next time you do that, you won't have a job. Do you understand?" I apologized and agreed. The "King" rejoined the regular rotation.

For my sales job at WVLK I reported to George Webb. When I first met him, he said, "I've got good news and bad news. The good news is I have a list of your accounts. The bad news is none of them have ever spent any money on the radio." As the new guy, I got the toughest list with regard to selling airtime.

Earning only $325 a month for my on-air work, I needed to make sales to improve my income. I took my list and divided it into columns for everyone who spent money on ads in the newspaper, in the yellow pages, or on TV. I also mapped all the potential clients into quadrants across Lexington. I decided to visit each business in person rather than call on the phone. I believed the key to sales was making clients buy into me as a person first. If they liked me, I had a chance. Kirk Jewelry was the first business I visited. I introduced myself to Lynn Luallen, who responded, "We don't buy radio advertising." I said, "I know Mr. Luallen. I just want to get to know you."

I visited Lynn regularly over several weeks, trying to make conversation, and learned that he enjoyed horses. Then one day out of the blue he invited me to a building near Cheapside. We walked through an office and another series of doors into what I realized was a full-fledged bookmaking operation. Bookies were yelling across the room; blackboards covered the walls, tracking racing odds; and phones were ringing. After we placed a few bets, Lynn and I became friends, and he eventually convinced his manager, Harold White, to buy some airtime from me.

This type of scene played out regularly, even though numerous doors were slammed in my face. I figured I needed to make one sale for every twenty businesses I visited. After each stop, I made notes about the clients. I determined which ones were financially unable to buy advertising and which ones could not be persuaded. I crossed them off my list and focused on potential clients. I ended up making one sale for every seventeen clients.

My biggest sales coup almost ended in abysmal failure. W. T. Grant & Company was a successful five-and-dime store like Woolworth's. Its manager, Ned Shapley, advertised in the newspaper but not on radio. I learned that Ned arrived every Monday morning at 8:00, stopped by his office briefly, and then walked to the lunch counter for a cup of coffee. Every Monday morning, I was at the lunch counter to have coffee with Ned. Each week he said, "I'm not buying radio." As usual, I responded, "I understand that, sir. I just want to get to know you." We would talk for a while, and then I would leave.

After three months, Ned mentioned that the company planned to open a new store in the Eastland Shopping Center across town. Ned looked at me and said, "You know something, I'm going to test radio. I want to use it for our new location. What can you give me for $15,000?" Nobody had ever made a sale like that at WVLK. Our lowest rate for the average client was $3.25 for thirty seconds. However, George Webb charged our best clients $2.60. I told Ned I could offer him $2.60 per thirty-second commercial. We shook hands, I wrote up a contract, and we signed it at the lunch counter.

I took the contract back to WVLK, and George immediately called a special sales meeting. He stood up in front of everyone and said, "Mr. Host made a big sale! Here is the contract, and this is what I think of it." He ripped it to shreds. He added, "He thinks he can sell spots for $2.60. We don't accept spots for $2.60—only $3.25." After a few more humiliating comments, he said I needed tell Shapley that the rate was $3.25. Lee Harper spoke up and said, "George, that's not right. You sell spots for $2.60." George retorted, "I'm the sales manager. I set the rates, and I'm not accepting a contract at $2.60 from him without getting my permission first." Obviously, Webb didn't like the new guy making such a big sale.

I devised a new plan and drove to the store to see Shapley. He wasn't there, so I left a message for him to call me immediately. He rang that evening and asked if there was a problem with our deal. I said, "Not really, but I think I might have a better opportunity for you." He agreed to meet me in the morning to discuss it.

That night I called Paul Warnecke, manager of WVLK's mobile truck. I asked if he could have the vehicle at the grand opening of the new store, and he agreed. I paid the truck fee out of my own pocket. The next morning, I told Ned that I could get him prime-time advertising plus the mobile truck for $3.25. He agreed, and I gave the revised contract to Webb, who never said another word about the ordeal he put me through. My boss, Ted Grizzard, was pleased with the way I handled Webb. I made the sale, kept my job, and gained the respect of my colleagues.

I thoroughly enjoyed working football games with Dee Huddleston and was excited to start traveling with the basketball team. Then, near the close of football season, Dee told me he was quitting because he couldn't spend so much time on the road. With Dee's sudden departure, I was doing the play-by-play, color commentating, and engineering for all the Kentucky Central Network broadcasts.

At that time, there were no exclusive radio rights for UK sports. Any radio station or network could broadcast games, and those that did competed for listeners. Cawood Ledford worked for WHAS in Louisville, Jack Lorri worked for WBLG in Lexington, and the other announcers worked for statewide networks: Claude Sullivan announced for the Standard Oil Network (owned by WVLK), and Earl Boardman broadcast for the Ashland Oil Network. Although their stations were competitors, these announcers developed a special bond. As the new guy, I was subjected to some mild hazing from my colleagues. The first time we covered a game on the road, some of us took a cab, and they sat me in the middle of the backseat. When the cab stopped, everyone jumped out and closed the doors, leaving me to pay the fare. Then, when I got to my hotel room, they had "short-sheeted" my bed. The guys played a few other pranks, but I didn't mind because I knew it meant I belonged in their fraternity.

Broadcasting games was just a small part of my job. In addition to working on the sales team and hosting my radio show, I became CEO of Kentucky Productions, a small subsidiary Kincaid formed to build the Kentucky Central Network. Don Horton, Fred Hensley, and Ken Hart managed the finances and other business affairs. I traveled throughout the state, signing stations to broadcast UK games.

Broadcasting UK basketball provided an opportunity to spend time with Adolph Rupp. Early in the season, I accompanied the team when it flew out to Southern California to play UCLA and USC. That Friday night, UK faced John Wooden's Bruins, and UK eked out a two-point victory. While returning to the hotel, our bus collided with a drunk driver trying to beat a red light, smashing the car into a street pole. I was sitting in the front row behind the passenger rail, and the impact threw me over the rail and into the bus's stairwell. I hit my head, and the jolt knocked me out cold. When I came to my senses, Coach Rupp was standing over me saying, "My Gawd! Is he dead?!" I spoke up to say I was alive and slowly made it to my feet. I had a bad cut and some bruises on my head, so they took me to a nearby hospital, where I was bandaged up and told to keep ice on my head.

The next night I called the game against USC wearing a massive bandage wrapped around my head. Thankfully, it was radio and not TV, because I looked absolutely ridiculous. The following week UK lost to St. Louis before taking a bus to Kansas. Rupp enjoyed giving us a tour of the campus in Lawrence, showing us where he had worked, studied, and lived while a student at the University of Kansas. Then UK beat the Jayhawks in overtime.

As the season progressed, I learned about Rupp's leadership style. Later in December we were in Philadelphia playing Temple University. Rupp instructed everyone to meet on the bus at the top of the hour. Fifteen minutes before the hour, he walked through the hotel lobby, donning his brown coat and hat. He stepped on the bus and, without checking to see who was there, looked at the driver and said, "Kick 'er, doc." All the players already knew what I was learning: "on time" for Coach Rupp meant fifteen minutes early. Arriving just in time was too late.

Rupp exhibited his brilliance in many ways. While other schools in the South focused on football, he built a basketball tradition at Kentucky. During his first decades as coach, other SEC schools employed football assistants to coach their basketball teams. Rupp was the full-time basketball coach, and he even had an assistant, Harry Lancaster. Rupp exploited this advantage by recruiting players nationally and refining his knowledge of the game. He also mastered media relations. My first season, we took a trip to Atlanta, where UK played the University of Georgia (UGA) and Georgia Tech. When UK lost to Georgia Tech, Rupp said little to the press. Then, after drubbing the Bulldogs by twenty-four points in Athens, he invited the press to his room at the Georgian Terrace Hotel in Atlanta. Rupp had a bathtub full of Lowenbrau beer for the sportswriters. As the rookie broadcaster, I was sent to buy a big sack of hamburgers for everyone. When I returned, Rupp was holding court with the press in his red silk pajamas. Everyone there was drinking beer except for Rupp. He had a tall empty glass and a bottle of bourbon next to him. He filled the glass halfway with bourbon, got up, and walked in the bathroom, where we could hear him add a splash of water to his drink. He came back in the room, sat down, and took big gulps of bourbon until his eyes started to water. Then he opened up for questions. One reporter asked him a question about Georgia and he said, "Shoot, Red Lawson [UGA's coach] is one of the best coaches in the history of the game." He loved to praise the coaches he could whip. He answered a few more questions before refilling his glass. Then, when he had given the reporters enough to fill their columns, he announced, "Okay you SOBs, this night is over. I'm going to bed!"

My time with the Kentucky Central Network in the early 1960s allowed me to experience the culture of other SEC schools. At that time, Coach Babe McCarthy at Mississippi State was one of the few who challenged Rupp's dominance. When the two teams met in Starkville, neither coach wanted to warm up with the other team, so the referees had to force both teams out on the floor. When Rupp returned to his seat, he found a dead skunk under it. The Mississippi State fans clanged their cowbells all game long. UK won, but I remember my head ringing all night.

From that season forward, I witnessed what made Rupp such a successful coach and leader. He demanded excellence from his players. Extremely harsh, he seldom used positive reinforcement. However, he expected perfection in both learning the game and executing on the court. He mastered public relations "spin" and knew how to set the narrative regarding his team. Rupp seemed bigger than his team, which made both UK fans and opponents' supporters even more interested in seeing the Wildcats play.

Back home in Lexington, I continued a relationship with a young woman I had met in college. During my time at UK, I had gone out on a double date with Carolyn Clark, and by my senior year, we were seeing each other exclusively. However, I had decided that being in a serious relationship while I chased my dream of being a pro baseball player was not an option. I knew that making it to the major leagues required incredible focus and commitment, and all that time on the road did not lend itself to a serious courtship. When I returned to Kentucky, Carolyn and I began to date again more seriously, and we got married at the Second Presbyterian Church in June 1960.

Soon after the wedding, I began my second year working for WVLK and the Kentucky Central Network. That fall, however, I was itching to do something else. After only one year, I was outselling all my colleagues at the radio station, doing UK sports broadcasts all alone, hosting my radio show, and turning the young Kentucky Central Network into the largest one in the state. Yet I had not received a promotion and was making just about the same salary. I wanted my hard work to lead to more opportunities for advancement.

After one experience at a football game, I decided to get serious about finding a new job. Since there was no exclusive network for UK, each week the broadcasters would draw straws to determine who got the best and worst locations to broadcast the games. Then the second-best spot was assigned, and on down the line. This particular day, UK's football team was playing Georgia Tech in Atlanta, and I drew the short straw. There weren't enough spots in the media booth, so I set up my broadcast table and equipment in the end-zone bleachers. It rained buckets nearly the entire game. From my vantage point, with no spotter, I was unable to see what was happening on the field, so I was literally making up some of the calls while getting drenched. Despite the small amount of notoriety I had gained as a radio personality and the satisfaction of building a radio network, I left that game determined to find something better.

I had a few offers to sell insurance, but I wanted an opportunity with a larger company. I contacted Jim Kaleen, who worked for Procter & Gamble (P&G). I asked him about job opportunities at P&G, and Jim arranged for me to interview with the company in Cincinnati, where I took several logic and aptitude tests. I must have tested well enough, because I was offered a job in sales. When I told Ted Grizzard and Claude Sullivan at WVLK that I had accepted another job, they tried to get me to stay. Although I enjoyed working for both of them, I had little respect for sales manager George Webb, and I had already made up my mind to leave.

Once I accepted the job at P&G, Pat Williams trained me in Lexington for the next six weeks. The company operated like a well-oiled machine. After my training, P&G sent me to Chattanooga, Tennessee—one of the worst sales zones for the case soap division. Both Colgate and Lever boasted a larger market share, which was not normal for P&G. When Carolyn and I moved to Tennessee, I soon learned that the situation was worse than I could have imagined. My predecessor had struggled with both his job and his personal life. He had committed suicide, leaving behind no company records.

Without documents to give me a feel for the sales situation, I decided to visit grocery stores and vendors in the region. Each day I left our duplex in East Brainerd and called on different vendors. I met Clyde Berke and Herbert St. Goar, who operated a large wholesale warehouse that supplied Dixie Savings Stores. Their stores dictated the local market, and they refused to buy most P&G soap products other than regular-pack Tide detergent. They also disliked P&G's payment schedule. I stepped out on a limb and convinced them to buy a train car full of regular-pack Tide and suggested the sale price at which they should advertise it. I assured them that they would see a spike in all grocery sales because of Tide's popularity, and if they didn't, I would buy back the inventory. Thankfully, the plan worked, or else I would have been in debt and out of a job.

I found my job both challenging and rewarding. I made $450 a month and had a company car. As sales increased, I earned several employee incentives, including company stock. Carolyn struggled being away from her parents in Lexington, but we managed to make regular trips to Kentucky. Within two short years, P&G led the soap market in Chattanooga.

One night, my division manager from Cincinnati, Wally Abbot, took me out for dinner and told me that P&G was promoting me to a position in Washington, DC, as the region's head salesman. At twenty-five years of age, I oversaw an area from DC down to Norfolk, Virginia, and as far west as Charleston, West Virginia. This included three sales units and more than twenty employees. Soon after moving to DC, we had our first child, Elizabeth. Carolyn found the move to DC especially difficult. She did not enjoy life in Washington, and we couldn't drive back to Kentucky on weekends, so we saved our money to fly home. She frequently stayed in Lexington while I worked in DC.

Though far from optimal, this arrangement allowed me to focus on work. I learned so much from my supervisor, Mike Hostage, whom I admired greatly. A brilliant manager, he taught me how to lead teams of people. A solid family man and a terrific person, Mike was everything I wanted to be. While working with Hostage to improve our team's sales, I noticed that most of the individuals being promoted at P&G were Ivy League graduates with MBAs. I worried that my efforts were being overlooked because of my résumé.

Then, during a period of about six months, a number of events caused me to shift my personal and professional goals. On November 22, 1963, I was in Mike's office when someone ran in and said, "Kennedy's been shot." In total shock, we drove over to the White House. All the lights were on, but we saw no security at all. When the president's funeral took place, we walked from our office to Arlington Cemetery and watched the procession of dignitaries. It was tragic and surreal. We witnessed people like Haile Selassie and Charles de Gaulle march by without any visible security. During those weeks, we entered the modern era of gun tragedy and violence, but the world's leaders had not yet responded with armored cars and security details.

In the following months, I did a lot of soul-searching. I was finally making a healthy income but remained dissatisfied. Carolyn stayed in Kentucky much of the time with our young daughter. Then Mike decided to leave P&G to become executive vice president at Marriott. One night, future P&G chairman Brad "OB" Butler came to talk with me. He said I had "broken the mold" by moving up the corporate ladder without an Ivy League education. I said, "Well, it isn't rocket science." He laughed and offered me a promotion to a unit manager's position in Philadelphia. I'm not exactly sure how or why, but I made an on-the-spot decision and replied, "Mr. Butler, I really appreciate the opportunity, but I'm not interested." He asked, "You don't want the promotion?" I said, "No sir, I'm going to leave the company." The following day, P&G executive district manager Chuck Jarvie, who had replaced Hostage, tried to convince me to take the promotion. Chuck later became president of Dr. Pepper, and I would work with him again many years down the road. At the time, I needed to move back to Kentucky, even though I had no idea what I was going to do.

Returning to Lexington without a job, I needed employment in a hurry. I discussed possible options with my father-in-law, Bill Clark. He had been a partner at Brock-McVey Corporation in Lexington but had sold his share of the company. He suggested that I go to work for his wife, Dorothea, who had a real estate business. Without any other prospects, I agreed.

I immediately enrolled in the Bemis Lawrence Real Estate School in Louisville and passed the real estate broker exam after only a few weeks. I wanted to do more, so I took insurance classes, and in less than a month I had passed the tests to sell fire, casualty, and life insurance. Covington Mutual asked me to be an insurance agent, so my mother-in-law and I opened up an office at 109 Walton Avenue, next door to Ray's Barbershop. We bought a sign that read: "Dorothea Clark Realty, Host Insurance."

I became very aggressive in both the insurance and the real estate business. I represented horseman John Gaines when he sold part of his Gainesway Farm to develop what is now the Merrick Inn (a development on the south side of Lexington). During that process, I got into the construction business too, building houses in the Gainesway development and in Cardinal Valley. Some of my former contacts in radio knew I was back in town, and Ken Hart hired me to broadcast games for WLAP. So, when I was not working in real estate or insurance, I was broadcasting UK, Transylvania, and high school games. My old high school coach George Conley actually became my football color commentator. Former UK standout Wah Wah Jones worked with me during basketball games.

John Gaines invited me to Keeneland (Lexington's upscale horse-racing track) and introduced me to what I called the "upper-crust" crowd. I did some good networking, and my businesses started to boom. Jack Crain approached me with a plan, and we formed Crain, Hardwick, & Host. Almost overnight, we became the second largest insurance agency in the city. Then Jack, Angel Levas, and Jim Shropshire convinced me to put up $5,000 to invest in Caribbean Utilities, which became the first utility company on the Cayman Islands. That investment started to pay dividends quickly and did so for a long time. By 1966, I was president of the Kentucky Mutual Insurance Agents Association, on the Board of Directors of the Lexington Board of Realtors, and active in both the Homebuilders Association and the Jaycees.

Life in Lexington was going well. Carolyn gave birth to our son David on June 30, 1967. We bought a house that backed up to UK's agricultural experiment farm (now the Arboretum). I woke up each morning and made a list of the three or four most important things I wanted to accomplish that day, and I made sure to complete those key tasks. By 1966, I was selling about ten houses a month, flipping houses on my own, selling insurance to anyone I could find, and doing radio broadcasts. Still in my twenties, I had amassed more than $250,000 in savings, which was rather substantial at the time.

Then Fred Wachs, publisher of the *Lexington Leader*, asked me to attend a meeting. When I arrived, I found myself among some influential local Republicans: county judge Joe Johnson, real estate developer Don Ball, my business partner Ted Hardwick, and Lexington sheriff and former basketball star Wah Wah Jones. They wanted me to run Senator John Sherman Cooper's campaign in Fayette County. I told them they had a problem because I was a registered Democrat; that had happened because Governor Happy Chandler used to come by and watch my baseball games at UK, and he was a Democrat. They told me that party affiliation was not a problem because Senator Cooper was such a bipartisan figure, but they did encourage me to switch parties. I agreed to do that and organized Cooper's campaign with Sally Stevens.

At the time, I did not give much thought to accepting the role of campaign organizer in Fayette County. I liked the senator, I appreciated what he stood for, and I thought it would be helpful to make some new business connections. However, it soon changed the trajectory of my professional life.

Although my college days were behind me, the years 1959 to 1966 proved invaluable to my lifelong education. The end of my baseball career taught me how to deal with adversity. My time at WVLK showed me that I was pretty good at broadcasting, but I had a natural gift for sales and working with people. While at P&G, I learned some of the most effective methods of running a company. My mentors in Washington, DC, were some of the best executives in the country. I still had one problem: at twenty-eight, I had no idea what I wanted to do when I grew up!

After returning to Kentucky to be with my family, I made up my mind to take everything I had learned and become the best businessperson possible. I built new relationships in Lexington and formed some of the personal business strategies I maintained throughout my career. I carried a notepad and jotted down any names or ideas that popped into my mind during the day. At the same time, I stayed focused and checked each day's goals off my list. By agreeing to assist with Senator Cooper's campaign, more political items began to appear on my daily checklist. Unaware of it at the time, I was beginning a new chapter in my life that I had never anticipated.

4

Exploring Life in Politics

Organizing Senator Cooper's campaign in Lexington provided my first official exposure to politics. Having no clue what I was doing, I observed, listened, and learned as much as I could as fast as possible. I invited seasoned politicians to speak on Cooper's behalf and utilized every business and social connection I had to ensure that all Republicans and a large minority of Democrats would vote for the senator.

Hosting Senator Cooper during his frequent visits to Lexington provided an opportunity to learn from him. On his first visit, I picked him up at the train station and took him to his hotel downtown. Upon entering his room, he leaned over, opened his luggage, pulled out a pint of bourbon, and asked me to pour him a glass. We sat and talked campaign strategy for a few minutes. Realizing my youth and inexperience in politics, Senator Cooper said, "I want you to watch me and learn how I operate politically." I responded, "Yes, sir," and I looked forward to learning from a legend in Kentucky politics!

Spending time with Cooper afforded me time to examine my own beliefs and develop a political ideology. Although a registered Democrat, many of my views aligned with the GOP. Moreover, Cooper taught me the value of being a centrist and working with others who held different opinions. He functioned equally well with Democrats and Republicans. Cooper believed that disagreements created opportunities for compromise and to show respect for others, regardless of their political affiliation—an essential lesson that stuck with me all my life.

Senator Cooper was far more progressive than some of his Senate colleagues, as well as many Kentucky Republicans. The people of the commonwealth accepted his stance on various issues because he was such a good statesman. For example, during one campaign, a woman supposedly came up to Cooper and told him how much she supported him but added, "Senator, please don't vote the way you think!" If he could win over constituents like her, I could learn a great deal from him.

Listening to Senator Cooper speak provided an education in itself. He began each address appearing to be a bit disheveled. He ruffled his papers and began to speak in a soft tone. As he mumbled his way through the speech, he literally made the audience lean in and concentrate on every word. He would then pick up the tempo slightly and organize his thoughts into clear and concise sentences. Finally, looking out over the audience, he would raise his voice so it nearly boomed through the microphone as he spoke to an important issue. After a short pause, he would boom into his next rousing and eloquent defense. Repeating this process, Cooper had the crowd completely focused on him by the end of his address. The audience might not remember the details of his talk, but almost everyone walked away saying, "What a great man. What an incredible leader!" They were correct.

After each speech, I was more worked up than anyone in the audience. Cooper's words motivated me to get back on the campaign trail with even more energy and dedication. Afterward, he would return to his soft-spoken self. Working the crowds at a rally, like any good politician, he looked each citizen in the eyes and listened intently to his or her concerns. He possessed a genuine concern for Kentuckians and viewed himself as a servant of the people. More than once he told me, "No matter where you end up, never forget the roots you came from." He was such a distinguished figure, possessing great command and humility at the same time. He exuded both energy and complete control.

Cooper and his Democratic opponent, John Y. Brown Sr., were both statesmen of a different breed. They simply refused to antagonize each other. John Y. Brown Jr. was working on his father's campaign, so he and I talked regularly about how much fun we were having campaigning for our respective candidates. My short time in business had taught me how to bring people together so that both sides could profit financially. Working with Senator Cooper taught me about leading people and inspiring them to buy into a vision.

Senator Cooper won Lexington and Fayette County on his way to a huge statewide victory. I developed many political connections across Kentucky during the campaign, including Marlow Cook, a Jefferson County judge from Louisville. After making a speech for Cooper, Cook invited me to dinner and told me he planned to run for governor. His opponent in the primary would be Barren County judge Louie Nunn. Cook told me how much I would dislike Judge Nunn and asked me to organize his Lexington campaign.

I accepted Cook's request, and in 1967 I started putting together an organization for him in Fayette County. By this time, I knew that proper execution was the key to a winning campaign. Without any computers to generate data in those days, I visited the Fayette County courthouse and studied all the precinct lists of Republican voters. I made note of everyone I knew in each precinct and ranked them by my ability to win their support for Cook. I met with Cook, and he agreed to my strategy of holding "precinct parties" that he would attend. I convinced people like Pat Freibert and Jack Trevey to create lists of supporters to invite to these parties. Although Nunn won the statewide primary election, Cook took Fayette County by more than 3,000 votes.

Cook lost the election, at least in part, because the results from Jefferson County and Fayette County were reported early in the evening. Nunn made sure that the results from counties in far southeastern Kentucky were delayed until he knew how many votes he needed to beat Cook. I have no idea how Nunn's team did it, but I do know that after Nunn lost the 1963 general election to Ned Breathitt, he had vowed, "Boys, we didn't get outvoted. We got outcounted! I'm never going to get outcounted again." To be sure, when the numbers came in from southeastern Kentucky, Nunn had the necessary votes to win the primary. I never heard Nunn admit to vote tampering, but he did say, "I never did anything in politics that hadn't been done to me."

The day after the primary, I returned to my office intending to go back to selling real estate and insurance. Then my phone rang, and a voice said, "Jim, this is Louie Nunn. You beat my ass in Fayette County." Somewhat startled, I replied, "No sir, Judge Cook beat you." He interrupted, "No, I beat him, but YOU beat my ass. Everyone tells me you are the hardest worker they have ever seen. You outworked us, outmaneuvered us, you out-everythinged us in Fayette County." I said, "I don't know if that is a compliment, but thanks." Nunn laughed and said, "Look. It's over. I want all Republicans to come together and I would like you to be for me in the fall." I told him he had my vote, and he interjected, "I want you to do the same thing for me that you did against me."

Before agreeing to work for Nunn, I needed to talk with my business partners Jack Crain and Ted Hardwick. My political work had been nearly all-consuming, and I wanted to make sure my associates were okay with it. I saw Ted across the hall first. I said, "Louie Nunn called me this morning. . . ." Before I could say anything else, he said, "It is more important to get Louie elected than it is to focus on this business." Clearly, Nunn had spoken to Ted before calling me that morning.

With Ted's blessing, I went to work for Nunn's campaign. I quickly realized that Louie wanted me to secure more than Fayette County, and he did not want to pay me. I met with Nunn regularly in Lexington, and I also traveled the commonwealth for his campaign. A crucial component of my job included convincing Cook's supporters to vote for Louie. This was challenging because Nunn's primary campaign had taken a negative tone, especially on the topic of religion. For example, when the two debated at Georgetown College (a Baptist institution), Nunn told the crowd, "I'm not going to make a big deal out of Marlow Cook's religion. He's a Catholic. I'm a Christian—a Baptist. I don't know why Cook wants to keep talking about religion." He regularly baited Cook with such statements.

In the general election, Nunn faced Democratic challenger Henry Ward. Ward was an upright man of integrity who had served as highway commissioner in the Breathitt administration, but he remained an outsider in his own party. He had defeated Happy Chandler in the Democratic primary, but that campaign had divided the Democratic base. Chandler was the more conservative southern Democrat who had already been elected governor twice (once in the 1930s and once in the 1950s). So Nunn made a deal with Chandler: Chandler would support Nunn, and Chandler's key operatives would be offered positions in the administration if Nunn won.

In early November Nunn asked me to meet him for dinner on the eve of the election. I sat for almost four hours with Louie and his right-hand man Warren Schweder, reviewing the odds in every county. We left knowing that Nunn had a good chance to be the first Republican governor in decades, but it would be close. The next day I drove to his campaign headquarters at the Brown Hotel in Louisville. John Duvall and I were news anchors reporting the election results for a statewide network I had put together just after the primary. While I remained nonpartisan on the air, the feeling of exuberance when we realized that Nunn would win was simply overwhelming. Nunn gave a brilliant acceptance speech, and I felt proud to have played a role in a winning campaign.

After Nunn's victory speech, I drove back to Lexington, ready to return to my business. The next morning I showed up at the office around 7:00 and went across the street to Clay's Diner for some coffee with the regulars. After talking about the hard-fought election for an hour, I headed back to the office. Shortly thereafter the governor-elect called and asked me to meet him at the Brown Hotel. When I said I needed to get back to work, he responded, "I've got something important to talk with you about, so go ask Ted if you think you need permission." When I asked what time I should be there, he said, "Any time you want, but I'd like you here at one o'clock."

When I arrived in Louisville, Nunn was there with Tom Emberton and Jim Watson. Louie sat me down and said, "Jim, I'll get right to the point. I'd like to make you the first member of my cabinet." Not sure what he had in mind, I pressed him for details. Nunn said he was organizing his leadership team in Frankfort and wanted me to be his commissioner of public information. He explained that I would oversee all of the state government's information services. When I said I thought his press secretary would assume these duties, Nunn replied that he wanted someone to dramatically improve communication among all branches of his office. I would have total authority on his behalf to interface with cabinet members and communicate his goals to the public. He wanted information services to provide a more coherent message from both commerce and tourism. The job would also entail overseeing photography, radio, television, and any audiovisual media utilized for state government.

Nunn was making a hard sell, so I said, "Don't you think I'm too young to do this?" He asked rhetorically, "Do you think you are too young?" I should have known better. Nunn had become Barren County judge at age twenty-nine—my current age. Nunn added, "I assumed you would take the job, so I've already prepared the press release." When I said I needed to run this by Ted, he answered, "I already have." Nunn essentially made it all but impossible to refuse.

When Nunn told me that my salary would be $18,000, I did some quick math and determined that I would still be able to make my home and car payments. Common practice at the time would have been to award state insurance contracts to my company, but I refused to do it. I told the governor-elect that I was worried about the conflict of interest. He asked, "What conflict?" When I asked if he planned to award state insurance contracts to Crain, Hard-

40

wick, & Host, he answered, "By God, that's how the system works!" I said I couldn't accept the contracts if I were involved in the government, so I would have to sell my share of the company. I still remember the look on his face when he said, "Well, that is very meritorious of you." I officially accepted the position before I left, becoming the youngest cabinet head in the history of the commonwealth.

After agreeing to join the governor's cabinet, I immediately began divesting myself of my business interests. I told Jack and Ted I needed to sell my share of the company. Ted looked at me and said, "Why would you do that? We are going to get a ton of business, and you will benefit from it!" I said it wouldn't be right and began to negotiate the buyout. I offered a price, and Ted said, "You're nuts, that's too much." He countered, and I said it was too low. So we agreed to meet in the middle. In one hour, I was out of the insurance business. I sold the homes I was building and my rental properties. Then I informed my friend Ken Hart at WLAP that I would no longer be available to broadcast games for the station. These sales provided a little extra financial cushion, which I needed with my new salary.

It is hard to imagine how busy I was even before assuming office. Each day I drove from Lexington to Louisville to help Nunn's transition team, even though I would not start earning a paycheck until after Nunn's inauguration on December 12, 1967. I attended the inauguration with my wife and parents. I remember the satisfaction I felt when I saw how proud my parents were. After the ceremony, there was much work to do. I had a steep learning curve since I had never held a government post. I surmised early on, however, that I needed to be in the good graces of Nunn's sister, Virginia. She served as his administrative assistant and, more important, was the gatekeeper for the governor. I got on her good side early.

I immediately learned about the role of political patronage in Kentucky. Governor Nunn had told me that I could hire whomever I wanted, and my first pick could not have happened in a more bizarre fashion. Early one morning, as I was driving from Lexington to Frankfort, I noticed a car stuck in the ditch on the side of the road near Versailles. I pulled over to see if I could help and found Ken Hart, my former boss. Ken was drunk—just plastered. One of the smartest and kindest people I knew, he simply could not keep his head when it came to alcohol and women. So I picked him up and said, "We're going to get you straight, and I want you to work in my office in Frankfort." Brilliant with communications, Ken was also good friends with Happy Chandler. Nunn had made an alliance with Chandler during the campaign, so I thought the hire would be a win across the board.

Ken had been working with me for a couple of days when Jim Watson, who worked in the governor's office, asked to meet with me. Watson brought along Loyd Murphy, one of the governor's aides. I did not know exactly what Jim and Loyd did for Nunn, and that was by design. They handled the cash and the backroom deals to get things done. Even the governor was in the dark in order to protect himself. They entered the room all stern looking, and Watson said, "Commissioner, you are off on the wrong foot." I asked, "Why?" He then asked, "Who is Ken Hart?" I explained how I knew Ken, and Watson informed me that he had not given his permission for me to hire Ken. I said, "The governor told me I could hire whoever I wanted." He retorted, "Nope. That's not how it works. Here is how you do it. . . ." The long and short of his explanation was that I had to clear every key hire through him.

After that meeting, I visited the governor, told him the story, and asked for an explanation. I will never forget what he said: "Let's get one thing straight. You can hire the people you want. I told you that. But don't hire the people you want." I said, "Governor, that doesn't make any sense!" He started laughing and said, "Nobody expected you to get this all straight immediately." Then he told me what steps I needed to take to navigate the patronage system and avoid any trouble. I told the governor that I had given Ken a job and I intended to keep him. He asked, "What happens if I say you can't?" I replied, "Then I'm gone." He grinned slightly and said he wanted me to stay, so I could keep Ken. From that point on, I followed the hiring protocol and had no trouble.

As I turned to leave, Governor Nunn added, "I do have a favor to ask of you. I want you to find an office for Happy, and I want you to take care of his people." Somewhat surprised, I said, "You want me to be the patronage head for Happy?" He answered in the affirmative. I had learned an important lesson regarding both Kentucky politics and Nunn's ability to manipulate situations and people to his advantage. I had agreed to a trade-off: keeping Ken Hart for accommodating former governor Happy Chandler.

I headed back to my office in the Capitol Annex to find space for Happy and his administrative assistant. I soon heard a commotion outside my office, and when I opened the door, there stood Chandler. He flexed his arm and said, "Partner, feel my muscle!" Then he grabbed me, gave me a bear hug, and asked, "Now, where's my office?" I showed him what I had in mind, and he said, "Oh, that's good. Now, I'm going to need an office for Bailey [his driver], and an office for Doris [his secretary], and an office for my friends when they visit." Before long, he had claimed nearly an entire wing. Then he handed me an extensive list of names and told me they all needed jobs. So, in addition to finding physical space for Chandler's posse, I had to infiltrate his people into the state government.

Having Happy around proved to be less of a burden than I anticipated. I enjoyed his larger-than-life personality. He came to my office during his first week and said, "Partner, I've got some advice for you." What he proceeded to tell me was somewhat vulgar, but it was valuable: "When people start throwing shit at you, just take your clothes off and let it slop all over you. Then get yourself a big terrycloth towel, wipe yourself off, put your clothes on, go on about your work, and don't worry about it." It would be many years before I fully understood the wisdom. When you try to lead transformative work, there will always be naysayers who trash you. The wisest course of action is to let it go and keep on pushing forward.

While the patronage practices frustrated me, I learned other lessons about "power politics" that actually benefited the people of the common-wealth. After only a few days in Frankfort, Louie called me into his office, sat me down, and said, "We have a problem. We aren't just broke. We are worse than broke, we owe money. We have a $24 million deficit that we didn't know about." During the era before computers, the governor's office maintained the budget on paper, and the public did not know about these fiscal woes.

Then the governor said he wanted to take me somewhere. His state trooper drove us from Frankfort to Kentucky Village, a correctional facility for juvenile delinquents that had been open since the turn of the century. The conditions were simply mortifying. The putrid stench of sewage permeated the place because of poor drainage. The bathrooms were covered in human waste and were beyond description. Overcome by the repulsive conditions, I actually vomited while touring the grounds. We spoke with several inmates who looked dirty and famished and smelled as bad as the facility did. Some of the young men reported that they had not eaten in days.

Before we left, Nunn started crying. I was too stunned to shed tears. I told the governor that these were the worst living conditions I had ever seen. He said he could show me worse and then stated, "I don't have any choice. I have to break my promise and raise taxes." He looked somber—even dejected. At the same time, I sensed a level of resolve in his voice when he said, "I've got one term to solve the horrible conditions in this state. I can't do it without raising taxes, but it will probably keep me from ever being elected to public office again."

I knew why the governor had taken me on that trip. I was the commissioner of public information, and he needed me to believe that a tax increase was the right thing to do. It worked. The governor planned to raise the sales tax from three to five cents. The next day, Nunn introduced me to Ivan Jett, a quintessential lobbyist who represented the retail industry in Kentucky. He sat down and stated matter-of-factly, "The governor says you and I are going to plot a strategy for selling the sales tax." Ivan looked and sounded like a soft-spoken country farmer, but he knew how to get things done. We made a list of the groups that would benefit the most from a sales tax increase and then determined which of those constituencies possessed the most political clout. Universities were at the top of the list, so we encouraged the governor to meet with all the presidents of the public colleges. Nunn showed them their estimated budget increases with the higher sales tax and then promised to cut their budgets if the proposed tax failed. They all supported the tax increase.

Ivan knew the legislators, and I learned about them quickly. We lined up the votes and then determined who needed to be pressured and what they could be given in return for a "yes" vote on the tax. For example, the Democratic representative from Madisonville, Bill Cox, had not agreed to support the increase. Nunn called him into his office and promised to put a community college in the budget but then asked rhetorically, "Do you know what a line-item veto is?" Nunn had the words "community college" written on a sheet of paper. He looked at Bill as he crossed out those words with a marker and said, "This is exactly what will happen if you don't vote for this." To pick up votes in northern Kentucky, the governor promised a public college that became Northern Kentucky University. For Louisville and Jefferson County he agreed to bring the struggling, municipally funded University of Louisville into the state system.

Sometimes the fighting got rough. I remember Representative Carroll Hubbard from western Kentucky coming to the governor's office. Nunn promised to use the line-item veto to cut every bit of "pork" that had been going to Hubbard's district. The son of a Baptist minister, Hubbard literally fell to his knees and begged the governor not to cut his funding. Nunn said, "There is one way for you to solve this. Vote for the sales tax!" Hubbard got on board, as did many others after intense meetings with the governor.

Ivan and I tried to stay out in front of the message. This included helping the governor spread the message in his speeches, which we had a hand in crafting. When he presented the official budget to the legislature in early 1968, he asked, "Would you have me do what is politically expedient or would you have me do what is best for the well-being of all our people?" He continued, "I have done what the time, circumstances, and conditions demanded I do. To do otherwise, I would not be worthy of the office I hold." That was the message in a nutshell. Nobody wanted a tax increase, but the state was broke. The governor got his increase because he knew when and where to pressure certain politicians, and we knew how to sell it. The two-cent tax increase allowed Kentucky to make tremendous strides in mental health, education, economic development, tourism, the penal system, and industry.

I had many other duties beyond selling the sales tax. When the governor fired his press secretary, he asked me to fill in and do "double duty." This was when I learned how to function on four hours of sleep a night, often crashing on a cot in my office. Each day had a full itinerary of events for both the governor and my public information office, and without the amazing help of some talented employees, we never could have achieved our goals. I eventually convinced Nunn to hire Larry Van Hoose as his press secretary, so I could go back to one job.

Some of the most important public relations reforms transformed the relationship between the press and the state government. We instituted a "message repeater," allowing reporters to stay current on what was happening in Frankfort. Each day, and up to three times a day, we recorded a two- or three-minute message about the most pressing issues in state government. All media members could call a phone number, listen to the recorded message, and immediately have something to talk or write about. Once we got the budget passed, we added a half-hour news briefing each week where members of the press had an opportunity to ask us questions on current issues. Although commonplace today, at the time it was an essential innovation. We also expanded the television and radio presence of the governor's office.

Called on to promote tourism and industry in Kentucky, I contacted *Fortune* magazine to see what kind of discount we could get if the state took out a large promotional spread. We initially agreed to pay *Fortune* a discounted rate for twelve pages and planned to sell ad space to Kentucky businesses to cover the cost. What seemed risky at the time became a huge success. What we were able to charge businesses amounted to more than the wholesale price we paid.

The state made money off the deal, and we made history by having the largest advertising spread in *Fortune*'s history. It was well over fifty pages by the time all the businesses had signed up for their individual advertisements. The idea paid dividends, leading to clear growth in business and tourism. It went over so well that we replicated the concept in *Forbes*.

I learned about the political manipulation and backstabbing that went on in government through personal experience. After a couple months in my role, I went over to the governor's office to see him. Virginia was not at her desk, so I walked in. When I entered, I found Nunn meeting with highway commissioner Bill Hazelrigg and Paul Fyffe, a radio station manager in Paintsville whom I had met while building the Kentucky Central Network. Louie looked stunned, so I apologized and left. I immediately put the puzzle pieces together. Hazelrigg had run as Nunn's lieutenant governor in the primary, and even though Louie had won, Bill had lost. The governor had rewarded him with a commissioner's post, but Hazelrigg wanted to bring his supporters into the cabinet to give himself more power. Bill disliked me because he wanted to issue his own press reports and get his name publicized. My job was to centralize such communications and make sure the governor's name was on them. I constantly told Bill "no," and he hated it.

I knew that Hazelrigg was trying to persuade the governor to replace me with Paul Fyffe. During the next few hours, I convinced myself that I was about to get fired and consoled myself with the fact that I could go back to Lexington and start making money again. Sure enough, the governor asked me back to his office. When I walked in, I just blurted out, "Governor, if you want me to leave, I'm prepared to go." He chuckled and asked, "How'd you know that's what we were talking about?" I said, "I could just sense it." To my relief, Louie said, "If you think I'm going to get rid of you, you're out of your mind. Hazelrigg will be gone in a few months. You are doing everything right. Your job is to promote the governor, and by God, you are doing it the right way. You aren't going anywhere!" He told me not to tell anyone about the conversation, to which I replied, "Who in the hell am I going to tell?" He laughed, and that was it. A few months later, Hazelrigg was out of a job.

Nunn was a master politician. Once the governor determined that Hazelrigg was interested only in self-promotion, he deflected criticism onto his highway commissioner. The governor would have a group of people in his office who wanted some highway paved, and he would call me in and say, in front of everyone, "Go tell Hazelrigg that I want that road built! I don't want it done in two hours. I want it built right now, dammit!" I would say, "Yes sir," and exit. Then a few minutes later he would call me and say, "I don't want that damn road built. Don't call Hazelrigg." This scenario played out repeatedly.

One of the greatest legacies of the Nunn administration came at the hands of my college professor and mentor Len Press. He had been an invaluable resource during my time at UK. Press had become active in founding and promoting Kentucky Educational Television (KET). Governor Combs had authorized the creation of KET in the early 1960s, and Governor Breathitt had funded the construction of a building, but KET had never become operational because nobody appropriated money to support the broadcasting work.

After I had been in office a short time, Len asked me for help. He and his wife Lil were die-hard Democrats from New England. He had had enough trouble dealing with Kentucky Democrats, and now with a Republican in the governor's office, he had no connections to keep things moving. I asked him to come down to Frankfort, and we outlined an argument for funding KET. He returned home and prepared a presentation.

When Len returned to Frankfort with his presentation, we walked over to the governor's office. Even though we did not have an appointment, Virginia managed to get us on the schedule. Before we went in, I grabbed Len and warned him, "We've got a shot, but I have no idea how the governor will respond." As usual, when I walked in Nunn greeted me by saying, "Host, what are you selling?" I asked, "Governor, do you know anything about Kentucky Educational Television?" He chirped, "I don't like it!" Then he explained his opposition to something that used taxpayer money and hurt commercial television in the process.

Undeterred by the negativity, Len sat down across from the governor with all his poster boards in tote. Louie walked around his desk, shook Len's hand, and said, "Why don't you go around and sit in my chair." Len took the governor's chair and started his presentation. Louie kept interrupting with questions, which Len took in stride. Len managed to share his three main points: KET would improve education in Kentucky by providing GED programs, it would make the legislature more transparent by televising its sessions, and, finally, it would provide Nunn and future governors the opportunity to address the people of the commonwealth directly on issues of key importance. Near the end of the brief presentation, the governor turned to me and asked, "Well, what do you think?" I said, "Forget the politics. He's one of the best people I've ever been around." I added that his wife was a key player in the mental health field, which Nunn wanted to transform. I said, "Len and Lil can do good things for Kentucky." Then he asked Len how much money he needed, and Press answered $5 million. Nunn said, "I'll see what I can do," and then he excused us.

Governor Nunn ended up putting $4.5 million in the budget for KET, and the legislature approved it. Later that year, on September 23, 1968, KET went live on the air, and Kentuckians across the commonwealth could tune in to their public broadcasting network.

One other important development involved the horse industry. During the summer of 1968, all the horse farm managers in central Kentucky decided to close their gates to visitors. Until then, private horse farms had graciously allowed people to come in and look at the horses and have picnics on the grounds if they desired. This was a huge part of the horse tourism industry. which attracted at least 125,000 people to central Kentucky annually.

I invited horse farm managers to a meeting and learned that they were closing their farms because an arsonist had been burning down stables. They had a clear problem, so I pitched an alternative: find a location off the interstate where tourists could park their cars or RVs and go on a tour of a horse farm. The private horse farms could rotate the days on which each one would be open. The newspapers ran articles about my proposals, and two important individuals contacted me. Fayette County judge Joe Johnson asked if I was searching for a farm that the state could purchase. I said, "Not yet, but we will need to." Johnson told me that L. V. "Harky" Edwards was in financial trouble and would be willing to sell his part of the Nichols family farm, Walnut Hall Stud. I visited Harky, and he confirmed this. I said we needed a state appraisal, and he replied, "I'll sell it for the appraisal price." This was a stunning offer, considering the storied history of the farm. It also provided an opportunity to expand the idea to include a model horse farm at the location.

When news spread about the possibility of a model horse farm, I received another important call from John Gaines (during my stint as a real estate agent, I had sold his Gainesway Farm a few years earlier). John said, "I'd like to talk with you about your idea for a horse park." We met for dinner at Pete Flynn's restaurant, just outside of Frankfort. John was a well-connected and intelligent visionary. However, he was very exacting and quite confrontational. If someone did not agree with his vision, he usually moved on to someone else. While we talked, John kept calling it a "Thoroughbred horse park." I interrupted and said, "This is not going to be a *Thoroughbred* horse park. It will be a park honoring *all* horses." Gaines retorted, "Well, I'm not going to be involved unless it's a Thoroughbred park." I said, "Well, that's too bad, because it's going to be the Kentucky Horse Park." He grinned, conveying that he was proud of my strong stance even though he disagreed. Then he said, "Okay, then, let's figure out how we are going to do it."

We spent three hours at a corner table strategizing about how to make this idea a reality. I wrote down what we needed to do on the back of an envelope. I envisioned a model horse farm and track where visitors could learn about the horse industry. It would also be a gathering place for group tours throughout central Kentucky, and hopefully it would attract various entities in the horse industry to move their national or international headquarters to the Bluegrass. We knew it needed to be in Fayette County and on a major highway, preferably along one of the new interstates around Lexington. Then we divided responsibilities to get the political backing we would need to fund the project.

The stars were aligning, but I needed to get the governor's approval, or else the project would die. When I slipped into his office, Nunn asked his regular question: "What are you selling today?" I said, "I've got an idea for you." But before I could continue, he said, "Well, I'm not listening unless you come with me." When I asked where he was going, he said, "Saginaw, Michigan, to give a speech on behalf of Congressman Gerald Ford." So we boarded a state-leased jet, and once we were in the air, the governor asked me to proofread his speech. He gave a great speech in support of Ford, and then we headed back to Kentucky. Still, he had not asked me what I wanted to discuss with him. After he had consumed a couple bourbons, I said, "Governor, I've got an idea that I think could be one of your crowning achievements." I told him about the model farm and then went through the steps needed to make it happen. Nunn did not say much about it until we got off the plane. As we were parting ways, he looked at me and said, "How much is this going to cost?" I said, "My best guess is between thirty and forty million." Without any hesitation he said, "Go for it." That was all I needed to hear.

I immediately called John Gaines and told him the governor approved. Gaines was going to discuss the plan with Kentucky House Speaker Julian Carroll. He got back to me a couple of days later and told me that Julian was on board, so we went to see Representative William "Boom Boom" Kenton. We had no problem winning him over, since we wanted to locate the park in Fayette County, where he lived.

Governor Nunn created the Horse Park Authority, which I chaired. We added numerous key members from the horse industry who served as advisers to the project. This group hired Ted Broida from Spindletop Research to conduct an economic analysis. We also managed to convince John Volpe, who had been governor of Massachusetts and was then serving as Nixon's secretary of transportation, to approve a spur off I-75 that would provide access to the Horse Park. Volpe had attended the Republican Governors' Conference in Lexington (discussed later) and had developed a close relationship with Nunn. When we visited him in Washington and asked for the spur, he looked across the table and said, "Consider it done." By the time the state legislative session took place, we had everything aligned, and the project went through with a bond issue. We started with 800 acres and eventually added another 400.

While I was working day and night on the Horse Park, Nunn summoned me to the governor's mansion, where I met him and his wife, Beula. Nunn, who had been the first governor to publicly support Nixon, played a leadership role in the Republican Governors Association and had used those connections to bring the next Republican Governors' Conference to Kentucky. He said, "I need you to plan and run it." First I needed to raise a quarter of a million dollars to host the event, because we could not use state money for the conference. We raised funds from wealthy Republican "power players," and even a few Democrats chipped in and offered assistance.

Then the governor decided that, since the governors would be in town for Derby Day, he wanted to add a fifth floor to the grandstands at Churchill Downs. I met with Lynn Stone, the president and CEO of Churchill Downs, who liked the idea. So we worked with business leaders at the racetrack to add another level to the historic grandstands that would meet the security needs of high-profile politicians and dignitaries. In future years, the fifth floor also elevated the luxury hospitality section of the racetrack, providing a new location for VIPs attending the Kentucky Derby or the Breeders' Cup.

With these two tasks well in hand, I turned my attention to the myriad details of the conference and its social events. For a few weeks I literally lived in the Campbell House, a historic hotel in Lexington that would serve as the event's headquarters. My staff and I worked on each day's itinerary, conference schedule, social events, and any specific concerns or needs of the individual governors. The overall conference had an itinerary, and each event had a logistics itinerary as well.

When the day of the conference arrived, we welcomed thirty-two Republican governors to Kentucky. Limousines adorned with their state flags transported the governors, and we also hoisted the flags of each state in front of the Campbell House. Ken Hart, my local go-to guy, and Lyn Nofziger, then Governor Ronald Reagan's director of communications, helped coordinate each day's political strategy sessions, breakout meetings, and keynote addresses. Vice President Spiro Agnew attended the conference and gave a speech. Governor Reagan provided excellent leadership for the conference. Everything went off without a hitch. We concluded the official meeting with a ball at the Phoenix Hotel.

Derby Day arrived with perfect weather as we took the governors to Spindletop Hall for a Kentucky-themed brunch with mint juleps and Bloody Marys. Then a long motorcade transported the group to Louisville for the Derby. We had host families traveling with each of the governors. As they entered the new fifth floor at Churchill Downs, each governor was met with a personal attendant for the day at the races. No doubt, the success of the conference played a significant role in developing new political connections for Kentuckians in Washington.

Those first months in Frankfort quickly turned into years. In addition to the high-profile reforms we made and projects we completed, each day offered a full slate of activities. I became involved with the Travel Industry of America, and we created the Southern State Travel Directors Association. At its first annual meeting in Lexington, we developed ways to promote tourism across the Southeast. Most of us were simply trying to get people from the northern states and Canada to stop in our various states on their way to the beach. We included tourism directors from Canada in every way possible, and that was a boon to the industry on both sides of the border.

Activities related to the civil rights movement and the Vietnam War placed great pressure on the Department of Public Information. The governor needed to address protests, and my department was at the forefront in articulating his message. In this regard, it was very important that we send the same message in our press releases to various media outlets. At the same time, we continued to move forward with Nunn's agenda. To help with these initiatives, the governor employed what he called the "Kitty Corps"—a group of young and ambitious liaisons assigned to the cabinet heads. My liaison was Bob Metry. These individuals kept the governor's office apprised of what was going on in each department. The Kitty Corps attended all cabinet meetings, but they also met with the governor almost every morning to report on each sector's activities. Because of this, Bob Metry and I spent a great deal of time together, and I developed relationships with other members of this group as well. Each of them had an incredible work ethic, and they wanted to get things accomplished.

When the governor learned that something was going on in a specific department, he would often call in the commissioner and ask for more details. When Nunn called me in, he often invited Larry Forgy, the deputy commissioner of finance. Larry was extremely bright and articulate. Both of us supported the governor and the Republican Party, but it seemed that we always took opposing stances on the issues. Nunn enjoyed pitting us against each other. I think he liked the entertainment value, but he also used our debates to better understand the contentious portions of any potential legislation or policy.

After two years of burning the candle at both ends, I visited the governor in his office and said, "I've been here two years, and it's time for me to leave." I explained that I had worked my staff so hard that they were simply out of gas. Louie said, "You think you are going someplace?" I tried to explain the situation, but he simply told me, "You can't leave." He said Bob Gable, the commissioner of parks, was leaving his position, so I could replace him. Once again, Louie's persuasion prevailed, and I agreed to the new job.

With the tax increase in 1968, the Parks Department finally had money to expand. My first order of business entailed visiting each state park to assess its strengths and weaknesses. I also visited potential sites for new parks. As I shared my plans with the governor, it became evident that he intended any expansions to be political in nature. He had a map of the entire state, and the counties that had voted for him were targeted for park development. In that first year we constructed Greenbo Lodge, the Barren River State Park Lodge in the governor's home county, and the Lodge at Lake Cumberland.

During this time, Beula Nunn invited me to the mansion to discuss her desire to save the Mary Todd Lincoln House in downtown Lexington. She explained that it was owned by a hardware store and was slated for demolition. After we visited the house, she said, "Young man, I will help you however I can, but you need to get the money to purchase and preserve that home!" Then she took me to Limestone Avenue and said, "That old building is Henry Clay's original law office. We need to save that too." She suggested that I create a foundation and added, "Young man, I know you will find a way to get the money." So we formed the Kentucky Mansions Preservation Foundation, raised money, and purchased the properties for preservation.

Mrs. Nunn also wanted White Hall, the former home of Cassius Marcellus Clay, renovated and added to the state parks system. The antebellum mansion was well known for its advanced plumbing and central heating system, not to mention the cannon on the second floor, which Clay had installed for protection from pro-slavery renegades trying to kill him. By the 1960s, the home had fallen into disrepair, and some of Clay's heirs, the Bennett family, donated the house to the state in 1968. So I did as Kentucky's first lady directed.

As I settled into my role as parks commissioner, two important developments occurred. The first involved contract bidding on state parks. I learned that Kentucky operated "force accounts" for projects that needed to be accomplished quickly. In our sector, this meant that for any emergency construction, contractors had only twenty-four hours to submit a bid. Looking at the list of force accounts for work done at the state parks, I realized that only three companies were making bids in western Kentucky. On each bid, two companies came in at about the same price, and the third company bid a slightly lower amount. After going through a stack of contracts, I saw a clear pattern: the first company would win a contract, then the second, then the third. The pattern repeated itself throughout the entire file.

I had a hunch there were some underhanded dealings, but I did not know where to look, so I called J. E. Owens, who oversaw finances for the state parks, into my office. He was a "nonmerit" employee, which meant that I could fire him. J. E. had been a fraternity brother of mine at UK, and he was an honest person. I asked him to have a seat and said, "Your job is safe as long as you tell me everything about the department, starting with these force accounts." He replied, "Why are you asking?" I told him that something seemed wrong and added, "If there is something going on here, I'm going to get rid of the cancer." He kind of chuckled and said, "I'll help you." So he told me what he knew and what he suspected: the district director for western Kentucky, Volney Brien, was doing something illegal.

Volney Brien had been a Democratic political operative in his region for years, but during Henry Ward's term as highway commissioner, Brien lost his job. When Nunn ran against Ward, he used Brien's disdain for Ward to his advantage, asking Brien to secure Democratic votes in the western part of the state. After Nunn won the governorship, Brien was rewarded with a job overseeing state parks in western Kentucky. District directors knew about the force accounts, and Owens believed that Brien was working with the contractors, allowing them to inflate the bids on force accounts and keep the money. Of course, this was only Owens's theory. Without my help and protection, he had no power to question or challenge this politically.

After listening to Owens, I met with state police commissioner Bill Newman, shared my concerns, and asked whether he would be willing to run an investigation without informing the governor's office. He looked at me and said, "You don't want Watson and Murphy knowing about this, right? I'll be glad to!" Bill understood that nobody challenged Watson and Murphy because those two operated as bullies. A few weeks later, while playing golf at a Republican fund-raising event in Owensboro, Newman drove up on a golf cart and said, "Commissioner, I've got your information. It's worse than we thought." Newman had secured evidence that Volney Brien was working with all three contractors. They were overcharging by 20 percent on all force accounts and splitting the profits.

I asked Newman if he had spoken with the governor, and he had not. So I immediately went to a phone, called Brien, and said, "Volney, I'm suspending you." He asked, "What for?" I answered, "You've been stealing." He said, "You don't have any proof," to which I replied, "I've got the evidence in my hand, and. . . ." He interrupted me and said, "It's not true. You don't have the right to do it." Raising my voice, I said, "I'm the commissioner of parks, so I can do what I want as long as it's honest!" I told him he had the right to appeal, but the suspension was solely my decision. Then he hung up on me.

Back in Frankfort, Jim Watson had called me. Before I called him back, I invited Ken Hart into my office to be a witness to the phone conversation. Once I got him on the phone, Watson started yelling, "You don't have the right to suspend Volney Brien!" I told him that I had requested an investigation and that I had evidence of corruption and fraud. Watson said, "You can't do that without my permission!" I asked, "Is that right?" He retorted, "Are you questioning me?" I replied, "No, I just want to make sure I understood what you just said: are you saying that if I don't put him back to work you're going to fire me?" He said, "That's what I'm telling you." I said, "Fine. Consider me fired, because I'm going to the third floor of the capitol [where the media congregated], and I'm going to tell the press exactly what happened. I don't care." Honestly, I wasn't playing around. If I couldn't control my own sector, I would leave. Watson backed off after that threat: "Well, just wait a minute,

Commissioner, before you do anything drastic." I told him, "If the governor wants to talk to me about it, have him call me."

The governor called me into his office a few days later and said, "Do you know what you've done? You've really upset a lot of people!" I asked him if he wanted to fire me, and he said no. However, he did say, "You may think you've done the right thing . . ." but he never completed the sentence. His tone clearly conveyed that he didn't like my actions making his political life more challenging, even if I had stopped corruption.

Before I fired Brien, I asked Don Harkins, director of the Legislative Research Commission, to meet with me. When he entered my office, I asked him whether he had a recorder on him, and when he said "no," I inquired whether he would be offended if I searched him. I was nervous the information I was about to share would somehow be spun to place the blame on me. He promised that he was not recording our conversation, and I took him at his word. Don was honest, but as a Democrat, his party could benefit if people lied about me. I needed him to keep the information confidential until I fired Brien, and he agreed. That trust led to a friendship that would benefit me later in life.

The next week I fired Volney Brien publicly and laid out all the reasons for his termination. Then the governor called a special cabinet meeting. When he walked into the room, he pointed at me and said, "I want everyone here to know that Commissioner Host kept this administration from a major scandal, and I want to applaud him for it." Murphy and Watson were seething with anger. The governor talked about my courage, and every insider in the room knew that I had taken on the corruption in Kentucky politics and won. That investigation helped the state, but it probably harmed my political career. After the meeting, Murphy came up to me and said, "If you ever try to run for office, we will bury you." I never even acknowledged the comment.

A few weeks later, Governor Nunn called a meeting with Tom Emberton, Gene Goss, Bob Gable, and me. He began by discussing some of the current items on his agenda, such as devising ways to get legislation passed. All at once Louie said, "One of you is going to be the next governor." At that time, governors in Kentucky could serve only one term, so incumbents often tried to choose their successors. Nunn concluded, "Whoever can go out and get the most support is going to get my support." We all discussed the matter for a while, expressing our deference to the governor and thanking him for his support. Then the meeting adjourned.

When Governor Nunn said that I had a chance to be the next governor, I took it to heart. I was thirty-two years old, and I couldn't imagine anything more exhilarating. All I needed to do was make sure I had the strongest support. Finally, it appeared that the decision to leave my business in Lexington for a government job in Frankfort might pay off.

5

Running for Office and Running a Business

After Nunn's comment about the possibility of me being governor, I called Ken Hart and a couple others into my office and said, "Let's put a campaign together right now." Ken devised a brilliant plan that involved finding influential individuals in key parts of the state and having them call the governor's office and express their support for me.

A few days later, while flying to a meeting in West Virginia, the pilot told me the governor wanted me to call him when we landed. When I did, Louie said, "What in the hell are you doing? All these calls supporting you for governor are melting the switchboard. I DID NOT tell you to do that!" I responded, "Governor, that's exactly what you said." He retorted, "Well, that isn't what I meant. You'll be on the ticket, but as lieutenant governor. I'm not telling you who's at the top of the ticket yet." I knew it was Tom Emberton and said so to Louie. He asked, "How did you know that?" That was all I needed to hear. After my uncovering of the parks scandal, it was clear to the governor that he couldn't control me, and at the time, I wondered whether that was why he chose Emberton for the top of the ticket and me for the second spot.

After a few weeks of campaigning, I realized that I couldn't run the way I wanted to unless I did it full time, so I resigned as parks commissioner. I had absolutely no problem winning the primary campaign for lieutenant governor (at the time, Kentucky still elected the governor and lieutenant governor separately). As we moved into the general election, I traversed the state, giving speeches on how Emberton and I would improve the commonwealth if elected.

Republican strategists quickly learned that Emberton was a gentle statesman, whereas I was a fighter. So they often sent me to debate Wendell Ford, the incumbent lieutenant governor and Democratic candidate for governor. Ford and I were both feisty, verbally fighting on the issues. Wendell nicknamed me "Bubbles" because I had put a bubblelike dome over the pool at General Butler State Park so that it could remain open year-round. In turn, I called him "Swindle Fraud." Both of us got pretty riled up during our debates, but we remained cordial after sparring. Happy Chandler cut into some of our support by running on his own Commonwealth Party ticket, but he would only play the role of spoiler.

I was thirty-three years old at the time, and the Democrats attacked my youth and inexperience. I tried to spin this to my advantage and argued that I had fought the corruption of career politicians. Ford effectively used the tax increase against us, even though he knew the state desperately needed the revenue it produced. He incessantly criticized "Nunn's nickel" and accused Republicans of raising taxes on hardworking people. It was a brilliant strategy because we spent much of the campaign on the defensive. Ford attacked us, knowing that, if elected governor, he would benefit from the additional funds.

The entire campaign felt like uphill sledding. The Republican Party brought in St. Louis campaign consultant Roy Pfautch, who tried to find some way to promote Tom Emberton. Since the governor and lieutenant governor were elected separately, we cooperated but communicated less than we should have. This became apparent when I walked into Pfautch's office and sitting on his desk was an Emberton-Carroll bumper sticker. Julian Carroll was the Democratic candidate for lieutenant governor, and Pfautch (with Governor Nunn's support) had tried to cut a deal with Carroll's campaign to support Tom for governor. I cannot prove this, but I believe Watson and Murphy pushed to divide the ticket so that I had no chance of winning.

Despite these deals, some people still thought I could win, and various moneyed interests were eager to try to buy my allegiance. For example, Garvice Kincaid invited me to his office during the campaign. When I arrived, Clyde Mauldin and Al Florence (Kincaid's personal money man) were in the room. Garvice said, "My people tell me you are going to win because you are working harder than anyone they have ever seen. They say you are going to run the governor's office. Is that true?" I said, "I don't think so." He said, "Well, that is what my people say." Garvice proceeded to lift a sack full of cash onto his desk. He said, "I know you don't have any money. I want you to take this. I don't want anything in return other than when you win, I just want to be able to call you from time to time." He reminded me that he had given me my first break on the Kentucky Central Network and asked whether I would be in my current position if not for him. I said, "I suspect I would not." Then he said, "Well, I want you to take this bag in appreciation." When I refused, he snorted and said, "Do you know how many people have been in this office and have graciously received money like this?" I just said, "I'm sorry. I am not like other people." He concluded, "No you are not. This meeting is over!" I was escorted out of his office.

With these various challenges, I didn't think I could win, but I still worked as hard as possible to get votes. On election night, I was in the lieutenant governor's suite hoping for the best. A large crowd had assembled, and my wife Carolyn joined me publicly for the first time during the campaign. As the results rolled in, it became apparent that I was going to lose, and people began to offer their condolences and leave. When the room was empty except for me, Carolyn, and my parents, Louie Nunn walked in. My dad, who had consumed a little too much bourbon, lit into Governor Nunn and told him off for not fully supporting me. Dad never really understood the political game. He was a tough old guy who was too honest and loyal. I jumped in and said, "Dad, that's enough. Governor, I really appreciate all that you have done for me." Then I went downstairs and gave my concession speech.

After I gave that speech, I decided that I was done with politics. I made up my mind never to run for office again. I had witnessed too many underhanded dealings, and I knew that I could never play that game. I wanted to do it the right way, and if I couldn't do that and still win, then I was done.

Nunn's support of splitting the ticket in western Kentucky bothered me, but I understood why he did it. A master politician, he wanted to preserve his legacy. The way to do that in Kentucky was to make deals to keep a Republican in the governor's office. The deals were made, but the Republicans still fell short because of the sales tax increase. Kentucky remained overwhelmingly Democratic, and Wendell Ford was the perfect southern Democrat; he tapped into the old "New Deal Democrat" votes in the state and won the governorship. As the national Democratic Party turned further left in the years ahead, Republicans gained in Kentucky and throughout the South. Maybe I ran two decades too early.

During those four years, I learned so much from Louie Nunn. He was one of the most charismatic figures I knew; he loved playing "the game" and was good at it. His incredible sense of humor complemented his biting wit. He could focus on the big picture and small details at the same time. He was also a master of people and personal relations. He knew how to work a room, he knew how to give a speech, and he knew how to get what he wanted from virtually every elected official. He used reason and force to get his message across. He was not afraid to spar with anyone, but he also knew when to back off. After losing the election, I was disenchanted with Kentucky politics and the prevalence of unethical deals to get things done. However, I still wanted to be able to cast a vision and sell it the way Louie did.

The sting of losing an election after working so hard is difficult to explain, but I'm certain others who have run for public office and lost understand this emotion. Even so, I learned important lessons that stayed with me for the rest of my life. First, it is virtually impossible to win an election on a ticket that has supported a tax increase. Second, successful leadership requires the ability to tolerate criticism, but in most political environments, one has to thrive on criticism and enjoy the fight. I love a challenge, but I have never been a fan of negativity. Back then, at my young age, I had the energy, but I lacked the wisdom. I did too much shooting from the hip and not enough work crafting my message. My running mate, Tom Emberton, was (and still is) a terrific human being, but I believe he was too gentle and kind to make it in politics. He ended up serving as a judge on the Kentucky State Court of Appeals, which suited him much better, and we remained lifelong friends.

While campaigning, I learned that the rural parts of the state are focused on finding the financial benefits (or "pork") to be gained from the growing urban areas. Generally speaking, the rural interests control the legislature. The "golden triangle" of Louisville, Lexington, and northern Kentucky provides the overwhelming majority of the state's revenue. For example, approximately forty cents of every tax dollar coming from the Louisville metro area goes to the rest of the state. The small amount of tax revenue provided by rural areas is unbelievably disproportionate to the money they demand in return. This is financially unsustainable, but people still vote for politicians with shortsighted plans to get what they can from the state's urban areas. This has hindered development. Promoting even greater growth of Kentucky's cities would expand the state's budget and allow for more spending across the commonwealth, but it is simply not an approach that wins elections.

Another life lesson I learned in politics is that when it comes to criticism and personal attacks, it is simply wiser to keep your mouth shut and go about your work. Since many good people feel differently about specific political issues, it is important to keep an open mind and learn that it is possible to disagree without being disagreeable. It is far easier to criticize and toss someone aside than it is to find common interests. Ultimately, it is better for people who find themselves at odds to learn to work together. It is better in personal relationships, in politics, and in business—but it is not easy.

I had decided at the beginning of my campaign not to ask people for money. If someone offered it, I accepted, but I never engaged in fund-raising. I simply did not like the idea of asking people to support me financially. Instead, I spent more than $200,000 of my personal savings and borrowed $75,000 from Jake Graves at Second National Bank in Lexington. After the election I owed him that money and had only $107 in the bank. This made me anxious, and I knew I needed to find a solution to my economic dilemma quickly.

Back home after my concession speech, Carolyn and I were sitting on the side of our bed. She asked, "What are we going to do? Are we going to take a vacation?" I said, "No, I'm going to work tomorrow." She inquired what I was going to do, and I answered, "Honestly, I have no idea." I needed to figure it out.

In the morning I drove down to Richmond Road in Lexington and ended up at Ray's Barbershop. He told me the tenants in the office above his shop had moved out, and he thought the landlord might give me a good deal. Since my father-in-law owned the space, he gave it to me rent free for one month, but he let me know that after thirty days I would need to start making payments. Then I asked Ray if I could list the pay phone in his barbershop as my office phone. With only $107 to my name, and I simply couldn't afford the deposit to have a phone installed. He agreed.

During that first week I accepted an offer to organize a special-election campaign. Congressman John Watts of Nicholasville had died in office, leaving the seat in the Sixth Congressional District vacant. Labe Jackson Sr., a Chandler Democrat who had become a Republican in 1968, was running against John B. Breckinridge for Watts's seat. Jackson paid me to run his campaign, which kept me afloat for a couple of months. We ran a good campaign but lost. However, those weeks bought me some time to make plans for the future of my business.

I still had my real estate and insurance licenses, even though I had sold my share of the insurance company I had helped build. One day as I sat in my office above Ray's Barbershop, I wrote out a list of my assets and liabilities. On the assets side I listed college sports, tourism, sales, and communications. On the liabilities side I had just one item: no money. Since I couldn't do anything about being broke, I decided to focus on the strengths I had listed and solicit business in those areas.

Fortunately, my first long-term job fell right into my lap. Newly elected Lexington mayor Foster Pettit and county judge executive Robert Stephens invited me to a lunch meeting and offered me a job as the first executive direc- tor of the Lexington Tourist and Convention Commission. The posted qualifi- cations included three years' experience with the tourism industry, and I was the only person they knew who met that stipulation. In an odd twist of fate, I had actually helped create this requirement when I worked in Frankfort be- cause I did not want such positions filled by nepotism or political patronage.

Pettit and Stephens offered me $18,000 annually, along with benefits, a car, an office, and funding for an administrative assistant. I told them they could not hire me, but they could hire my new company. I said I would take the $1,500 a month as a retainer for my company, but they did not have to provide anything else. I proposed that they hire me for six months and then, if they were not pleased with my work, they could hire someone else. However, I requested the first $1,500 immediately because I was broke. They agreed, writing the first check that day. This arrangement allowed me to pursue addi- tional business clients.

I immediately took the check to Jake Graves, who had loaned me $75,000 during my campaign. Jake was a southern country gentleman. When I walked in, he had his feet up on the desk. He wore high-laced shoes and a button-down shirt with a diamond stickpin through his tie. A spittoon sat next to his desk. He offered his typical greeting: "Hey, podner! How are ya?" I handed him the check and said I was ready to get back to work and pay off my debt. He asked what I planned to do, and I told him that I had no idea. He opened up the top drawer of his desk and pulled out an old deposit slip with the carbon paper underneath. He said, "I'm going to give you a $10,000 advance, so you can get your business going. I'll give you six months before you need to start making payments on the interest." He simply asked me to provide weekly updates on my accomplishments and what I intended to do in the week ahead. Then he told me that I needed to incorporate my business for liability protection. I didn't know what to do other than thank him for his generosity and wisdom.

I walked out of Graves's office and down the street to Don Harkins's law office. Don had become a close friend and confidant when he was working at the Legislative Research Commission and I was uncovering corruption in state government. Don walked me through the paperwork of incorporation and then said, "All we need to do is name your company. What is it going to be?" I admitted that I was the lone employee but wanted to sound influential, so I decided on Jim Host & Associates. He smiled and said, "Okay, I will put it down."

A few days later, my old fraternity sponsor and mentor Jim Shropshire took me to lunch. He said he hadn't donated anything to my campaign because he didn't want to see me in politics. He added, "I am truly sorry you lost, but I believe it will end up being the best thing that could have happened to you." He proceeded to hand me a $1,000 check to get me on my feet. I told him I couldn't accept the check as a gift but I would take it as an investment and make him the first outside shareholder in my company.

I then set out to develop a strategy for my work with the Lexington Tourist and Convention Commission (LTCC). Most of the LTCC board members were hotel owners looking to expand Lexington tourism. I called our first meeting and handed out an agenda. Then my old insurance partner (and Kentuckian Hotel owner) Ted Hardwick spoke up. "Jim, let me tell you why we hired you." He explained that Lexington had a multimillion-dollar federal grant for urban renewal, which former mayor Fred Fugazzi had secured. The urban-renewal grant stipulated that HUD would provide 75 percent of the funding, and the city would contribute 25 percent of in-kind expenses. A friend of Vice President Hubert Humphrey, Fugazzi had traveled to DC and devised an arrangement whereby Lexington would be forgiven its 25 percent of the grant if it constructed a convention center and arena in a zone targeted for urban renewal. Now, the city had used the funding to demolish the old train station, remove the tracks, and knock down several dilapidated buildings. If Lexington failed to build a convention center, it would owe HUD $3.5 million to cover its 25 percent of the grant. The hotel owners wanted the convention center for business, and the city needed the project started to avoid the penalty, which it could not afford.

A bit stunned by the dilemma, I realized that it offered an opportunity to help the city. Lexington's downtown had spiraled downward since the late 1950s, and a convention center would bring people back to the city. The primary challenge involved creating revenue sources to borrow enough money to build the convention center. Various LTCC board members shared ideas, but nobody knew how to bring the various constituent groups together to support a funding mechanism. So they told me I had one year to get the project moving.

Determined to make this work, I remembered a financial plan I had discovered while working in state government. The Kentucky Fair and Exposition Center in Louisville, which included Freedom Hall, was state owned. While serving as Governor Nunn's representative on the Fair Board, I learned of an interesting financing scheme. The state had allowed a hotel, the Executive Inn East, to be built on government-owned land next to the Exposition Center. The hotel paid a 6 percent ground rent (instead of a property tax) on its revenue to cover the debt service on Freedom Hall. Ground rent allowed the funds to be allocated in ways that property taxes could not be. I wanted to replicate this in Lexington. I spoke with attorney Earl Wilson, who had established the original state statute allowing a ground rent in lieu of a property tax, and he thought we could use a similar plan for a convention center in Lexington.

I also consulted Don Harkins to ensure that we could utilize the ground-rent plan. Once he confirmed that it was legal, I contacted my fraternity brother Bill Hughes, who had worked his way into an executive position at Hyatt Hotels. I also met with my former boss and mentor from P&G, Mike Hostage, who had become a vice president at Marriott Hotels. I asked both of them what they thought of the ground-rent plan. I also hoped to lure one of their big-name hotels onto the property. Both of them liked the idea, so I started leveraging the two against each other.

I had been serving on Governor Nunn's cabinet when a group of individuals, who called themselves the "Alleycats," began agitating for a new on-campus basketball arena. These were successful UK fans and alumni in Lexington who could not secure season tickets to the always-sold-out Memorial Coliseum. The Coliseum held 12,000 people, and Coach Rupp's success made tickets extremely difficult to obtain. The Alleycats got their name by hanging out in the alley beside the Coliseum before games in the hope of finding extra tickets. They had convinced Governor Nunn and UK president Otis Singletary to meet with them and discuss the possibility of state funding for a new on-campus arena.

President Singletary had come from the University of Texas. He loved sports, but football was his passion. During the meeting with Governor Nunn and the Alleycats, Singletary said that he intended to direct any state assistance for construction toward a new football stadium. The Alleycats then began lobbying city officials for an off-campus arena. Of course, the city did not possess the resources to fund a new arena, but the Alleycats, who were led by Dr. Roy Holtzclaw and DeWitt Hisle, had made their voices heard in the local community.

I shared my idea for a convention center, a new arena, and a hotel with Mayor Pettit and Judge Stephens and the LTCC board. I pointed out that a 6 percent ground rent on the hotel and a fifty-cent bond fee on tickets to events at the new arena could help pay the debt service on the convention center. But to make this happen, we would need to get multiple constituencies on board. They all liked the idea and suggested that we create a new board to guide the project to completion.

First called the Lexington Civic Center Board, the name was eventually shortened to the Lexington Center Board (LCB). We strategically selected individuals who could win support from various groups in Lexington. We needed William T. "Bill" Young Sr. and Garvice Kincaid on the board. They both had money and influence, and Garvice controlled major radio and TV outlets in Lexington. Unfortunately, they detested each other. I pleaded with Bill to join the board, and he agreed to serve. Then I asked Garvice, who begrudgingly conceded under one condition: the meetings had to be held in his Kentucky Central boardroom in the old Lafayette Hotel (now City Hall). We invited Alleycat DeWitt Hisle as well as Linda Carey, who had tremendous influence with the arts and culture element of the community. Mayor Pettit and Judge Stephens added their own delegates to the board. Accountant Bill Jackson was an important addition. We asked Jake Graves to chair the LCB because he got along with everyone, including both Young and Kincaid. The board then hired me as its first executive director.

During the first LCB meeting, I explained the entire situation to the members. The city desperately needed to construct a civic center to enhance downtown and avoid the $3.5 million federal penalty on urban renewal. A large group of citizens wanted a new basketball arena for UK to accommodate bigger crowds, and a small bond fee on ticket sales would provide a revenue stream to help fund construction. We had a green light on charging a hotel a 6 percent ground rent on revenue to help pay debt service on the convention center. The board members liked the plan, and they hired my company to execute the strategy.

I organized a trip to Hartford, Connecticut, for the LCB so that we could study that city's new convention center and learn lessons that might help our endeavor. The trip was well worth the time and money. Hartford had included a retail element in its convention center to attract shoppers. We returned knowing that a retail mall in our complex would provide additional revenue to fund the project. We finally had a rough draft of the necessary elements for the Lexington project: convention center, arena, retail mall, hotel, and parking space—all of which would generate money to fund the project.

Wanting to include all segments of the community, I met with Howard White, who was considered a leading spokesperson for the African American community. I asked him whether he had any concerns about the project and if he would be willing to support it. He wanted black members of the community to be hired to work on construction of the facility. I said, "I assure you this will happen."

For the project to work, we needed UK to move its home games downtown. One key element of that move was naming the arena. Nearly everyone wanted it named in honor of Coach Rupp, but there were a few detractors, primarily Garvice Kincaid. At the beginning of one meeting, I handed out an agenda that included an item listed as "naming the arena." As the meeting progressed to that item, Garvice looked at me and said, "What's your suggestion?" I said it needed to be named for Adolph Rupp. Almost immediately, DeWitt Hisle made a motion to name the new facility the Rupp Arena. Garvice exclaimed, "Over my damn dead body!" I asked why he objected, and he went into an expletive-ridden tirade about how arrogant Rupp was and vowed that he would never support naming the arena for him.

Howard White was the first one to speak up and say, "Mr. Kincaid, I respectfully disagree." Kincaid shouted, "Oh, you disagree! Well come to my bank again and you won't get anything." Then Bill Young chimed in: "Garvice, you are wrong." Young was the only one who could stand up to Garvice and not fear any retribution. Garvice turned to me and said, "You staged this!" I had prepared for the meeting as usual, but there had been no "staging" involved. When we took it to a vote, everyone except Garvice voted for Rupp Arena. Garvice then spoke up again and said that although he had made his protest known, he wanted a unanimous vote, so he withdrew his opposition to naming the facility Rupp Arena. He did not want it to appear that he had lost.

Of course, naming the arena mattered only if UK agreed to move its games there. President Singletary had the ability to make or break the whole deal. I visited Singletary with LCB members DeWitt Hisle, Bruce Glenn, and Bill Jackson to pitch the idea. Singletary basically blew us off. He didn't believe we could deliver. He didn't think we could fill a 25,000-seat arena with Wildcat supporters, and he seemed skeptical about our pledge that UK would not have to pay any money toward construction of the facility. We all left the meeting dejected.

I returned to see the still-skeptical Singletary about a month later. I asked him whether he would approve the plan with the following conditions: We would build the new arena at no cost to the university, and UK would receive all the revenue it was currently earning at each home game at Memorial Coliseum before the Lexington Center Corporation received a single dime for expenses. The Lexington Center would guarantee to pay that amount to UK up front, but once this threshold was met, 14 percent of all ticket revenue would go to the Lexington Center as rent for UK's use of the arena. In short, UK assumed no risk with regard to construction costs, and it was guaranteed all the profit it was currently making on basketball games. Singletary must have said twenty times, "Host, you are out of your mind," but he eventually admitted, "I would be a fool not to take that offer." I said, "Yes, you would be." He added, "If you guarantee to give us what we get now, we will agree on something, but I don't think you can do it, so you have to prove it to me."

We had hired Spindletop Research to conduct a feasibility study to ensure that all the funding strategies were sustainable. The study's projected cost-revenue analysis determined that we could afford to build a complex costing around $25 million if we could secure the revenue streams we had listed. This was enough to get the reticent Singletary on board. It also provided an additional tool as we entered the project's next phase.

The LCB asked me to find contractors to bid on a "design-build" project. To keep costs down, I wanted to seek bids in a nontraditional way. Usually, architectural firms charged 6 to 7 percent of the total project's cost, with part being paid up front and the remainder collected throughout the project until completion. The architectural firm would design the building before seeking bids from contractors. These general contractors would regularly charge change-order fees, increasing the costs. Then a development company would be brought in to attract a hotel and private businesses for the mall. Instead, I asked each large engineering and architectural firm to team up with a construction company and a development company and make only one bid for the entire project. I then connected these firms with local architects who could work on the project. We called each grouping a "consortium," from which we wanted a single bid. In this way, the LCB and the city government could be reasonably certain that cost adjustments would be minimized. I also wanted local architectural firms to be on board with the project so that when we issued bonds, the city would have additional local support.

The board asked me to research national firms that would accept this strategy and to promote the idea to them. I traveled the country promoting what we eventually called the "design-build" model, whereby large firms worked with developers, construction companies, and local architects for a single bid. I always brought a concept model of the arena, the hotel, and the shopping center to these meetings. I also had an attorney with me to ensure that everything complied with local, state, and federal laws. We had more than fifty applicants for the job, so some of the board members and I flew around the country, learning about these firms and their vision for the Lexington Center. We eventually asked three firms, all of which had experience building major sports facilities, to make proposals: Winmar Company out of New York, Finch-Heery Company out of Atlanta, and Ellerbe Associates from Minneapolis.

I spent the next three months communicating with each firm, making sure it was going to bid on the whole project in association with its construction crews, development teams, and local architects. We had multiple meetings with the LCB, which brought in Tom Dupree Sr. to sell the bond issue. I met personally with the leaders of each consortium a few weeks before the bid presentations, and they all promised a competitive bid following the design-build model.

When each group arrived in Lexington, I took its representatives out to eat to get a feel for their plans. I met with George Heery from Finch-Heery, along with his local architectural partner Hugh Bennett. I had connected these two men because they were both Georgia Tech alums. After a couple of drinks, George looked at me and said, "Jim, I hate to be the bearer of bad news, but we are not going to be able to get this done." I asked, "What do you mean?" He responded, "Nobody is going to do this. We are an architectural firm. We are going to take an architectural fee and show you how it can be done the right way." Hugh followed me out of the restaurant and said, "I'm embarrassed. I know how hard you've worked and I'm just flabbergasted by this." I said, "Well, if he presents it that way, you won't get the job." When I took the Winmar representatives out, they said they were still on board. Ellerbe Associates said the same thing, so I still felt confident on the morning of the bids.

George Heery presented first. He produced all the designs and said nice things about me, but he never looked at me. He summarized by stating that his company knew how to get the job done but my model was wrong, and if the Lexington Center Corporation wanted to work with Finch-Heery, it would have to be done on a traditional bidding model. I had expected this, so when Heery left the room I said, "I'm sure the next presentations will go much better than this one, and we will have a team to work with."

When the second consortium organized by Winmar made its presentation, it too did an about-face, contradicting what it had promised the night before. Winmar said we could not complete the project with the bid structure I proposed. When the Winmar team exited, the air left the room. Garvice Kincaid raised his voice and said to me, "Young man, you have sold us a pig in a poke. You have wasted all of our time with this cockamamie design-build bull. You will regret this the rest of your life!" He carried on and dressed me down in front of everyone. My heart sank into my stomach, but I tried to keep it together. "Mr. Kincaid, I have saved the best for last. I think we are all going to be impressed." We had spent nearly eighteen months organizing this project, and we needed an acceptable bid.

Fearing the worst, I went to the Ellerbe team and bluffed, saying, "We've seen two solid proposals. I hope you're ready to step up to the plate." They said, "Our presentation is going to blow you away." I hoped it was true and prayed for the best. They entered the room, opened up their presentation boards, and went through their proposal item by item. The Ellerbe architects were going to work with Huber, Hunt, and Nichols Construction out of Indianapolis. That firm had collaborated with Finch-Heery on Riverfront Stadium in Cincinnati; it was constructing the Superdome in New Orleans and had just completed Commonwealth Stadium at UK. The local architects would be Johnson and Romanowitz, and the Ellerbe-owned Landmark Development Corporation would provide the investment dollars to secure a hotel and tenants for the retail shops. Before they finished, board member Doc Ferrell said, "Where do we sign?" and some of the board members started applauding. I was giddy beyond belief but also upset at their enthusiasm. I didn't want Ellerbe to know it had no competition.

When the Ellerbe team left the room, I said to the committee, "We couldn't have done a better job if we had written the proposal ourselves!" They had presented architectural renderings of an arena seating nearly 25,000 people. They had proposed a retail mall and were willing to take responsibility for renting the space while guaranteeing a minimum of $245,000 in rent for the Lexington Center. They had planned a hotel that included this gem: the 6 percent ground rent would be based on gross profits rather than net. Garvice looked at me and said, "By God, you pulled it off!" I was so relieved. Then the board granted me permission to negotiate with each group. The first two were stunned when I informed them that we had a successful bid. Then I told the Ellerbe group that the board had voted in principle to accept its offer, but we needed to negotiate some of the details. Ellerbe was satisfied, and the project moved forward.

The next challenge involved the bond issue. Tom Dupree Sr. had no trouble getting approval from the newly merged city-county government because otherwise, it would owe the federal government more than $3 million. The challenge was convincing investors in New York. When Dupree laid out all the revenue streams, they exceeded $30 million, but investors feared that these estimates were based on the success of a college basketball team. Moody's first rating was in the B range, which would have been impossible because of the high interest rates. So Tom asked Mayor Pettit to fly with him to New York and convince Moody's that this was a top-notch investment. The mayor did just that, leading to a change in the bond rating. Revenue from UK basketball tickets ended up being the least of their worries. The local government then approved a $37 million bond issue for construction of the Lexington Civic Center, approximately $25 million of which funded Rupp Arena—none of which the city was liable for.

Involved with the project through the various phases of construction, I eventually transitioned from executive director of the LCB to a public relations consultant for the board. The way the contract was written, we were able to address multiple challenges on the fly. For example, we originally wanted a 25,000-seat arena. We realized, however, that the available land was too small, so we scaled back to fewer than 24,000 seats.

We hired consultants to make sure that everything was constructed in the best possible way. For example, when building the entryways to Rupp Arena, one consultant advised, "Build all of these large enough to get the elephants inside!" So we did, in order to attract the circus to town. Now, whenever a UK team wins a national championship, they can drive a bus onto the floor at Rupp Arena because we took that advice.

Although constructed before the advent of ESPN, Rupp Arena's design included camera platforms as well as cables for television, so TV trucks can park at a platform and plug in their equipment with one simple cable-cord outlet. Consultants also told us that if we wanted to host NCAA events, we needed adequate room for a national press corps. So we included plenty of space for the media where Heritage Hall connects to Rupp Arena. Since then, Rupp Arena has regularly hosted NCAA tournament games.

As construction progressed, I asked the LCB to hire an in-house executive director. The board asked me to stay on, but I refused. With other developments in my own business, I could not give it the proper attention. David Peterson served as an interim director, and then executive director Tom Minter did an excellent job for the next three decades. When he accepted the job, he asked me to continue to serve as a public relations consultant on the project. He wanted me to be available to answer any questions concerning the individual personalities and the political implications of all the important decisions.

As Rupp Arena and the Lexington Center were being developed, it became clear that we desperately needed more parking. When the city condemned the area north of the Civic Center to create a parking lot, there were some protests about the houses being taken through eminent domain. Many were poorly kept rental properties, and the area had been infamous for its brothels, bars, and illegal gambling houses. I was concerned that land speculators would try to buy the rundown rentals and then make quick profits on the resales.

When the demolition began, there were a few protests, but the board and the newly merged Lexington–Fayette County urban government handled the situation very well. Those who were removed from their homes were given fair-market value plus moving expenses. Renters were also provided with moving expenses. The city made sure that everyone was in a better situation than they had been in originally. The excellent treatment provided to the displaced families was largely thanks to Councilwoman Pam Miller and Mayor Foster Pettit. Miller, a New Englander and Smith College alumna, was the first woman elected to the Lexington–Fayette County Council. She had initially hoped that the Lexington Center Corporation would build a parking garage, but that option proved too expensive. Because of her advocacy, Lexington's urban renewal avoided some of the mistakes made by other cities during that era. Of course, urban renewal remains a controversial issue, and hindsight has taught us important lessons about preservation. Some will disagree, but I still believe that the city and the remaining neighborhoods were better off.

The project brought people downtown and allowed adjacent neighborhoods such as Woodward Heights and Davis Bottoms to develop an even stronger identity.[1]

Behind closed doors, there were other conflicts. We collaborated with a national design team, a construction firm, a development group, and UK. This created multiple opportunities for disagreement. For example, Dave Warner headed up Hunt Development and worked with the Hyatt chain on hotel construction. Dave and I had some disagreements concerning the design and cost of the hotel. At one point, he got so upset that he took his shoe off and beat it on the table like Nikita Khrushchev. Once he cooled off, we found a solution and moved forward. The LCB's construction committee (Bill Jackson, DeWitt Hisle, and Bruce Glenn) spent countless volunteer hours over the next few years to make sure everything proceeded as smoothly as possible. Hisle chaired that committee and played a key role in making Rupp Arena a reality.

An often overlooked part of the Lexington Center project was the renovation of the Lexington Opera House. Early on, we had determined that to make the most of this urban-renewal grant and win the support of the arts community, an Opera House renovation needed to be included in the project. Three blocks north of the Lexington Center, the historic nineteenth-century Opera House had fallen into disrepair. Board member Linda Carey, a patron of the arts, helped lead the Opera House renovation. This became a substantial challenge because the entire roof needed to be replaced.

As we neared completion, Bill Young Sr. initiated an endowment campaign for the Opera House. We ended up raising $2.5 million, and since then, the Opera House Fund Board has grown that endowment. The Opera House has given $12 million in subsidies to local art groups to rent the Opera House and has attracted national touring acts that otherwise wouldn't have come to Lexington because of the limited seating capacity of the Opera House. Despite these distributions, at the beginning of 2019 the fund had nearly $7 million from investments made on the original $2.5 million raised. Nearly a half century later, Linda Carey and I are the only two founding members still on the board. Bill Young Jr. has done an excellent job carrying on the legacy of his father, serving as chair of the Opera House Fund Board.

With the completed Lexington Center project, UK had a new home for basketball, the renovated Opera House was attracting national acts, the downtown area gained the luxury Hyatt Regency and a new retail mall, and the Heritage Hall convention center was hosting exhibitions and conferences of all kinds. The revenue streams existed to pay the debt on the construction, and the city of Lexington had made good on its original urban-renewal grant from the federal government. All my work stemmed from contracting with the Lexington Tourist and Convention Commission. Jim Host & Associates had grown busier. It was time to turn toward new adventures.

6

Business in the Bluegrass and Beyond

Fortunately, both the Lexington Tourist and Convention Commission (LTCC) and the Lexington Center Board hired my company rather than me personally. This allowed me to look for other business opportunities. Before long, new prospects in Kentucky and beyond presented themselves. When something looked good and fit with my core values, I jumped at it.

I could not have imagined that a casual conversation with a friend would change the trajectory of my work. Norman Tice, general manager of the Phoenix Hotel and member of the LTCC, showed me a photo and asked, "Do you know who this group is?" I had no idea the photo had been taken at the National Tour Brokers Association (NTBA) inaugural meeting in Atlantic City in the 1960s. I did not know a single fact about the NTBA. Norman explained that it was a small organization comprising family-owned and licensed tour brokers. He asked me to attend the next NTBA meeting on behalf of the LTCC.

I agreed, even though I barely knew the difference between a travel agent and a tour broker. I intended to pitch Lexington as a tourist destination. I phoned ahead of time to register, but I was asked to wait until I checked into the hotel. Arriving at the newly opened Hyatt Regency in Atlanta during the middle of an ice storm, I was directed to Bob Shenk, owner of Ridgeway Tours in Lancaster, Pennsylvania, and treasurer of the NTBA. He said I needed an association membership to register for the conference and get the discounted hotel rate, so I wrote a check and joined the NTBA.

I attended an "icebreaker" social event that evening and met Rick Etherson, owner of Roger Q Tours in Knoxville, Tennessee. He introduced me to John Penler, manager of Paragon Tours in Massachusetts. They cochaired the planning committee for the next year's conference in Roanoke, Virginia, and asked the LTCC to sponsor a luncheon at the event for $2,500. Seeing an opportunity to promote tourism in Lexington, I agreed.

After attending various conference sessions, I wanted to meet NTBA president Joe Casser, owner Casser Tours in New York. Rick introduced us, and when I had the chance I said, "Mr. Casser, I would like to host a board meeting in Lexington for your group." He replied, "Well, we don't do that. We always hold our meetings in New York City." I said, "If you can get to Lexington, we will pay all your other expenses." He raised his eyebrows and asked, "Can you afford that?" I mustered as much confidence as I could and responded, "Sure, we can afford it." Casser thought for a minute and then said, "If that's true, I can make it happen."

I grew anxious on the way back to Lexington thinking about all the money I had committed to hosting the NTBA board. When I told Norman Tice what I had done, he asked, "Will Arthur Tauck, Jim Spencer, and George Talmage come?" I said they would but added, "We are really going to have to impress them." He agreed, and we began working with the LTCC to plan a special event.

Using my experience from the Republican Governors' Association, we developed a top-notch itinerary. We picked the members up at the airport in limousines. I called in some personal favors and provided private tours of the horse farms around Lexington. The members of the LTCC offered critical assistance because this was a once-in-a-lifetime opportunity to put the Bluegrass region on the national tour map.

I knew the event impressed the NTBA board members when they invited me to attend their next meeting in New York. Ecstatic, I saw this as an opportunity to get "inside" the group. Nothing really important happened at that first meeting, but I listened intently and learned as much as possible about the organization and how I might help it.

While profitable, the NTBA operated like a family business without any focused organization. Reid Price, an organist at a Washington, DC, church, served as a part-time executive vice president. The group paid him $10,000 annually to lobby Congress and other DC entities involved with the travel industry. But as an untrained, part-time lobbyist, Price was less effective than the NTBA board had hoped.

After attending the board meeting, I began to prepare for our luncheon at the annual meeting in Roanoke. We organized an entire team of "redcoats" from Kentucky who wore red blazers and worked the crowd, promoting the commonwealth. Lexington mayor Foster Pettit agreed to speak, and he blew them away. Then Preston Webber, Doug Breeding, and J. D. Crowe played bluegrass music while the attendees sipped on Maker's Mark bourbon. Everyone loved it.

After the luncheon, the board invited me to sit in on the tour brokers' meeting. During the meeting, Joe Casser introduced a filmmaker who had been hired to create an NTBA promotional film. This guy started talking about having a bus driver describe the attractions while driving the bus. The group immediately realized that he didn't understand their business, and they began to boo. Then somebody shouted, "Throw the bum out!" An embarrassed Casser sent someone to ask me if I had a copy of the promotional video I had shown NTBA board members. It was a Bluegrass tour promotion in which the ghost of Henry Clay showed people around Lexington's historic sites. Apparently, Casser had liked it. I happened to have a copy of the 16mm film with me, but as I fumbled around, trying to feed the film into the projector, the crowd started to get unruly. I gave up on the projector and approached the microphone instead. I raised my voice and said, "I want everyone's attention. I've been invited to speak to you. I'm not a tour broker, but I know how to make a high-quality film. I also understand the difference between a tour broker and a bus operator. I don't think you need to see the film right now to know that I can do this and do it well." Well, the crowd started cheering. I said a few more things, and then Casser invited me upstairs to negotiate a contract to produce the NTBA promotional film.

After speaking with the board members, we agreed in principle that my company would make a promotional film about the NTBA for $50,000. They asked me to attend the next board meeting in New York to hammer out the details. When I arrived in Manhattan, I checked into the hotel they had reserved for me. At breakfast the next morning, if I had turned the plates upside down, the eggs would have stuck to them. I survived the meal, and we started the meeting. I shared my vision for the film and said we needed someone famous to provide the necessary impact. I told them Chill Wills, a western actor, was available. They were all surprised that I could secure him, and they approved it.

A month later, Arthur Tauck asked me to meet him, George Talmage, and Mary Lee in Pittsburgh to discuss the future of the NTBA. They took me to an Allegheny Airlines club room at the airport and eventually asked me if I could run the NTBA. I told them they could hire my company to run the association. When they asked if I had any employees, I told them I had one: law-school student Darryl Callahan. Despite this, they agreed in principle to hire Jim Host & Associates, but Tauck said I would have to finalize the details with Joe Casser.

I met Casser in an old dilapidated building in Manhattan. His office was full of dusty typewriters and brochures. When I walked in, he said, "Young man, everyone thinks you should be the new executive director of the NTBA. Quite frankly, I don't think we need to spend a lot of money." I replied, "Mr. Casser, how much is a lot of money?" He asked me what I wanted, and I said $25,000. I simply wanted a one-year contract, I added, and if the association was not impressed, it could hire someone else.

Casser told me I needed to resign my position on the LTCC because it would be a conflict of interest. I agreed to do so once I had completed my current contract. Then he asked me how much the LTCC paid me. When I told him $18,000, he interjected, "The NTBA will pay you $19,000." I countered, "You mean you think I should only get one thousand more for quitting that post and taking on more risk?" He responded, "I do. That's the offer. Take it or leave it." It was a gamble, but I saw the potential in the NTBA, so I agreed to do it.

After I accepted the job, Art Tauck called me and said, "I think you need to hold a board meeting." So I set up a meeting, and when everyone arrived, I handed out an agenda. Jim Spencer immediately said, "I see we've got a new sheriff in town! We actually have a meeting agenda." During the meeting, the group voted to elect themselves to serve on the board for another year. Then Bob Shenk reported that the association had paid all its bills and stated how much money it had in the bank. I asked whether he had a financial statement, but he did not. He said he would hand out the auditor's report when it was available. Tauck looked at me and raised his eyebrows. After the meeting, he said, "Jim, we need to get a handle on the books."

At the next board meeting, I shared two ideas to improve the NTBA. The first focused on the need for broader representation on the board. I worried that my suggestion might offend some members of the tight-knit group, but I told them that rotating the board would create greater buy-in for the association. Second, I needed a better understanding of the organization's finances.

Shenk, who had been the treasurer for more than a decade, exclaimed, "You don't trust me?" I said, "This has nothing to do with trust. If I'm responsible for the NTBA, I need detailed knowledge of the numbers to set financial forecasts."

Tauck convinced Shenk to let me take over financial management of the association, so I flew to Lancaster to look at the books. Tauck flew in as well, and Shenk picked us up at the airport in his big Cadillac. We headed to Shenk's office, but he parked three blocks away because he didn't want his employees to know he had a luxury car. Once we were in the office, he said, "Okay, let me get you the money." He went into a safe and started pulling out grocery bags and cardboard boxes full of cash and checks, some of which had been written a year earlier. After setting the last bag down, he looked up at me and said, "It's all here."

I told them I would go through every penny and get the books organized. I transferred all the money into one big box and wrapped it with tape and twine. I had no other choice but to check the box on my flight back to Lexington. Thankfully, when the plane landed, the cash had arrived as well. I called my friend and accountant DeWitt Hisle and asked him to meet me at my office. I did not want to count all that money without a witness. When I opened the box, DeWitt just stood there, stunned. We dumped it out on the floor and organized it. Once we were done, Hisle wrote an official witness letter stating that all the money had been accounted for. I now knew that the NTBA generated its revenue from the annual meeting, membership dues, and security deposits. That made devising a new business plan pretty easy: the way to grow the association was to increase membership and conference attendance.

Shortly after organizing the finances, I received a call from Rick Etherson from Knoxville, who was cochairing the annual NTBA meeting in San Diego scheduled for January 1975. He asked me to fly out to Southern California and meet him at the San Diego Sheraton Harbor Island Hotel, which would be hosting the convention. He walked me through the standard operating procedures for the annual event and then said, "Now it's yours. Put it together." I didn't have the first clue about planning an NTBA convention. I didn't have the mailing lists or a list of the previous year's attendees—nothing. I requested and eventually received enough information to get me started. Then I barely slept for the next few months as I tried to manually create a record of all the attendees' reservations and details. Thankfully, Etherson recommended that his friend, Dr. Oscar Fowler from the University of Tennessee, visit me in Lexington. Fowler was a computer professor, and he offered to design a program to help organize the event. I thought that might be beneficial, so we decided to work together.

I learned that at these events, tour operators always reserved tables for themselves in a large convention room. Suppliers hoping to sell goods or services approached the operators at the tables to make their sales pitches. However, the suppliers had no idea when companies would have representatives at the tables, so they spent much of their time trying to hunt down the tour operators, who would come and go as they pleased. This created a wildly disorganized marketplace.

Oscar and I met multiple times and figured out how to computerize everything. I told him what I wanted to plan, and he programmed it into his system. We asked the suppliers to list the tour companies they wanted to meet with, and we asked the tour operators which suppliers they were most interested in dealing with. Then we coordinated specific meeting times so that everyone received a personalized agenda upon arriving at the conference. We charged more for the conference because we were providing more value, and I wanted to show the NTBA that I could make the conference both more efficient and more profitable. By promoting the conference more aggressively, we doubled the number of participants from the previous year, despite raising the cost.

As members arrived, we gave them their individualized itineraries and invited attendees to an opening dinner reception sponsored by the Florida Travel Commission. By the time the head of the Florida Travel delegation, Morrie Ford, got up to speak, a large number of attendees had consumed too much alcohol, and the room had become rather rowdy. President Joe Casser unsuccessfully attempted to quiet the crowd. Finally, I stood up and began pounding on the podium, shouting, "I want everyone's attention!" I introduced myself and said, "I may be the shortest-lived executive vice president in the history of any association, but I know one thing for sure: the Florida Travel Commission sponsored this nice dinner, and you should honor them by listening to what they have to say." I added emphatically, "If you cannot abide by these simple rules, then leave." I worried that my heavy-handed approach would kill the happy vibe of the meeting, but my fears subsided quickly when almost everyone in the room started applauding. They went on and on. When Morrie came to the podium, the crowd silenced, and he gave an excellent speech.

After the successful annual meeting, the NTBA had a couple hundred thousand dollars in the bank. With that news, the board asked me to continue.

We made other substantive changes with the presidential election process and instituted a rotating board based on voting. These reforms increased interest in NTBA leadership and led to a boom in membership. Within a matter of years, we turned it into a multimillion-dollar operation. I stayed in that position for more than a quarter century, and my company's retainer increased with the NTBA's growth.

Around the same time, I received a call from Don Wheeler, manager of UK's radio station WBKY. I had worked with Don years earlier at WFKY in Frankfort. Now he chaired the committee that contracted the radio rights for UK football and basketball. In the late 1960s UK, along with other universities, began to offer exclusive rights to broadcast athletic events. UK now contracted with one company that paid the university to be its exclusive broadcasting voice on the radio for football and basketball. Don asked me to bid on UK's radio rights because he knew I understood how to build a radio network in Kentucky. I asked for a copy of the RFP (request for proposal) and learned that the G. H. Johnston Agency of New York was paying UK $44,000 annually for radio broadcast rights.

As a former athlete, I had a lot of history with UK sports. I had been involved with the K-Men, a service organization for student athletes, during my time on campus. After graduating, I worked with a number of other former athletes from UK and helped form a letterman organization for alumni. Our original goal, as UK lettermen, was to raise funds to provide scholarships for former student athletes who had not completed their degrees and wanted to return to school. We eventually changed the name to the K-Club and included women in the organization. I served as president of that group in 1966–1967 and also served on UK's Athletics Association Board at that time. I loved UK and wanted all its sports programs to be the best in the nation.

In 1967 UK's athletic director (AD) Bernie Shively died unexpectedly. "Shive," as we called him, had been an incredible mentor to me. People involved in intercollegiate athletics across the state and the nation held him in the highest regard. He had done an impressive job navigating UK through the point-shaving scandal that hit the basketball program in the early 1950s and was considered one of the best and most honest ADs in the country. Though busy, he regularly gave me advice regarding personal decisions in my own life. Because I traveled with the team, broadcasting games, in the late 1950s and early 1960s, Shive and I often played gin rummy. We claimed to have the world's longest-running game. We kept track of every card game, and at the end of each year, one of us would pay out a few dollars to the other. Then we continued the game into the next year. His passing was a great loss for UK and for me personally.

Following Shive's funeral, Ralph Angelucci, chair of the UK Athletics Association (UKAA), called and asked me to serve as UK's next AD. At the time, I was busy building up my insurance and real estate businesses, so I asked for few days to think about the offer. I was finally making some good money and wasn't sure I wanted to quit my businesses. I also worried that becoming AD would not be the best move for my wife and young children. I ended up thanking Ralph for the offer but declined. However, I assured him that I would help the program in any way I could. My former baseball coach Harry Lancaster ended up becoming AD. I was happy for Lancaster, even though it caused a rift in his relationship with Coach Rupp. Because of Rupp's proud personality, he disliked having a former subordinate become his boss. At that point, Louie Nunn approached me about serving in his cabinet, so that is where I spent my next four years.

When Wheeler presented the opportunity to get involved in UK radio broadcasting in the 1970s, I jumped at the chance. I had organized the Kentucky Central Network years earlier, but I didn't know all the costs involved— whether stations paid to broadcast games, and how much advertisers paid for commercials. I did know this: if I could get my foot in the door, I would figure it all out. I met with my friend and attorney Don Harkins to discuss my bidding strategy. We thought that if the Johnston Agency knew I was bidding, it would probably increase its bid to just above $50,000. So I decided to bid $52,850. As it turned out, the competition bid $44,000 again and didn't even sign the RFP with the offer. This meant that UK had received only one legitimate bid—mine—but it delayed in awarding me the rights.[1]

While I was anxiously awaiting news about the contract, Ray Hornback, UK's vice president for university relations, called and said that some people at UK had questioned my ability to cover the bid. The call frustrated me and infuriated Don Harkins. He encouraged me to take legal action against UK. Even though I had offered the highest (and only signed) bid, I did not want to sue my alma mater. In addition, I thought I could do some good for UK if the university accepted my offer.

I visited Harry Lancaster and shared my story. He knew that some people had questioned my ability to pay the fee, and I learned that others were worried I would use the broadcast rights to promote myself and run for political office again. So I met with some of the UKAA board members and offered to provide a letter of credit guaranteeing that the university would get paid. Everyone liked this approach, so I visited my friend and mentor Jake Graves and asked him to provide a financial guarantee to UK. He said, "You're a risk taker, Host, but you haven't failed me yet!" He gave me a letter of credit, and UK awarded me the broadcast rights.

At this point, I had transitioned to consulting work for the LTCC, but I remained under contract with the Lexington Center Board and was running the NTBA. Despite these obligations, I knew that I needed to travel the state and meet individually with station managers if I wanted to build the UK Radio Network. Even though it was time-consuming and sometimes frustrating work, visiting at least one radio station in nearly all of Kentucky's 120 counties helped me to form strong relationships that made the network successful. I met with almost every manager at virtually every radio station in the state to share my plan for building the network.

Before selling the network statewide, I needed to develop a financial model to keep my company afloat. The greatest challenge turned out to be selling statewide advertising to companies that didn't want it. Multiple businesses wanted to divide their advertising between Lexington and Louisville, while others wanted to advertise in only one region of the state. Keeping all the advertising markets together when possible, while allowing other businesses to run commercials in select markets, was an incredible challenge. For example, South Central Bell included Louisville and much of western Kentucky, while GTE covered eastern and central Kentucky. Neither company wanted to pay for advertising in parts of the commonwealth where it had no chance of increasing profits. To solve this dilemma, I determined a statewide standard rate for advertising. Then I offered a percentage discount off the statewide rate for companies that did not benefit from advertising across Kentucky. In essence, we developed a large statewide network, but local stations followed their own special formats. Individuals working at those stations had to know when to run the commercials on their local stations. This was not easy, and local stations occasionally made mistakes, which upset clients. We were constantly sending affidavits to stations to sign off on exactly which commercials they ran during the games.

The second challenge involved deciding how much to charge stations to carry UK games. After considering the possible rates, I decided not to charge anything during those first years. It was more important to me to build the size of the network than to collect fees. I hoped to change this, but in the short run, I could not afford to have the network shrink on my watch. I also knew that I needed to acquire powerful stations in order to sell advertising. Louis-ville's 50,000-watt clear-channel WHAS could broadcast out into the western states at night. Cincinnati's clear-channel WCKY could be heard throughout the eastern United States. I created radically different deals for those stations than for the smaller ones that barely covered three counties.

WHAS in Louisville proved to be a relatively easy sell because Cawood Ledford stayed on as the play-by-play announcer and Ralph Hacker contin-ued his color commentating. These two were longtime personalities on the network, and Cawood actually worked for WHAS at the time. The backlash from listeners would have been horrible if they had given up their spot on the network.

I also wanted to make a deal with WCKY in Cincinnati, so I met with manager Dave Martin and offered to pay the station to carry UK games. No-body had ever given the station money to broadcast games before, so the ex-ecutives were eager to sign a contract. Because I paid them, I managed to keep all my advertising inventory on the air. This meant that if I paid WCKY $250 to broadcast each game, I had to sell that amount of commercial airtime to break even. However, the coverage WCKY provided across the eastern United States was incredible for UK athletics.

Broadcasting UK games on WCKY meant that the University of Cincin-nati's Bearcats were bumped to another, less powerful channel. Gale Catlett, a former assistant to Adolph Rupp, had become the University of Cincinnati's basketball coach. He called me after the deal was announced and chewed me out in the most offensive manner possible. I took it in stride because I knew I had just removed his team from WCKY, one of the most powerful stations in its home market. But I don't think he ever forgave me for winning those broadcast rights.

Because Kentucky is a basketball-crazy state, some Kentucky stations I visited wanted to broadcast only basketball games, not football. The G. H. Johnston Agency had not monitored this situation closely, and a number of stations along the southern border of the state carried Kentucky basketball and Tennessee football. University of Tennessee (UT) football had a strong following in southeastern Kentucky. I visited UT officials to discuss my con-cerns, but they blew me off. So, I decided to place UK games on stations in places like Oneida, Jellico, and Harrogate, Tennessee. That quickly got the attention of the UT Athletics Association, and we agreed to clear our radio networks only in our respective states.

While marking out territories, I told stations that if they wanted to broadcast UK sports, they needed to carry both football and basketball games. Some station managers pushed back, but I held my ground. By keeping football and basketball together, the network could advertise from September into March. We gave stations 50 percent of the advertising time to allow them to earn their money back, and I sold the other half to companies across the state. The key to making this work financially was the fifteen-minute pregame and postgame shows, providing more airtime for commercials. This arrangement gave me enough airtime to sell statewide sponsors on the network and pay UK what I had promised it. In fact, we eventually increased the pre- and postgame shows to thirty minutes because they were so popular.

I did not make a single penny during my first year broadcasting UK sports, but I almost broke even. However, in one year I created the largest college sports radio network in the nation. Additionally, the two clear-channel stations allowed night games to be broadcast into forty states. In subsequent years, the businesses seeking airtime realized the value of this, and selling UK game rights became a profitable part of the business. Stations started to pay to broadcast the games, and my company began to keep a larger percentage of the airtime for commercials.

My new contracts with the NTBA and UK came almost simultaneously. I spent my first year working with the UK Radio Network while preparing for the NTBA annual meeting in San Diego in 1975. After a successful convention, I headed back to Kentucky for the final months of the basketball season. As fate would have it, UK made a run in the NCAA tournament, and I was back in San Diego for the finals in March.

When UK made it into the NCAA tournament in 1975, I learned that I had to pay the NCAA additional fees to broadcast tournament games on the UK network. The tournament then consisted of thirty-two teams. UK played its first game at Coleman Coliseum in Tuscaloosa, and I met with Charlie Thornton, Alabama's sports information director (SID). Charlie and I had first crossed paths when I was working at the Kentucky Central Network in the 1950s and he was the SID at Tulane. During our conversation in Tuscaloosa, I handed him a sheet of paper listing all the UK affiliate stations and what I owed the NCAA for broadcasting the first-round tournament game. He looked at me and said, "My God, Jim, that's more money than everyone else put together. Nobody ever reports all their stations." Somewhat stunned, I looked at him and said, "Well, I do." Then I asked him for a copy of the amounts the other broadcasters had submitted to the NCAA. I wanted to learn what the other university networks were doing. He agreed and gave me the list, which proved to be very enlightening.

UK managed to advance to the second round by soundly defeating Al McGuire's Marquette team. The regional tournament in Dayton, Ohio, consisted of two games, leading to the Final Four. UK beat Central Michigan by seventeen points in the first game. The regional final promised to be a difficult task against Bobby Knight's undefeated Indiana Hoosiers. The Hoosiers' 34–0 record included a twenty-four-point beatdown of Kentucky in December. Few pundits gave the Wildcats a chance. UK's balanced attack from Rick Robey, Kevin Grevey, Jimmy Dan Conner, Mike Flynn, and Jack "Goose" Givens gave the Wildcats an 89–81 lead with just over five minutes to go. Indiana mounted a furious comeback but fell just short. Kentucky won by a score of 92–90 in one of the greatest basketball games I had ever witnessed. A year later, Knight told me that he thought his 1974–1975 Hoosiers were probably a better team than his undefeated squad the following year. When the UK team crossed the Ohio River back into Kentucky, fans holding signs and cheering the team lined the highway. It was absolute euphoria.

Advancing to the finals meant that I would finally break even on the broadcast rights, but the NCAA broadcast fees kept me from making a solid profit. I headed back to San Diego for the semifinals, where UK beat Syracuse, and John Wooden's UCLA team won a nail-biter against Wooden's former assistant Denny Crum and his Louisville Cardinals.

Following his team's victory over Louisville, Wooden announced that he would retire after the game against Kentucky. The news stunned the basketball world. Years later, I spoke with his daughter, who said that Wooden had not told anyone he planned to retire. I might be wrong, but I think that after almost losing to one of his former assistants, he decided to hang it up while he was still on top.

Before the championship game, I was courtside preparing for the matchup with our broadcast team Cawood Ledford, Ralph Hacker, and Rick Edwards. Sitting next to us were broadcasters for the Mutual Radio Network, which held the national rights for championship broadcasts. Hacker looked at me and said, "I wonder if you would have a chance to get the broadcast rights for the NCAA championship." So I walked onto the court before the tip-off to speak with Tom Jernstedt and Dave Cawood, the two individuals who over-saw the NCAA tournament. At the time, Jernstedt, Cawood, and two staff members organized the entire Division I NCAA tournament. I pointed over to the Mutual Network's broadcasters and asked, "How much do they pay the NCAA for their national broadcast?" One of them answered, "$3,000." I said, "You've got to be kidding me! How much do you take in from all the rights for the tournament?" Jernstedt replied, "I'm not sure, but probably around $20,000." Cawood looked at me and admitted, "You're paying us more than we are getting from Mutual." Since UK played in every round of the tournament, I had paid the NCAA $7,500. After studying the data Charlie Thornton had given me, I believed that UK was one of the few schools, if not the only one, that listed all its broadcast stations. I told Jernstedt and Cawood that they were losing substantial revenue, in my opinion, because nobody else reported all their stations. This meant that the UK Radio Network provided fully one-third of the revenue the NCAA made on radio broadcasting. Then I decided to ask the big question: "Would you guys like me to take over the national championship radio broadcasts? If I can replace them [pointing at Mutual], I will give you a $30,000 guarantee or 50 percent of the profits—whatever is greater. I'll also take over the administration of radio rights, so you don't have to do it." Organizing the network and collecting the rights fees required a lot of work, and I thought my offer to take it off their hands while paying them more money was a deal they couldn't refuse. They looked at each and smiled but did not give me an answer.

UCLA went on to beat UK in what would be one of the most important games for basketball superiority in the country. The officials called an unusu-ally tight game as the Bruins stayed in front of Kentucky for most of the con-test. Foul trouble limited Mike Phillips's and Rick Robey's playing time. UCLA had a nine-point lead with ten minutes remaining. A UK run closed the gap to 76–75 with five minutes remaining. At that point, UCLA's Dave Meyers fouled Kevin Grevey. Meyers reacted to the call by slapping the court, and the officials called a technical foul. The usually calm Coach Wooden lost it. He stormed onto the floor, yelling at officials Hank Nichols and Bob Wortman. They begged Wooden to return to the bench but refused to call a technical foul on the legendary coach in his last game. UK missed the free throws, and on the ensuing inbounds play the officials called an offensive foul on James Lee. The momentum shifted back to UCLA, and the Bruins closed the game on a small run. The "Wizard of Westwood" went into retirement with a tenth

NCAA title, and UK's team left dejected. While speaking with Hank Nichols years later, he said that if it had been any other coach in any other game, they would have called another "T." Although it doesn't matter now, I will always believe it cost UK a championship banner.

A week after the game, I got a call from NCAA executive director Walter Byers. He said, "Dave Cawood tells me you are the real deal. I've checked you out, and I want to meet with you in my Kansas City office tomorrow at 9:00 a.m." Then he said good-bye. I took a flight that evening. When I walked into Byers's office, he offered a kind and soft-spoken greeting. He was wearing one of the worst toupees I had ever seen, and he had long sideburns and a wandering left eye. He asked me to take a seat and pulled up a chair next to me. He began, "I understand the following . . . "—repeating almost verbatim the offer I had pitched to Jernstedt and Cawood in San Diego. I agreed, and he added, "Here is the deal: I will offer you a one-year trial, and we will find out if you can perform. If you do, we will talk about an extension. Now, go build a network." I said, "Mr. Byers . . . ," but before I could continue, he said, "It's Walter." So I said, "Walter, what about a contract?" He stated, "Just send me a confirmation letter, and that will be our contract." As I started to get out of my seat, he said, "I didn't dismiss you yet." So I sat back down and he said, "Let me give you some advice about running your business. I see some good qualities in you, but you have got to understand discipline. I mean all the way down to whether or not people leave old coffee cups on their desk." Then he gave me a handbook he had written for the NCAA and said, "This is the world as Walter Byers sees it." Then we were done. Even with his lecture, the entire meeting had lasted only fifteen minutes. I left knowing that this guy did not mess around. I had spent time in front of some strong personalities, but Byers was the most intimidating. He offered no pretense. He was hard-nosed but soft-spoken. He knew what he wanted and used every word to effectively convey it. He was an absolute genius. To this day, he is the only person I have ever been in awe of.

I left Kansas City motivated to prove that I could be a success in college sports. Returning home, I was excited and a bit apprehensive. I had one employee and an administrative assistant. I needed to build a national network, so I decided to follow the template I had developed for the UK Radio Network. I studied national standard rate and data booklets, which provided information on advertising rates for radio stations in every state. Each day I chose a different state and spent the first half of the day calling radio stations and trying to sell them on clearing the NCAA basketball championship broadcasts. If they said yes, I sent a follow-up letter confirming the agreement and listing the specific rights, conditions, and guidelines. The NCAA had provided me with no information or instructions on building a radio network, so I developed a handbook on how to recruit stations. The NCAA liked it so much that my manual became the official NCAA publication for building a college radio network.

I stayed in communication with Tom Jernstedt, sharing the challenges I encountered. I wanted him to know that despite the slow going, I was developing a template that would accelerate the growth of college athletics in the future. The Mutual Network had just over 70 stations, so I set a personal goal to secure 200. I started with Kentucky because of my connections there. Then I plowed through every other state, getting what seemed like hundreds of rejections weekly. I managed to reach my goal, but I had not considered how many of those stations were in large cities with top-tier markets. That was what potential sponsors wanted to know before they would agree to buy advertising.

As I contracted with each station, I stipulated that if its local collegiate team was in the NCAA tournament, it could broadcast on the university's existing network. But once that team lost, the station would use the NCAA Network. Three or four months into securing stations, I needed to start selling advertising. Otherwise, the whole venture would be a colossal failure. I called potential sponsors but struck out at every turn. I was a much better salesman in person, but the national scope of this operation required sales calls by phone. Finally, out of nowhere, Dolan Walsh called and said, "I'm with D'Arcy MacManus [Budweiser's sales agency], and I want to buy something on the NCAA Network." I could not recall anyone ever reaching out to me about buying advertising without me making the first move. I flew to St. Louis to discuss advertising options. Dolan, a short guy who smoked incessantly, took me to lunch at a private club overlooking the new Busch Stadium. He consumed three Budweisers during the meal. I suppose he was testing out the merchandise! He had requested a list of all the stations in the network, which I provided. We ended up agreeing to an advertising contract totaling $30,000.

By the time the 1976 national championship game was played in Philadelphia, I had signed only one other sponsor: the NTBA. Thankfully, my work with that organization secured its partnership. The NTBA paid between $6,000 and $7,000 for advertising spots. Had it not been for Dolan Walsh at Budweiser and the NTBA, I could have lost my shirt. Jake Graves loaned me

$30,000 to pay the NCAA before I received my checks from the sponsors. Once again, he kept my business afloat.

Since UK did not even make it to the NCAA tournament that year, I hired Cawood Ledford to do the play-by-play. I handled all the engineering, production, and stats myself to save money. Before the championship game, I had my headphones on and was busy getting ready for the broadcast, when I felt a tap on my shoulder. It was Walter Byers, who said, "You did a hell of a job, but you didn't make any money, did you?" I said, "No sir. As a matter of fact I didn't." Before walking off he said, "Call me when you get back home. We'll schedule another meeting."

Back in my office, I thought, "He's gonna tell me to take a hike." He knew I had worked hard, but at the end of the day, I needed to turn a profit. I picked up the phone and called him, ready for the axe. But when Byers got on the phone, he said, "Jim, I've decided to give you a three-year deal. You paid us $30,000, which is fine, but I know you didn't make any money." He said our new deal would be a fifty-fifty partnership with no rights fees. Taken aback, all I could say was, "What?" He said, "I know you heard me, but I want you to make me one commitment. I want you to devote your life to college sports. I don't want you doing any pro sports. If you devote your life to college sports you will be successful, because I will make sure you are successful." That was it. Another fifteen-minute talk, and he gave me an amazing opportunity. To this day, I believe he offered me the deal for two reasons. First, he knew I was honest. I had paid all the fees due to the NCAA when others had short-changed the organization. I had also paid the $30,000 I promised the organization, even though I lost a few thousand dollars on the deal. Second, he knew I loved college athletics and was passionate about expanding its commercial appeal. Regardless, he trusted me before I produced any tangible results.

During 1976–1977, my company had three employees: Darryl Callahan, Lucy Demaree, and my administrative assistant Helen Johnson. We were expanding locally and had consulting contracts on several projects. Our three big accounts consisted of the UK Radio Network, the NTBA, and the NCAA Radio Network. We were all putting our hearts and souls into these businesses to make them the best in the country.

As we entered into the next year of UK's contract, I blanketed the state with radio signals covering all 120 counties. We had finally figured out a standard template for advertising to make sure our company turned a profit, albeit a very modest one. It did not help that in 1975–1976 UK had had mediocre seasons in both football and basketball, so I decided to focus on what I could control: the broadcast quality. We worked to make the fifteen-minute pre-game and postgame shows more engaging and informative so that we could sell more airtime. We experimented during football games with a sideline reporter to describe the activity on the bench. We actually stuck a coat hanger outside the broadcast booth to transmit a two-way signal. We also tried placing a reporter in the stands with the fans, but that flopped. There was too much noise and not enough action to report. The sideline reporting, however, added to the color of the game. Over the next few years, employee Rick Edwards improved the two-way radio model and developed a clear signal. To my knowledge, we were the first in the nation to use sideline reporters, now a mainstay for both radio and television broadcasts.

During the NCAA Radio Network's off-season, we stayed focused on adding stations and sponsors. By the 1977 national championship, we had more than 300 stations, including a number of important additions in large markets. I knew that Kentucky basketball had a unique culture, but I was still somewhat shocked that radio stations in certain markets did not care at all about college basketball. I got the network to cover cities in the Northeast, but marketing firms, most of them in New York, remained disinterested in buying advertising. This was frustrating, but it opened my eyes to the potential for college sports marketing. Millions of fans wanted to listen to the games, and I knew I had a shot at being one of the first to tap into that market. I also learned that "affinity" markets like college basketball and football had intensely loyal fan bases. Millions of alumni around the country considered their college years the best or most formative time of their lives, which created undying loyalty.

Both Budweiser and the NTBA expanded their contracts for the 1977 championship, held at the Omni in Atlanta. I convinced the Georgia Division of Economic Development to run commercials as well. We added a number of other smaller accounts. Even with the fifty-fifty split, the NCAA received a bit more than the $30,000 it had earned the previous year, and it turned out to be a successful investment for my company as well. We also improved the production side of the broadcast, making the games much more appealing for both the avid fan and the casual listener.

While sitting courtside with our broadcast team before the semifinal games, I noticed Big 10 commissioner Wayne Duke talking with Dave Cawood from the NCAA right in front of me. They were paying no attention to me, but I heard almost every word they said. They were discussing the game-day program's cheap pages, the low-quality printing, and the alcohol ads, which were a violation of NCAA policy. I walked up to them and said, "Would you like me to take over the programs?" Duke said, "You're doing a great job with the radio. Why don't you try doing it next year?"

Al McGuire's Marquette team defeated Dean Smith and the Tar Heels in the championship game. The next week, I got a letter from Dave Cawood offering me a contract to produce the national championship programs on the same basis as the radio network deal. I agreed to pay all the up-front costs and split the profits with the NCAA.

As fate would have it, UK made it to the 1978 championship in St. Louis. I called Smoot Falgren, whose ad agency Falgren and Ferris had Ashland Oil as a client. Ashland owned gas stations all across Kentucky, so I asked if we could sell official programs exclusively at those stations and promote it on the radio. Ashland agreed to the deal. In the championship game, Jack "Goose" Givens led Kentucky with forty-one points to defeat Duke in an exciting matchup. After the tournament, I sent the NCAA a check for $48,000, its 50 percent cut for the programs. As soon as the NCAA received its share, Walter Byers called me and said, "Jim, come back out here. We need to have another conversation." I explained my deal with Ashland, and Byers learned that a basketball venue was not the only place where people would buy NCAA national championship programs. The NCAA assigned Jim Shaffer to assist with program development the following year.

The NCAA Radio Network became more profitable as well. Each year I sent the NCAA a detailed report of the work we had done, the stations broadcasting the games, the sponsors that bought radio time, and the profits the NCAA earned. After 1978, Tom Jernstedt asked me to present the data in person to the NCAA Division I Basketball Committee. With an opportunity to make a good impression on a large group of NCAA representatives, I put together a detailed report on the NCAA Radio Network and the championship programs and distributed it at the meeting. I spoke for about five minutes and had nothing but good news. I directed the attendees to a few key pages of the report that contained executive summaries of expenses and profits. I told them they could find all the minute details they needed in the report and asked if anyone had any questions. Nobody did, but a few commented on the report's effectiveness and how much they appreciated my valuing their time.

We had another solid run with the NCAA in 1979 that culminated in the most watched and listened to championship game in history. Larry Bird's Indiana State team squared off against Erving "Magic" Johnson's Michigan State Spartans. The high-profile game boosted the NCAA's ratings on both TV and radio, which in turn improved future sales. This was good news, because the NCAA had asked me to take over radio rights of the regional games as well.

When I attended the 1979 summer meeting of the NCAA and presented my report, I thought things could not be going any better. Then North Carolina State's AD Willis Casey slid one of our championship programs across the table and asked, "Do you like this?" I looked up and said, "Yes sir." Then he slid some other programs across the table from the first-round tournament sites. They were horrible looking. Some of the ads had been printed upside down, and the cheapest quality ink and paper had been used. Without my saying a word, Willis looked up and added, "If you want to keep doing championship programs for the NCAA, you need to start doing all the programs for every round."

This would be a vastly more challenging undertaking because the NCAA was getting ready to expand the field to forty-eight teams in 1980. The game sites would be spread across the entire country, and I would need data on all forty-eight teams instead of just four. In addition, the NCAA announced the field on a Sunday evening, and the games started four days later, on Thursday. Printing had not yet been digitized, so the labor involved seemed almost insurmountable for my small operation. But for whatever reason, I just sputtered, "Yes sir, I will do it." Almost everyone around the table was elated, but I left rather perplexed. When I walked out into the hall, Tom Jernstedt found me and said, "I didn't have anything to do with that. I know you said you would do it, but I don't know how you can." I responded, "We will figure it out. I will find a way to do it."

After the meeting, I met with my banking friend Jake Graves and shared the story of how I had ended up with this new job. He had always been loyal to me and remained my go-to source for quick capital, so I always kept him apprised of my business ventures. I knew I wanted to keep the entire project in-house to manage quality control, but this meant I needed to invest in printing equipment. Fortunately, I had already started publishing programs for UK sports and had been looking into expanding my printing operation. I hired Ken Adams, a fraternity brother who had worked at IBM. Ken knew the printing business, so we researched purchasing options. We decided to buy a used six-color Harris printing press from Rees Printing in Winchester, Kentucky, and then rented an old warehouse in Lexington where we could run the press.

Right after we agreed to make this purchase, Jake Graves told me that a client of his, Gene Tharp, owned Adcraft Press. Gene had been diagnosed with cancer and needed to sell his business. Jake encouraged me to buy it because it would both help Gene and give me the resources I needed for a large-scale printing operation. While I was still pondering the decision, Jake came to me and said, "I will give you 100 percent financing if you will buy Adcraft." I didn't have the first clue about running a full-fledged printing operation, but I agreed anyway. Jake loaned me the money, and we got everything from the business—including a little Honda that became my second car. I even hired Mike Wells and Arthur Short who had worked at Adcraft Press. We moved the entire printing operation into a newly rented warehouse.

As we prepared to go into the printing business, Ken Adams asked me, "How in the world are we going to print all these programs and still get them delivered to all the host sites?" I said, "I have no idea, but we are going to sit down together and find a solution." That is exactly what we did. As the basketball season started, we determined that we needed to collect information on 100 teams that might make the NCAA field. As certain teams floundered, we shrank the list to the teams that had a legitimate shot at making the tournament. Then we called the SIDs at these schools and asked them to provide the rosters, statistical data, and pictures they wanted in the program. I followed up personally with each SID, either thanking them for providing the information or asking them to get us their materials as soon as possible. We set up a "war room" where we collected the information on all the potential tournament teams.

By "Selection Sunday," we had all the potential team information set in galleys and ready to roll. Before the NCAA announced the teams publicly, Dave Cawood called me with the brackets, giving us a three-hour head start. We took the pairings from the NCAA and made a long list of which teams were playing each other. We also determined which programs needed to be printed first in order to make it to the venue on time. Then we ranked each additional tournament site and lined them up to hit the press as soon as the first group of programs was printed. We worked through Sunday night into Monday and did the same thing on Monday night. As the first programs came off the line, we had a series of proofreaders making sure that the quality met our standards. We examined every line to verify that all the team information was correct and that all the advertising was in place. I was the final person on the proofing team, and I read every word of each program to make sure everything was perfect.

Once we printed the programs for each individual site, we took them to the post office in Lexington. I had contacted the post office weeks before and devised a plan to have all the packaging set before the programs arrived. And once the programs arrived at the post office, we wanted them to be shipped immediately. As soon as the programs left the post office, we informed NCAA officials at each site to let them know the estimated time of arrival and how many programs had been shipped.

We set up a separate "war room" for the NCAA Radio Network, which was now broadcasting all rounds of the tournament. This meant that the contracts were far more complicated because we had to determine which broadcasters needed to work on their own institution's radio network and which broadcasters were free to call games for us. We also determined which radio stations would be allowed to broadcast on their "home school" network and which stations needed to utilize the NCAA Radio Network. As we made all these decisions, we sent programs to the broadcasters at each site. We also mailed contracts to all the affiliate stations, letting them know how much they owed the NCAA for the games. If we did not hear from the affiliates immediately, I would call and let the station managers know that if they we did not receive their broadcast fees, they would not be allowed to carry the tournament games.

The small team at Jim Host & Associates did amazing work. We never missed a program delivery, and we cleared all the stations slated to carry NCAA tournament games. We improved both the programs and the radio broadcasts. All this made selling advertising on the radio and in the print programs much easier. I have always remained intensely loyal to this group of people because they stuck with me in those early years.

I learned an important lesson during that time: no matter how bleak the situation, there are solutions as long as people are willing to communicate, compromise, and adapt. We did a whole lot of that during our first couple of years, and it slowly began to pay dividends. However, my lesson in facing challenges became much more acute the following year.

7

Working in an Ever-Changing Environment

I began the 1970s in politics and ended the decade with a marketing and promotion business focused on college sports and association management. Soon after the 1980 NCAA men's basketball championship, our contract to broadcast UK sports came up for renewal. Since gaining the rights in 1974, we had built the largest collegiate sports radio network in the country. In 1977, when the rights were up for bid again, I had offered $83,500 annually—over $30,000 more than what we had been paying—and retained the rights. By 1980, the network blanketed the state with coverage, and the two clear-channel AM radio stations in Louisville and Cincinnati allowed UK games to be heard in forty states. No other collegiate broadcasts possessed such a national reach.[1]

Prior to submitting an offer, I learned that John Casey's American Network Group (ANG) would also be bidding. A businessman from Boston, Casey and Celtics basketball legend Tom Heinsohn had purchased the Nashville-based ANG with an eye on Kentucky. Realizing that I would need a strong bid to beat the competition, I made an extremely generous offer of $135,000 a year. Casey and the Kentucky Network Group (KNG), as ANG was called in the state, outbid me by $33,750 annually, or just over $100,000 for the three-year deal, and the UK Athletic Association's Press, Radio, and TV Committee, in a 5–4 vote, recommended that Casey's bid be accepted.[2]

I could not have been more stunned or disappointed. I understood the network's finances, so I knew that KNG could not afford to maintain the network with Casey's offer. UK granted me an appeal, during which I told UK president Singletary and the Athletic Association board how much I loved Kentucky and shared my desire to promote the university. I reminded them that we had built the largest college radio network in the country with more than 120 stations, two of which were 50,000-watt stations that covered forty states. I warned that this would be jeopardized if my company did not get the contract.

The full board deliberated and issued an 8–6 decision in favor of KNG. The board members in private business favored me, but UK employees voted for KNG. Everyone knew that Singletary loved athletics, and if he was involved, he was in charge. This meant that the UK president did not want me to get the broadcast rights.[3]

The RFP for control of the UK network's rights called for the highest and best bid. I knew I had the best bid, because we were committed to keeping 50,000-watt stations WHAS and WCKY and supporting the university. However, Singletary and his supporters were clearly set on accepting the highest bid, which I had not offered. Someone later told me that Singletary had been named to ANG's Board of Directors, which would have granted him financial benefits. I never attempted to verify that rumor, but years later, a lawsuit against the company listed Singletary as a "director." Though I was still an admirer of Otis Singletary, learning of his association with ANG changed the manner in which I approached him. He accomplished many great things for UK, but I believe this decision harmed the promotion of UK and its athletic programs for years.[4]

I was devastated that after laboring to build the UK Radio Network, it was now controlled by an outside company. I watched the network regress under KNG, losing key affiliate stations during the next six years. Losing the UK network was a bitter disappointment to me. However, I took my medicine and was determined to remain positive about UK. I continued to speak highly of my alma mater and help the institution in any way possible.

The only positive spin I could find for my company was that losing UK would force us to expand our reach into new business opportunities. I held a meeting with all the staff and said, "I want you to know that everybody here in this room has a job. You are all going to stay, and we are going to start building this company." Then I stressed, "This loss is going to be the best thing that has ever happened because it is going to force us to do what I should have done a long time ago: take the knowledge we have learned here and expand on it."

Then I closed by saying that there were new opportunities out there, and we were going to seize them. I am not sure whether anyone believed me at that moment, but I intended to make it happen.

I anxiously explored expansion opportunities, hoping we could work with other universities and athletic conferences. I had recently made a small inroad with the Southeastern Conference (SEC) in 1979, when it decided to revive its basketball tournament. Several individuals at SEC universities served on the NCAA Basketball Committee. They understood my work and had approached me about publishing programs for the event. This small contract generated minimal revenue, but I hoped that working closely with conference sports information directors and athletic directors (ADs) might create additional opportunities. However, a big conference deal simply fell in my lap when I least expected it.

That same year, Charlie Thornton, who was now the associate AD at Texas A&M, called me. I had first met Charlie when he was Tulane's sports information director. Bear Bryant later hired him for the same position at Alabama, where Charlie provided me with the information that led to my work with the NCAA tournament. He called me on a Friday night and said, "I need a favor from you. Would you fly down here to Dallas for a Southwest Conference meeting tomorrow?" He told me that the Southwest Conference (SWC) schools were not pleased with their radio network and needed some advice on how to proceed. I said, "Charlie, I don't have the time to come to Dallas." He countered, "Look, I'll pay your expenses, and I'm not going to hang up until you agree to come." I was determined not to give in, but then Charlie added, "Jim, how long have we known each other? I need this as a personal favor." So I agreed and took the first flight out the next morning. I arrived just as the meeting was starting.

As soon as I entered the room, they gave me the floor. I began by asking a number of questions to better understand the situation. I learned that the Humble Oil Network had sponsored SWC football broadcasts for years before it became the Exxon Radio Network. Exxon utilized the Mutual Radio Network to organize the broadcasts, which included only one SWC game each week that reached listeners in Texas and Arkansas. The other schools then jockeyed for stations across Texas. The University of Texas and Texas A&M carried the most station affiliates, while schools like Houston, Southern Methodist University (SMU), Texas Christian University (TCU), and Rice University struggled to expand outside their own communities. Each SWC school received $3,000 annually for the conference broadcasts. We had an honest and productive discussion about their grievances and the challenges they faced. Then they asked me what should be done. I had not prepared anything, so I began by outlining a business plan for the SWC while I spoke. I told them, "I don't want to offend anyone, but I'm going to rank all the SWC universities based on your value to advertisers." I wrote on a paper flip chart:

1. Texas
2. Texas A&M
3. Baylor
4. Texas Tech
5. TCU
6. SMU
7. Houston
8. Rice

I left Arkansas off the list because its sponsorships and radio stations looked totally different. When I asked the ADs if I was correct, they all thought I needed to flip Baylor and Texas Tech, but otherwise, the rankings were spot on.

I recommended creating a radio network that broadcast every conference game. It was easy to get stations to broadcast Texas or Texas A&M games but virtually impossible to sell Rice or Houston games outside of the Houston market. The same held true for TCU and SMU in the Dallas–Fort Worth market. I suggested that they sell the SWC Network by allowing each radio station to choose one primary university whose games it would broadcast. However, if a station's team was not playing, it would be required to broadcast another SWC game. The SWC also needed a funding formula based on each university's ability to generate sponsorships and radio advertisements. The small schools would receive less than the large ones, but they would still receive substantially more than they could ever earn independently. In addition, the smaller schools would benefit from increased radio exposure.

As I neared the end of my remarks, the two most influential ADs in the conference casually strolled into the room. Darrell Royal from the University of Texas and Frank Broyles from the University of Arkansas had been conspicuously absent, but I had been assured they would attend. It was obvious that they had just returned from golfing. When they sat down, Coach Broyles looked at me and said, "Young man, take five minutes or less and explain that again." I still remember John Conley from Texas Tech grousing under his breath, "Well, if you would have been here you so and so. . . ." I said, "Yes sir," and explained it again. When I finished, Coach Royal said, "How much are we paying you to be here?" I said, "Absolutely nothing. I agreed to do this as a favor for my friend Charlie Thornton." Charlie spoke up and said, "That's right! We aren't paying him a dime. I asked him to come help us out, and he graciously agreed."

Broyles then asked a series of questions, and I answered each one as best I could. Royal just sat there and listened. All at once Broyles yelled across the table, "Darrell, this sounds good to me. Why don't we hire him?" Royal agreed, and everyone else in the room followed suit. I knew that Broyles and Royal influenced the conference, but I had no idea the extent of their control. They basically dictated their will to the other ADs.

I had arrived that morning to offer some free advice as a favor to a friend. I had no idea they were looking to hire someone. So I finally spoke up to clarify my position: "Before we go any further and you hire my company, I need to know if you all will help set up a studio in Dallas to run the operation." They agreed. I then said, "I also want permission to hire each university's broadcaster. I will give you right of refusal, but I want the best voices I can find." They agreed to that as well. In fact, a number of ADs said it would be a blessing because they weren't happy with some of their longtime radio announcers but couldn't fire them.

Within twenty-four hours, I had been tasked with creating an entirely revamped SWC Football Radio Network. The first task involved hiring the best broadcast crews available. I asked every AD in the conference if they were pleased with their play-by-play announcers. I requested game recordings to evaluate them. Then I posted jobs all over Texas so that new voices could apply. I spent hours in my home basement listening to announcers and searching for the right people. I started by interviewing broadcasters at a Holiday Inn off I-35 in Dallas. I let some people go, and I recruited new voices to fill the broadcast booths across the conference.

The SWC agreed to a novel idea I had pitched to reduce costs and create a unique broadcast experience. For conference home games, each university's announcer would do the play-by-play, and the visiting team would supply the color commentator. This allowed for one "voice" of each individual university. Shuffling personalities around to find the best voices changed the trajectory of various university radio networks for decades. For example, Dave South was doing color commentary for Frank Fallon at Baylor. Fallon was a legend in his own right, but Dave was too talented to keep in a supporting role. I recommended that he take the play-by-play position at Texas A&M, but I warned him that he would have to be intensely loyal to that institution. This was not a problem for Dave, who continued as the voice of the Aggies until he retired at the end of the 2017 season.

While we were organizing our broadcast crews, we started building the SWC studio in Dallas. I hired Dick Gabriel, who worked at CBS affiliate channel 27 and WVLK radio in Lexington, to organize the studio operation. He prepared everything and kept me apprised of nearly every detail. I also appointed Bill O'Connell, producer of the University of Texas broadcasts, to oversee all game productions. Each team had its own production crew, but Bill made sure everything ran smoothly through the Dallas studio.

With all the office and studio staff, game announcers, and production crews in place, I called another meeting at the Holiday Inn. I opened by proclaiming, "We are going to make real change with this network!" I then outlined each new innovation to be implemented. I explained that we would pair the home announcer with the visiting team's announcer for color commentary and utilize sideline reporters. I described how the Dallas studio would switch to the most competitive games when appropriate. I concluded that we would build the best and most exciting college radio network in the country. Unfortunately, some of my new colleagues did not share my enthusiasm, and you could almost feel the air leave the room. The negative vibes were palpable because nobody wanted to give up their individual school approach. Nevertheless, we moved forward with our plans.

As we established the new network, I flew to Dallas almost weekly to make sure everything was progressing smoothly and in a timely fashion. After reporting to the central office and studio, I would hit the road and visit individual SWC universities and meet with ADs to assess their needs and discuss the network's progress. I developed good relationships with all the ADs during that first year. I enjoyed getting to know these leaders and learning about their individual schools. However, none of these friendships turned out to be more important personally or professionally than the one I developed with DeLoss Dodds, Darrell Royal's successor at the University of Texas.

The network's success ultimately depended on advertising sales, and I knew exactly who we needed for that important task. I had recently hired Ken Adams to help Host Communications Incorporated (HCI) with the NCAA, so I asked him to lead the sales team for the SWC Network. Ken worked closely with Marc Kidd to devise a plan, and they immediately sold a key sponsorship. Although I was not there, the two of them met with Bill Cahill of Fina Oil. He was interested in the sponsorship but thought the $290,000 price tag was too high. So Ken said to Bill, "Why don't we flip a coin? Heads the sponsorship is $270,000, tails it's $290,000." Bill said, "I like you guys. Sounds like a plan!" They flipped the coin, and it was tails, so our first key sponsor paid $290,000. That provided a much-needed financial cushion, allowing us to sell more sponsorships and commercials to other companies.

When football season arrived, we had everything in place. I had clear lines of communication with all the ADs, coaches, and sports information directors, our network sponsors, and the local affiliates. Every Saturday afternoon we saturated the Texas and Arkansas airwaves with SWC football. Our command center in Dallas monitored each game, and when one team was about to score, we briefly cut into that game. Fans heard more than 95 percent of their own games, but they were also updated about other action throughout the conference. A few critics objected and wanted to listen to only their team's game, but collectively, the strategy helped build a conference loyalty that I believe was unmatched in the history of the SWC.

After our inaugural season in 1980, I drove to every school and personally handed a revenue check to each AD. The smallest checks I delivered that first year were for $30,000. When I handed SMU's Russ Potts his check, he exclaimed, "You have made a friend for life!" Most responses were similar. The larger schools received around $60,000. The only non-Texas institution, Arkansas, had a separate marketing strategy, but I gave Broyles more money than he had ever seen from broadcast revenue. From then on, he was always trying to pick my brain for new marketing ideas. Working with Arkansas also taught me that, with regard to radio, it was better for my company to contract with individual universities so that we could blanket the state with radio networks. Regardless of the school or the amount, we radically improved on the $3,000 paid to SWC schools the previous year. It solidified the trust of the ADs, who were quick to let me venture into new areas.

Operating the network created a natural path into other media and marketing ventures. We created an SWC highlights television show and added coaching shows at the member schools. In addition, the ADs sought my advice about marketing and promotion at their own universities. Before long, we were producing game-day programs at almost every school in the conference.

The rapid growth of my company's printing business began taxing the space and equipment we had purchased a few years earlier. Hayden Kirkpatrick, owner of Thoroughbred Press, which did most of Keeneland's printing in Lexington, provided a solution. Years earlier, I had subcontracted out some printing work with Hayden, and I still owed him $10,000. When the bill finally came due, I told him I didn't have the money but promised to pay him in a few weeks. Kirkpatrick looked at me and said, "Young man, I think you are going to make it. Why don't you keep the money and give me some shares of your company in return?" I thanked him profusely, and we agreed that ten shares in the company would settle my debt.

By 1983, I had purchased more printing equipment from Rees Printing in Winchester, and we secured new printing orders when we were not producing college sports programs. One day Kirkpatrick came by my office and complained, "You're cutting into my business!" I said, "I'm sorry Mr. Kirkpatrick. I didn't know that, but it will improve the value of your shares." He looked unconvinced and added, "It's not worth what I'm losing. Why don't you just buy my company?" He had about seven acres of prime real estate on Broadway in an old building that had served as a hospital during the Civil War. General U. S. Grant had spent time there rehabilitating during the war. So my company bought Kirkpatrick out, gaining some much-needed space and equipment for our expanding enterprise.

Each year, our work with the SWC grew more profitable as more sports fans tuned into the network to cheer on their teams. I delivered larger checks to the schools, and my company profited as well. We received a management fee for running the network, the conference covered our costs, and we also made a percentage of the total profit. This gave us a huge incentive to expand the network and generate additional revenue.

Over time, I learned that the success of the SWC and the radio network was due in large part to Darrell Royal and Frank Broyles. They understood that the conference's success depended on the larger schools sharing a healthy portion of their profits with the smaller schools. Royal had implemented this philosophy at Texas with regard to gate-receipt revenue long before I entered the picture. For example, Texas might give Rice $100,000 for a game played in Austin, but when Texas played at Rice, the Longhorns would not collect a check. This arrangement kept the small schools competitive enough to play big-time football but weak enough for the powerhouse universities to get a win in most years. The same philosophy made the SWC Network a success as well. The larger schools allotted more than their "fair share" of profits to the smaller schools.

This approach faced a challenge a couple of years later. Eventually, De-Loss Dodds replaced the retiring Darrell Royal at Texas, and Fred Jacoby replaced longtime SWC commissioner Cliff Speegle. Both Dodds and Jacoby were content to continue the sharing philosophy, and neither leadership transition created a problem. However, in 1982, Texas A&M, tired of athletic mediocrity and always losing to rival Texas, hired Jackie Sherrill and sought to transform the Aggies into a national powerhouse. Everything seemed fine during Sherrill's first year at A&M. Then, after the 1983 season, I gave my standard address to the SWC football coaches and ADs that outlined the revenue and profits each school would receive. Everyone seemed pleased with their share of the money and the trajectory of the conference. Near the end of the meeting, Coach Sherrill stood up and proclaimed, "I am opposed to this. I think Texas should keep its own gate receipts and all of its broadcasting revenue. I think A&M should do the same thing. I think every school should rise or fall on their own merits." Sherrill had clearly spoken with the representatives of the larger schools prior to the meeting, because none of them seemed surprised. Those from Rice, Houston, TCU, and Baylor looked completely shell-shocked.

The announcement stunned me as well. I looked around the table and said, "If this is what you want to do, then obviously the Southwest Conference as we know it cannot survive." No vote was taken at that meeting, but everyone could see the writing on the wall. Afterward, Sherrill chased me down the hallway and tried to appease me. "Jim, I know what I'm doing," he said. "You're the best in the business. I want you to control the broadcasting rights for Texas A&M. That's why I'm doing this." I looked at Coach Sherrill and said, "I am not interested." Then I turned and walked away.

After that SWC meeting, DeLoss Dodds asked to speak with me. He let me know that if the conference decided to disband the radio network, he wanted me to control the broadcast rights for the University of Texas. However, he had one stipulation: "If you work with us, you can't work with Texas A&M. It's one or the other." This was a frustrating predicament because I loved the culture at both schools. The breakup of the SWC Radio Network would be a loss for my company. However, I told Dodds I understood and informed him that I had already turned down an offer from Sherrill.

In March 1984, a few months after Coach Sherrill made his comments,

Lowry Mays, the founder of what became Clear Channel Communications, asked me to meet with him and Sherrill in Birmingham. I knew him well because our sons attended the same prep school in Connecticut. Lowry owned the 50,000-watt WOAI in San Antonio, along with other radio stations across Texas. A brilliant businessman and A&M alum, Lowry would take a seat on Texas A&M's Board of Regents in 1985. He was an integral piece of Sherrill's plan for the Aggie network.

Lowry's request came during the NCAA men's basketball tournament, and I agreed to meet with them one night after the day's games had ended. It was long past my bedtime when we sat down in a hotel bar around midnight. Lowry explained that he, Sherrill, and the Board of Regents were seriously considering leaving the SWC. They sought to control their own destiny and escape the shadow of the University of Texas, and they were willing to join the SEC or another conference to do so. As Sherrill had already done, Lowry asked me to organize Texas A&M's radio network. I shared my own thoughts about the wisdom, or lack thereof, of such a move. We had a candid conversation about what all this would mean, but it was clear that Sherrill had made up his mind and had the support of the university administration.

At the next conference meeting, the athletic directors held a vote regarding Sherrill's proposal. The four larger schools—Texas, Texas A&M, Texas Tech, and Arkansas—clearly favored breaking up the network. Rice, Baylor, Houston, and TCU opposed the move. SMU was the swing vote. While I cannot prove this, I believe that SMU had been told that if it voted with the larger schools, those institutions would lobby the NCAA to impose only minor sanctions on the SMU Mustangs, who were being investigated for serious and repeated recruiting violations. Cheating was nothing new to the conference, and during the 1980s, only Baylor, Rice, and Arkansas avoided some sort of controversy or scandal. SMU ultimately voted with the larger public institutions to dismantle the conference network and have each university create its own network. Despite this, SMU still received the NCAA's "death penalty" and did not play football in the 1987 and 1988 seasons.

Arkansas left the SWC to join the SEC in 1991. Three years later, Texas, Texas A&M, Texas Tech, and Baylor left for the newly created Big 12 Conference. Rice, Houston, and TCU were left to fend for themselves. Much has been written about what led to the dissolution of the SWC, which had been in existence since 1914. Everyone has their own interpretation, but I believe that Jackie Sherrill's successful push to have Texas A&M control its own network and profits led directly to the conference's downfall. I think he would probably agree and would have no problem with what happened.

That vote marked the end of my company's work with the SWC Radio Network. We finished one final season as all the universities scrambled to put their own networks together. Our short time working with the conference had been wildly successful. We developed a media model that generated healthy revenue streams for the conference and created an opportunity to rapidly expand the radio network. This, in turn, grew the fan bases of each university and fostered conference loyalty. It helped me grow my company after losing the UK broadcast rights and made it far more profitable. I developed lifelong relationships with ADs and other sports donors across Texas. Finally, it taught me some valuable lessons regarding the market and the value of corporate sponsorships for college athletics. I would use this knowledge during the rest of my career in sports marketing.

In retrospect, it is hard to overestimate the importance of timing in leadership and entrepreneurial decision making. Sometimes the right timing is the result of strategic planning, and sometimes it is simply blind luck. For my company in the early 1980s, it was a little bit of both. We started the SWC Radio Network at the height of radio broadcasting in football. It was not the golden age of radio, but from the 1950s through my time with the SWC in the 1980s, the NCAA controlled all football television rights and strictly limited the number of games on TV. This obviously boosted the radio market.

That arrangement soon changed dramatically. In the late 1970s a group of coaches and ADs from "big-time" schools organized the College Football Association (CFA) to address their collective concerns. Shortly after its formation, the CFA focused on winning TV broadcasting rights for individual "power" conferences. While the NCAA argued that too many televised games would diminish game attendance and gate receipts, bowl game attendance provided hard evidence to the contrary. Tens of thousands of fans followed their teams across the country, even though they could stay home and watch the games on TV. A growing number of institutions believed that the NCAA was more interested in maintaining a monopoly on the TV market (and its profits), rather than simply protecting gate receipts.[5]

The battle between the CFA and the NCAA put university presidents in a serious predicament. The presidents were involved with the NCAA, where they set policy governing intercollegiate athletics. At the same time, the presidents of universities with "big-time" athletic programs were interested in keeping more of the revenue generated through television broadcasts. Many presidents were clearly conflicted, and UK's Otis Singletary was chief among them, because he was very involved with both the CFA and the NCAA.

For me and my business, this meant that SWC football fans had access to only one regionally televised and one nationally televised game each week. Because of this, nobody's team was on television regularly. It also meant that fans had to go to the game, where my company sold the programs, or they had to listen on the radio, where my company sold the advertising. The NCAA's TV policies created a much larger market for radio broadcasting.

In 1980 Chuck Neinas resigned his post as commissioner of the Big 8 Conference to assume leadership of the CFA. He had worked for Walter Byers from 1961 to 1971 as assistant executive director of the NCAA before accepting a job with the Big 8. Now he was challenging his former boss over television regulations he had worked to maintain earlier in his career. He had help from NBC, which had recently lost the contract for the NCAA basketball tournament. Upset by that loss, NBC was eager to get back at Byers and the NCAA by working with the CFA. In August 1981 Neinas brokered a deal with NBC worth $180 million over four years to broadcast football games for CFA teams, which would reap the profits. Byers, who had just negotiated a four-year deal with ABC and CBS worth more than $263 million, threatened to expel any NCAA team that participated in the CFA contract. Then Neinas and the CFA sued the NCAA through a lawsuit brought by the University of Oklahoma and the University of Georgia.

The *Regents* case, as it became known in the college sports management world, went through a number of appeals before being heard by the US Supreme Court. The highest court upheld earlier rulings that the NCAA was in violation of the Sherman Antitrust Act of 1890 because it restricted free trade and commerce. The Supreme Court ruled that the NCAA's practices of price fixing and restricting televised games constituted an unfair monopoly or "cartel," as one district judge had concluded.

Few people realized the full implications of the *Regents* case. It took a number of years, but this ruling (along with the advent of ESPN and other sports networks) has allowed almost every football game at any "big-time" university program to be televised. New television contracts took money away from the NCAA and funneled it to the conferences or, in a few instances, to the institutions themselves. So, I got out of conference-wide radio broadcasting just before television would have severely cut into my profits. However, radio remained an important part of the revenue scheme for individual universities. Many older fans never signed up for cable television, and others actually preferred to listen to their team's radio announcer rather than television broadcasters. It would take another two decades for television contracts to completely dominate the landscape of college football, but the process began in the 1980s.

Operating the SWC Radio Network changed the nature of my company. Rather than dealing with UK sports and the NCAA basketball tournament, we developed a national perspective and became involved with many more institutions. Because of this, HCI developed two distinct sectors: (1) college sports broadcasting and marketing, and (2) association management and the NTBA. As my work with UK and the SWC revealed, the college sports side involved a great deal of risk. However, the NTBA and the tourism business offered greater stability. It provided a steady cash flow that allowed us to more accurately forecast revenue.

Thankfully, as the SWC Radio Network came to an end, events in the tourism industry elevated our work with the NTBA. One essential lesson I had learned as executive director of the NTBA was the value of a tour broker's license. The US Constitution gives the federal government regulatory control over interstate commerce. For decades, companies that wanted to conduct tours across state lines needed a tour broker's license to do so. Licenses were difficult to obtain, and having one was essential to running a large-scale tour company. Licenses also gave tour brokers the right to lease motor coaches from companies such as Greyhound or Trailways, which had regular route authority.

The first such license had been issued to Arthur Tauck Sr., who conducted tours through New England and into Canada. By the time I got involved with the company, Arthur Tauck Jr. was running the family business, and it was still the industry's gold standard. Tauck, along with other key members of the NTBA, wanted to restrict licenses for two reasons. First, a license served as a status symbol or indicated recognition as a leader in the business. Second, a license requirement limited competition from upstarts hoping to make money in the industry.

After only a few years as executive director of the NTBA, I listened to board members' growing concerns that the federal government might "deregulate" the industry and not require a license to operate a company that conducted multistate tours. This frightened the leadership, and they asked me to develop a plan to fight deregulation of the industry.

In 1977 we hired the legendary Clark M. Clifford and his law firm to help in the fight. Clifford, the quintessential Beltway Brahmin and DC insider, had worked with multiple presidents on various issues, and by the late 1970s, he had become one of President Carter's advisers. Although we had no pending litigation, we basically hired Clifford to lobby on the NTBA's behalf. This strategy worked well until Ronald Reagan became president. At that point, I saw that we were not going to defeat deregulation, so we needed to try to delay it. I told the NTBA board that I would continue to fight deregulation, but we needed to devise a strategy to move forward when deregulation of the industry inevitably took place. Failure to plan for deregulation, I warned the board, would be disastrous for the NTBA.

Clifford assigned attorney David Granger to promote our interests. An impressive attorney, Granger helped us slow deregulation. This gave us time to devise a plan for operating in a deregulated industry. David and I developed a close friendship while working together, which would prove to be a huge blessing to me years later.

Several NTBA board members still hoped to defeat deregulation, but any realist who was paying attention saw the writing on the wall. Congress finally acted while the NTBA was holding its annual meeting in Toronto, Canada, in 1982. I explained to the board that it was time to embrace the change. I had already prepared a new name and a new logo, which the board voted to approve. The group's name changed from the National Tour Brokers Association to the National Tour Association (NTA) that week.

In addition to these changes for publicity and marketing purposes, we instituted our own standards and screening process for NTA membership. Although these were not as stringent as licensing requirements, we had multiple stipulations for joining the association, the most important of which was evidence of liability insurance. Because of my background in insurance, we also started offering tour operator protection packages.

We publicized our new operating plan, and almost immediately the NTA started to grow exponentially. The organization had approximately 300 members when I first came to work for it. By the time of the Toronto convention, that number totaled nearly 800. One year later, convention attendance nearly doubled to 1,500, and the year after that, we exceeded 2,000 attendees at the convention. Our team worked with what we called "destination marketing organizations" in nearly every state. Subscriptions to the association's *Courier Magazine* skyrocketed as well. We charged healthy rates to advertise in the promotional publication, and we also raised the cost of association membership. In short, although the licensed tour brokers I represented had lost their protected market, I wanted to make sure they gained something in return.

This work brought in substantially more revenue for the NTA and made my company more profitable. Less than a decade earlier, I had agreed to serve as the NTBA's executive director for a $19,000 annual retainer. However, I had also built in bonuses for my company as the NTBA reached various revenue thresholds. As the association made more money, my company benefited as well. I wanted to make sure that when I grew the tour brokers' business, they helped me grow mine. That is exactly what happened.

Another windfall from deregulation and the growth of tour companies stemmed from the expanding list of allied members. I used the organization's size to leverage better deals for the tour brokers. The NTA secured official sponsors that paid money to have access to members of the association. This was huge because with one stroke of a pen, a tour operator could send thousands of tourists to a particular hotel chain or airline. Airlines, hotels, and restaurant chains all wanted to sponsor events so that they could sell their products or services to the tour brokers.

We created additional demand by telling sponsors and suppliers that if they paid their fees at least six months in advance, they would be guaranteed a specific spot or time at the convention. When sponsors paid their fees in advance, this allowed us to make money on early deposits because of the crazy interest rates in the early 1980s. Simply putting money in six-month CDs generated a lot of interest income.

Operating the NTA was a far less visible part of HCI's business than sports, but it continued to be a key component. It was a low-risk endeavor that afforded us the opportunity to expand the much riskier college sports marketing side of the business. Thankfully, as the NTA business boomed, my work in athletics kept me more than busy. Operating the SWC Network had taught me that a group of universities working together could command a larger share of revenue when securing media sponsors, and I thought it was worth replicating at the NCAA.

I was working the finals of the NCAA men's basketball tournament in Philadelphia in 1981 when Walter Byers invited me to a reception he was hosting for a number of close friends and colleagues. Walter held these receptions each year on the Sunday night before the championship game on Monday. At the reception I took Byers aside and commented, "Walter, I think it is time to have corporate sponsors for the NCAA tournament. There is incredible opportunity, and you're missing out on a lot of revenue." I had reached this conclusion because it was becoming increasingly difficult to sell radio advertising for the NCAA tournament. We had cleared all the top markets, but when I tried to sell commercial time, people continually told me, "Jim, we are looking at TV advertising." I was constantly trying to find ways to generate revenue, and I thought corporate sponsorships would be mutually beneficial for both the NCAA and my company.

I went on to explain to Byers that I was not talking about small amounts of money to hang banners around the arena. I wanted a few large corporations that could obtain a competitive advantage by offering, for example, two free tickets to the championship-weekend tournament games. Then the companies could advertise their official sponsorship of the NCAA on the side of a soap package or a cereal box. Corporations would also be able to advertise across the multiple media outlets that had sprung up during the previous decade. With the growth of the tournament, television coverage, and the radio network, I thought it made perfect sense. I will never forget Walter looking me in the eyes and telling me, "Host, over my [expletive] dead body."[6]

Not one to be easily dissuaded, I replied, "Walter, I'll tell you what. I'm going to send you a letter explaining the strategy." He quipped, "Don't waste your time or the paper!" I simply said, "I hope you will consider this, because it can change the entire trajectory of the NCAA and college athletics." We didn't speak again that evening. I spent an inordinate amount of time crafting the perfect letter, making sure that it explained my position clearly. I noted the importance of building the NCAA "brand" as well as the tournament. I argued that major corporations could pay the NCAA, build the NCAA brand, and promote the tournament, all while avoiding commercial signage at the event. I sent the letter, and a few days later I received a note from Walter that simply read, "Duly noted." However, about six months later, Walter called me and said, "You know that corporate sponsorship idea you mentioned to me. Why don't you come out here and we can talk about it."

As I started pitching the corporate sponsorship concept to Byers, the NCAA simultaneously began an aggressive expansion. The tournament first grew incrementally from forty-eight teams in 1980 to sixty-four teams in 1985. Each expansion created new challenges, but we calculated ways to make it more profitable. Two individuals were key to the quick success of NCAA tournament expansion. Dave Gavitt had been the head coach at Providence before helping to create the Big East Conference and becoming its first commissioner. Vic Bubas had been the head coach at Duke University and served as the first commissioner of the Sun Belt Conference. These two people, along with Duke AD Tom Butters, worked tirelessly to expand and promote the NCAA tournament. They were led by NCAA executive vice president Tom Jernstedt, who did a superb job organizing the tournament for nearly four decades.

As the NCAA expanded the tournament field, it also became increasingly interested in enhancing promotion of the tournament. People started using the term "Final Four" in the 1970s, but it is generally accepted that John Chay of the *Cleveland Plain Dealer* first printed it years earlier. After noticing the growing popularity of the term, I suggested to Tom Jernstedt and Dave Cawood that the NCAA should trademark the phrase, which it did after the championship in 1981. This seemingly small move transformed our marketing strategy.

The NCAA made other important decisions and improvements as well. In 1981 the NCAA replaced NBC with CBS, which started televising the tournament in 1982 and brought new life to the event. CBS broadcast a selection show for the first time and, unlike NBC, televised the regional games. Although my work involved radio and printed programs, CBS's promotions helped my business as well. In addition, the NCAA selected the New Orleans Superdome as the first official dome site of the Final Four. Moving the semifinals and the championship game into the dome seemed like a risky proposition. The NCAA did not want nationally televised games played at a half-empty venue. As it turned out, the move to the Superdome was a resounding success, and it nearly tripled the number of fans who purchased programs.

As we prepared for the Final Four in New Orleans, I spent a great deal of time working with the NCAA and Dr. Mervin "Merv" Trail to make sure the new location would work. Trail served as chancellor of the LSU Health Sciences Center in New Orleans and tirelessly promoted the Crescent City. He was the first person to include weekend festivities that involved more than just basketball games. Rather than diminish the games, it made the entire Final Four experience better. When Dean Smith's North Carolina Tar Heels beat John Thompson's Georgetown Hoyas 63–62 for the title, a crowd of 61,000 saw the game in person, along with a huge television and radio audience. The Division I men's basketball tournament had changed forever, and the NCAA started to realize the tournament's untapped potential.

The SWC, NTA, University of Texas, and NCAA all played vital roles in the expansion of my company. When I lost the radio rights to UK sports, many thought the company would fold. As the cliché goes, when one door closes, another one opens. In this case, multiple doors opened. Thankfully, we made the most of the work that was right in front of us, and we were prepared to take the next steps when the opportunity presented itself.

Me (left) with my brothers Jon and Jay in 1943.

My parents, Bea and Will Host, had an indelible impact on my life. They were strict and sacrificed a great deal to ensure that their sons had an opportunity to succeed in life.

The Ashland High School baseball team in my senior year. I am in the back row, the second player on the right.

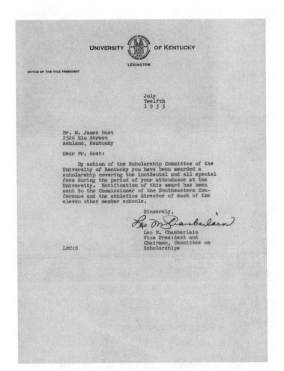

This official letter offering me a scholarship to UK changed my life. I did not receive it until mid-July, less than two months before the beginning of the fall semester.

As an NCAA scholarship athlete, I was not allowed to play intramurals, so I coached Delta Tau Delta's basketball team. I am on the far left with the clipboard.

During the summer between my junior and senior years, I knew I needed to improve my pitching if I wanted to play professional baseball. Thankfully, I managed to do so, and during my senior season I posted a 1.52 ERA.

The UK baseball team in my senior year. I am in the back row, sixth from the right. We had won more games in the history of UK baseball up to that point, despite falling short of an SEC championship.

Putting on the White Sox uniform felt like a dream come true. Unfortunately, a shoulder injury ended my dream of making it to the big leagues.

After Dee Huddleston resigned as play-by-play announcer for the Kentucky Central Network, I served as its lone broadcaster for UK athletic events. At the time, no company owned exclusive broadcasting rights, but ours was the largest network in the state for UK broadcasts.

Herbert St. Goar (left) and Clyde Berke (right) of Dixie Savings Stores in Chattanooga, posing with me and their first train-car load of Tide from Procter & Gamble. Convincing them to purchase that much product changed the trajectory of P&G in the area and led to my promotion.

After I agreed to register as a Republican and to chair John Sherman Cooper's Senate campaign, the Fayette County Republican Party presented me with this elephant.

This photo was taken shortly after I became commissioner of public information in Governor Nunn's cabinet. In 1967, cabinet heads were called commissioners; today, they are called secretaries.

Governor Nunn at the press conference announcing my new job as commissioner of state parks.

Kentucky first lady Beula Nunn and I developed a close relationship when we worked together to preserve historic landmarks during my time as commissioner of parks.

Cawood Ledford (right) and me broadcasting an NCAA tournament game. Whenever UK lost in an early round, I hired Cawood to call the Final Four.

I hosted Bill Cahill (left) of FINA Oil and golfer Jack Nicklaus (center) at an NCAA convention in New Orleans during the 1980s. FINA Oil's sponsorship was one of the primary reasons the SWC Radio Network was such a success.

UK offered the men's head basketball coach position to PJ Carlesimo (right), but he turned it down and returned to Seton Hall.

Van Florence (left) was the chief aide to multiple basketball coaches, as well as chair of the Committee of 101, a service group for UK athletics. Rick Pitino (right) was a challenge to work with, but he masterfully resurrected UK basketball after the dark years of scandal in the late 1980s.

Roy Kramer (left) was gracious and unassuming and, I believe, one of the most underestimated conference commissioners in intercollegiate athletics. He and I developed a lifelong friendship when we worked together to promote the SEC.

SEC commissioner Roy Kramer (left) ushered in an era of unparalleled success for the conference. He was a visionary who understood the changing media landscape of intercollegiate athletics. We are pictured here with Mark Shapiro (center), who was running ESPN's programming at the time.

Duke AD Tom Butters (left) next to his wife, Lynn, with Pat and me. Tom was visiting Lexington to invite UK to join the ACC.

(*Left*) Despite our schools' rivalry, AD Doug Dickey (left) and I signed a deal that was profitable for both the University of Tennessee and Host Communications.

(*Below*) The University of Tennessee had one of the longest institutional relationships with HCI. Bob Kessling (center), who succeeded John Ward as the voice of the Vols, and Steve Early (right), general manager of the Vol Network, were key to the success of this partnership.

(*Left*) Pat and me at the Kentucky Derby.

(*Below*) After we were married, Pat took on the important but unpaid role of event planner for HCI. She organized the annual Kentucky Derby party we held for our most import-ant clients and served as a valued adviser as I made key decisions regarding the direction of HCI.

Left to right: Baylor's former football coach and then executive director of the American Football Coaches Association Grant Teaff, Tennessee's Phillip Fulmer, and Georgia's Vince Dooley at one of HCI's Kentucky Derby parties.

Cawood Ledford and his wife, Frances (left), posed with Pat during his last broadcast season at UK in 1992.

David and Bean Granger, with me between them. David helped save HCI during the Bray Cary fiasco.

Closing the deal with GE Capital. Left to right: HCI CFO Jerry Moore, GE Capital executive Dave Kelsey, me, HCI partner Chuck Jarvie, and attorney Joe Terry.

HCI's senior leadership team in the 1990s. Although the team changed over the years, this photo includes some of the longest-serving members. Chuck Jarvie and I are seated. In the back row (left to right) are Mark Dyer, George Ackerson, Marc Kidd, T. J. Nelligan, Rick Ford, Jerry Moore, and Hank Phillips.

CM Newton (center) with me and legendary sports executive Jerry Colangelo (left) during Newton's induction into the Naismith Basketball Hall of Fame in 2000.

Me with NCAA president Ced Dempsey (center) and Sean McManus of CBS (right) during one of the high points of our negotiations.

HCI operated the NCAA Radio Network for more than a quarter of a century and worked with many amazing announcers through the years. Some of the best were (left to right) Dave Sims, Bill Raftery, and Marty Brennaman (with me on the right).

Pat took this photo with Ann and Terry Holland, AD at the University of Virginia (front left), and University of Texas AD DeLoss Dodds and his wife, Mary Ann (front right), when the two schools' football teams played in Charlottesville. UT was one of our oldest clients, and HCI gained the media rights for UVA athletics in the 1990s.

One of my best moves while working in the Fletcher administration was appointing UK football great Derrick Ramsey (left) as my deputy secretary in the commerce cabinet. He went on to serve as Kentucky's secretary of education in the Bevin administration.

Key players in bringing the Alltech World Equestrian Games to Kentucky in 2010 (left to right): Alltech founder Pearse Lyons, Princess Haya Bint al-Hussein, my wife Pat, Catherine Keogh (our point person for Alltech), Pearse's wife Deirdre, and Mark Lyons (now CEO of Alltech).

The announcement that the World Equestrian Games would be coming to Kentucky and that Alltech would be the title sponsor. Governor Fletcher is on the left in the front row, and Pearse Lyons of Alltech is on the right.

Our delegation to the World Equestrian Games in Aachen, Germany, brought back ideas to improve the games. Jack Kelly (left) served as CEO of the Alltech World Equestrian Games in Lexington. Lexington mayor Jim Newberry (right) provided much-needed support that helped the games run smoothly.

Alltech founder and CEO Pearse Lyons (left), former governor John Y. Brown Jr. (center), and myself during the Alltech World Equestrian Games at the Kentucky Horse Park. The event went off without a hitch, solidifying Kentucky's standing as the equestrian capital of the world.

At the opening of the KFC Yum! Center, Governor Steve Beshear (right) and Louisville mayor Jerry Abramson (left) surprised me with this plaque that would hang in the new arena's atrium.

Completion of the KFC Yum! Center during the Great Recession was an incredible accomplishment that required the hard work of many civic-minded leaders.

Pat and me attending an event at the governor's mansion.

After completing my term as executive director of the National Tour Association, I posed with all the past presidents I had served with. Although my work with the NTA was not as public as my work with college sports, the association played a central role in the growth of group tourism in the United States.

Pat with two of my closest friends in college sports: Tom Jernstedt (left) and DeLoss Dodds (right).

This photograph, taken during the weekend of Charles Barkley's enshrinement into the Naismith Basketball Hall of Fame in 2006, shows (left to right) Larry Hayes (Mayor Abramson's chief of staff and vice chairman of the Louisville Arena Authority), me, Dave Gavitt (founder of the Big East, past chair of the NCAA Division I men's basketball tournament, chair of USA Basketball, and one of my closest friends), Charles Barkley, and William Summers IV (a key administrative aide to Mayor Abramson).

Left to right: Pearse Lyons, Senator Mitch McConnell, Pearse's wife Deirdre, and son Mark Lyons at a McConnell campaign event in 2008.

Pat and her daughter Tiffany at my induction into the University of Kentucky Athletics Hall of Fame in 2009.

The inaugural class of "Champions of Sports Business" presented by the *Sports Business Journal* in 2010. Left to right: me, Jerry Colangelo, Tony Ponturo, Donna Lopiano, Ron Labinski, and Neal Pilson.

Me with Dick Vitale (center) and Denny Crum (right) when Vitale was inducted into the Naismith Basketball Hall of Fame in 2008. Vitale and I developed a friendship around basketball, even though I worked in radio and he announced on television. Crum, who coached UK's archrival Louisville, couldn't have been more gracious to me.

Joe B. Hall (right) and I entered the College Basketball Hall of Fame together in 2012. Hall served as Adolph Rupp's assistant for many years before succeeding the legendary coach and doing a great job.

Me (left) with two college basketball legends I am fortunate to call friends: John Calipari (center) and Tom Jernstedt (right).

Legendary television broadcaster Tom Hammond (right) and I were honored together when the Bluegrass Sports Commission named two awards after us in 2012.
Despite Tom's success, he is one of the most unassuming and kind individuals in the
sports broadcasting business.

Left to right: Mannie Jackson, owner of the Harlem Globetrotters; former governor
John Y. Brown Jr.; me; and PG Peeples, president and CEO of the Lexington Urban
League since 1969.

Left to right: renowned Kentucky journalist Al Smith; Dr. Terry Birdwhistell, former dean of the UK Libraries who conducted my original oral history interviews; Len Press, UK professor, my mentor, and founder of Kentucky Educational Television; and me.

At an awards banquet, Pat and I posed with the legendary Muhammad Ali, his wife Lonnie, and Dr. Richard Lapchick, an influential visionary who has used athletics to promote racial and gender equality.

Me (left) with some of my closest friends (left to right): Tom Jernstedt, longtime NCAA executive vice president; Big 10 commissioner Jim Delany; and longtime Duke AD Tom Butters.

Me (left) with two of my dearest friends who are now deceased: UK's athletic director CM Newton (center) and Baseball Hall of Famer and former US senator Jim Bunning.

My best friend from high school Jon Zachem (left); attorney Terry McBrayer (center), one of Kentucky's leading citizens; Wayne Martin (seated), former manager of Lexington's CBS affiliate WKYT; and me. We all have eastern Kentucky roots, and we still meet regularly to talk about politics, sports, and life.

Executive director of the Lexington Urban League for nearly half a century, PG Peeples (center) posed with me and Kentucky football legend Derrick Ramsey (right) at a recent fund-raising event for affordable housing. Under Peeples's leadership, the Urban League has raised more than $26 million to put Kentucky residents in homes.

Five of our grandchildren when they were young.

Left to right: my brothers Jay and Jon, our parents Will and Bea, and me.

My two brothers, my mother, my son David, and me.

Pat and me with (left to right) my daughter Elizabeth Host Dupree, her husband Tom, and our two grandsons James and Clark on my eightieth birthday.

Pat with her daughter
Tiffany's two sons.

Left to right: Pat's daughter Tiffany, me, my daughter Elizabeth, and Pat.

8

The NCAA and Corporate Sponsorships

Despite losing the UK rights, the first few years of the 1980s were very successful for our company. However, I had been unable to get Walter Byers to even engage in a discussion about corporate sponsors for the NCAA tournament. Then, out of the blue, Byers called me. I remember picking up the phone and exchanging greetings. Immediately Walter asked, "Host, remember the idea you had about corporate sponsors that you shared with me at the Union League in Philadelphia?" I said, "Yes sir." He responded, "Be in my office tomorrow at nine. I want to talk about it." As usual, he didn't give me an opportunity to plan ahead or arrange my schedule. As always, I said, "Yes sir." I caught the first flight out of Lexington that afternoon so I could be in his office the next morning.[1]

I knew that the College Football Association had challenged Byers and the NCAA over football television rights. I was unaware, however, that Byers had secured a CFA bulletin written in January 1982 in which the CFA's head, Chuck Neinas, suggested changing the name to the College Sports Association to allow the organization "to address issues related to basketball and other sports." As Byers stated in his own memoir published years later, "The CFA strategy centered on removing the NCAA football from television and then undercutting the NCAA in basketball. Since about 75 percent of its income was generated by the . . . tournament, the NCAA would be fatally crippled." Byers saw signs of a potential coup and needed corporate sponsors to make basketball too valuable for NCAA institutions to defect. NCAA tournament teams already received healthy payouts, but Byers was ready to up the ante.[2]

When I walked into Walter's office, he was holding the letter I had written about corporate sponsors—the one he had told me not to bother writing. He looked at me and said, "Host, let me get this straight. Are you telling me that we are not talking about putting any company signs in the venues of the NCAA tournament?" I said, "No sir." Walter had always made it clear that he wanted the NCAA tournament to resemble the Olympics or the Master's golf tournament, without any banners or advertisements at the events. Then he asked, "How can you pull this off? It sounds like you're trying to sell air." When he said that, I knew I needed to reframe my argument. So I said, "Walter, this is a way of building the brand of the NCAA and the Final Four. We can actually get large corporations to pay you and, at the same time, go out and promote the NCAA tournament." I explained that that companies would be willing to use the NCAA logo and the term "Final Four" to promote their products.

Walter looked at me and asked, "How will putting the logo of the NCAA on some label help sell a product?" I told him that when I worked for Procter & Gamble, everyone in sales was always looking for some sort of promotion to secure a competitive advantage. I suggested to Walter that Gillette might be a prime target for NCAA sponsorship because it spent a lot of advertising dollars during sporting events. My friend Gordon Wade, whom I had helped train at P&G, had contacts at Gillette. If I could get an "in," I thought I could convince Gillette to sign on as the first corporate sponsor because of the marketing edge it would offer. Walter asked me how much I thought a corporate sponsor would pay. I said, "My best guess is that I could sell a three-year sponsorship for $250,000 per year." I also emphasized that each sponsorship would be subject to NCAA approval. When Walter asked how much it would cost the NCAA or my company, I reemphasized, "Walter, they are going to pay the NCAA to use your logo and fan base to sell their own products!"[3]

I explained again that a corporate sponsorship would not cost the NCAA anything. For instance, if a company wanted ten tickets as part of each deal, it would pay the sponsorship fees and the ticket costs. I thought the tickets would be an essential selling point for the corporate sponsors. They could put "Win a trip to the NCAA Final Four" on their product packaging. They could tell a grocery store chain like Kroger that the store that sold the most Gillette razors during the month leading up to the event would win an all-expense-paid trip to the Final Four. In addition, I would give sponsors airtime for radio commercials on the NCAA Network as well as key print ads in the official programs. Walter said, "That might work." I replied, "I think it can work, but I need your permission." Walter said, "I tell you what we'll do. You go out and get the first sale, and we'll split the proceeds fifty-fifty. However, you need to pay your expenses, and whatever sponsors you do land, you will be required to service them." I said, "That sounds fair to me."

I planned to contact Gordon Wade first. When I worked for P&G in the 1960s, it operated a fast-track management program for young, talented Ivy League graduates whom the company intended to promote to corporate headquarters. P&G assigned several trainees to me during my time at P&G, but Gordon was probably the brightest. Gordon later became a leading consultant for major global corporations. He had connections with everyone, and I knew he would provide sound advice.

Before I could call Gordon, he called me just before I left for the Final Four in New Orleans. He wanted to take some friends to the horse races at Keeneland and asked if I could get him some good seats. He liked to invite friends to attend the races at Keeneland during the day and play poker at night. I promised I would find him some seats and then shared my plan to develop corporate sponsors for the NCAA. He said, "That's a hell of an idea. I'm going to be staying at the Marriott in Lexington when we visit Keeneland. Come see me and we can discuss the details." So I agreed to visit.

We spent a few hours at the Marriott one morning, and I elaborated on my strategy. Gordon provided some excellent advice for negotiating with Gillette. The company ran promotions with Major League Baseball through the World Series and spent money on marketing with the NFL through the Super Bowl. However, the company had "dead time" on the calendar during the spring, and an NCAA corporate sponsorship would fill that gap. That would be my selling point. Gordon then connected me with Bill Ryan, who oversaw the personal care products division at Gillette. After sharing my plan with Ryan, he invited me to Boston to make a sales pitch.

Before I made the trip, I called my friend and longtime NTBA colleague Bruce Beckham. Bruce lived just outside of Boston and was a huge Red Sox fan. He said, "You need to see a game with me!" I had never been to Fenway, so I gladly agreed. As an interesting aside, when I was standing in the hotel lobby waiting for Bruce to pick me up, I saw Phil Niekro. I went up to him and said, "Phil, I'm Jim Host." He looked puzzled, as clearly that meant nothing to him, so I said, "I beat you in a fifteen-inning game between Holdrege and McCook. . . ." He interrupted and said, "I remember that!"

The day after the game at Fenway, Bruce accompanied me to Gillette's headquarters, where we met with Bill Ryan and two of his associates from Gillette's razor division. These were the days before PowerPoint, so I started pulling out some whiteboards while providing some background on the NCAA's basketball tournament. All at once Bill interrupted me and said, "Jim, why are you here?" So I cut to the chase: "I want Gillette to be the first-ever corporate sponsor of the NCAA tournament." Bill asked, "What does that mean?" I went through my sales pitch about Gillette needing a marketing strategy during the "dead" spring months and how the growth of the men's basketball tournament and the official advent of the Final Four provided evidence that a corporate sponsorship was a wise financial investment.

They seemed to be with me up to that point, so I said, "You will get to use the NCAA and Final Four logos, be the exclusive product in your sales category, and you can purchase twenty NCAA Final Four tickets for promotional purposes. All your artwork will have to be approved by the NCAA." Bill asked, "How much will it cost?" I responded, "Half a million dollars per year with a three-year contract, which will increase slightly along with the consumer price index." He said, "Fine, we'll take it." I was elated but wished I had started with a higher asking price. We shook on the deal, and I said I would get a contract drawn up and send it to them.

When we walked out, my friend Bruce Beckham, who had witnessed the whole thing, asked, "Do you think you undersold it?" I said, "I have no idea. Nothing like this has ever been done, so I'm not sure." Then he asked, "Who else are you going to try to get?" I said, "Come with me to my hotel room, and let's see if I can sell another one." I then called Carl Frey, who was the senior vice president for marketing at Valvoline, a Lexington-based oil company that sponsored a lot of motor sports, including NASCAR. I basically gave Carl the same pitch I had just made to Gillette. I added that the 1985 Final Four would be in Lexington, so Valvoline would have an opportunity to capitalize on the event. With virtually no hesitation he said, "I think I'll do it." I told Carl that Gillette was the one corporate sponsor ahead of Valvoline, but the two companies were in no way competitors. Then I asked him to be patient while we hammered out all the details with the NCAA.

When I got back to Lexington, I called Byers and said, "Walter, I've got two sponsors!" He immediately asked me, "How much money did you get?"

I responded, "Half a million dollars annually for each one with a three-year contract." Byers said, "That's more money than I ever imagined!" I let him know that I would hire an attorney in Lexington to help us draft the contracts. Soon thereafter I sent the documents to Walter, but I didn't hear anything from him for months. I kept calling his office, and he wouldn't take my calls. So I started calling Dave Cawood, begging him to get Walter to return my calls. More than six months had passed since my initial agreement with Gillette. Now, in the beginning of 1983, I was getting nervous. My contact at Gillette, Dick O'Hearn, kept telling me that his supervisors were growing impatient and we needed to close the deal.

I believe the primary reason for Byers's inattention stemmed from his focus on the *Regents* lawsuit. The NCAA had lost its initial case as well as the appeal. Byers and the NCAA were now appealing to the Supreme Court. Walter viewed the case as a fight that went beyond a television contract. He was engaged in a war for the NCAA's survival, but part of his strategy included corporate sponsorships. When he finally reengaged, I worried that the months of delay might cost us the Gillette and Valvoline deals.

During this time, I was working by phone with Derek Coward, a brilliant but superior-acting Englishman who was the vice president for marketing of Gillette's safety razor division. Derek was getting fed up with the lack of response from the NCAA, and I understood his frustration. However, according to Dave Cawood, Derek had offended a lot of people at the NCAA, and he didn't know whether the deal could be made. Finally, Derek wrote a scathing letter to Walter Byers, stressing how good the partnership could be if not for the ineptitude of the NCAA and its tangled maze of bureaucracy. That apparently got Byers's attention because Walter called and asked me to bring Derek Coward to Kansas City for a meeting.

Since I had never met Derek Coward in person, I flew to Boston before the Kansas City meeting, hoping to get to know him a little better. After some small talk, I thought we were on the right track, but then, in his proper British accent, Derek said, "Mr. Host, I don't believe this is going to work. I have never experienced anything like the intolerable behavior shown to me by the NCAA." He went on about the lack of efficiency and said he could not imagine partnering with such an organization. I looked at him and said, "Derek, you are working with a different group of people, but I promise that if you can break this barrier, it will be the most meaningful marketing strategy you can imagine." He responded, "I know it has potential, but that doesn't matter if we can't make a deal." Getting a little nervous, I suggested that I call the NCAA right there in his office and make sure our meeting was going to happen. He agreed, so I called the NCAA and confirmed the meeting. I said, "We're in, and I'm telling you this is going to work." It was obvious to me that Walter Byers had finally put Gillette on his priority list.

I flew out to Kansas City and met Coward for dinner the night before the meeting. We got to know each other better, and I learned that he liked Beef-eater gin. I hoped our conversation would make us both more comfortable the next day, but as it turned out, that probably didn't matter. When we arrived the following morning, Walter Byers immediately took over the meeting. We walked into the room, and he had copies of the contract ready to hand out to everyone. He looked at us and said, "All right, let's get this deal done. Mr. Coward, would you tell us about Gillette and what you do?" Derek obliged, and when he was done, Walter said, "Okay, you have convinced me that Gillette will be a good partner to the NCAA and will help enhance the experience for student athletes across the country." Then he went through the contract line by line.

After Coward's scathing letter about the NCAA, Byers wanted to make sure Gillette knew that the NCAA was a top-flight organization. Byers also wanted to make it clear that he was in charge, not me. The marketing contract was actually between Gillette and my company, since I controlled the rights to NCAA radio broadcasts and programs. However, Coward left knowing that Byers made the decisions for the NCAA. In 1984 Gillette became the first college corporate sponsor in history by partnering with the NCAA.

Meanwhile, Valvoline was also getting anxious about my ability to deliver a contract. Carl Frey kept warning, "If you don't get this done soon, I'm going to pull out of the deal because we want our sponsorship in full swing when the Final Four comes to Lexington." Once we closed the deal with Gillette, we simply used the same template and filled in the details for Valvoline. Valvoline's deal was complete in time for the 1984 Final Four in Seattle, which gave us two corporate sponsors for the event.

Seattle proved to be an amazing host city, but that first Final Four with corporate sponsors was quite a challenge for me. Taking a cab from SEA-TAC into downtown Seattle, I noticed huge billboards advertising shoes, soft drinks, food, and services, and they all read something like, "Welcome to the NCAA Final Four." I immediately met with Bob Walsh, the Seattle native in charge of organizing events, and learned that the city had sold advertising to various companies to fund all the special events held around the Kingdome. I told him he had ambushed the NCAA sponsorships, and he didn't take kindly to my challenge. As our argument escalated, I thought he was going to punch me. Thankfully, he did not. Bob and I eventually became good friends, and I learned that the NCAA needed to inform host cities that they couldn't sell advertising with the NCAA logo or Final Four trademark without negotiating through the NCAA. In the future, we also set up "clean zones" near the arenas where only NCAA sponsors' advertisements were allowed.

After our first tournament with corporate sponsors, I wanted to find out how the promotion had gone and whether the NCAA partnership had paid off. I asked Gillette, which had decided against putting the promotion on the razor-blade packaging, opting instead to utilize free-standing inserts that went into newspapers across the country. The insert had a coupon for Gillette products and an advertisement promoting a contest to win a trip to the Final Four. When I asked Derek Coward if the company was pleased with the results, he let me know that Gillette had generated more than $140 million from the coupon and promotion—or nearly 7 percent of its revenue. This told me that we were on to something big that could revolutionize the NCAA, college athletics, and my company.[4]

With two corporate sponsors in place, I focused my efforts on expanding into new industry markets. Our first soft-drink sponsor was Coca-Cola. Then I brokered a deal with American Airlines as a corporate partner, because I knew its head of marketing through the NTA. I pulled him aside during one of our breaks at a travel conference and told him that the NCAA Final Four was coming to Dallas in 1986. I thought a corporate partnership would make sense with the Final Four being held in one of American Airlines' hub cities, and we managed to close the deal.

I also wanted to ink a deal with a hotel chain, and I had an obvious partner in mind: Hyatt. During the building of the Lexington Center and Rupp Arena, Hyatt had won the negotiation over Marriott for space in the complex. Tim Lindgren became the general manager of the Hyatt Regency in Lexington and did such a good job there that he was promoted to other Hyatt hotels in larger markets. By the mid-1980s, he was the general manager of the Hyatt in Kansas City. I connected Lindgren with the NCAA, hoping to establish a partnership between the two organizations. Then we convinced Hyatt to become the official hotel chain of the NCAA. That deal included some perks for NCAA officials, who were able to get preferred bookings and room upgrades.

Not every sales pitch I made was a success. Gatorade was an example of a deal that just didn't work out. Initially, I went after Gatorade as a separate drink sponsor, arguing that it was a sports drink and wasn't in competition with soft drinks. Nobody ever called a time-out during a game to chug a Coke or a Pepsi. So I went to see Bill Schmidt, an Olympic javelin thrower who became a marketing genius for Gatorade. His plan was simple: he supplied free Gatorade to sports teams, but they had to drink it out of the Gatorade coolers on the sidelines. It was a brilliant idea, because Gatorade was suddenly everywhere on TV. Bill agreed to purchase a sponsorship for three years, but because Byers refused to allow courtside product placement or logos at the NCAA tournament, Gatorade ended its sponsorship after the initial contract. Our first soft-drink sponsor, Coca-Cola, also ended its sponsorship after the first contract expired, opening the door for Pepsi.

Probably the greatest success story in the early years of NCAA corporate sponsors involved Pizza Hut, which we started negotiating with in 1986. I set my sights on Pizza Hut because the pizza business was booming among college-age students and families with young children, two demographics that were likely to watch the tournament. Pizza Hut was interested in signing on, but it was looking for a new marketing strategy that would separate it from the competition. I needed a unique sales pitch to close the deal, and Marc Kidd, the head of our sales team, helped me devise a strategy.

At the time, Rawlings was an official licensee for NCAA athletic equipment, and it had bought the rights to have sporting goods, including basketballs, displaying its name and the NCAA logo. I researched the topic and discovered that Rawlings was making its basketballs in Taiwan. I asked whether the company could make mini-basketballs and how much it would cost to produce two to four million of them. The answer was $2.19 per ball. We developed a plan, and Marc Kidd and I went to see David Novak, who had recently become the chief marketing officer for Pizza Hut.

When we met with Novak, I told him that if Pizza Hut became a corporate sponsor, we could produce four million basketballs with the Rawlings, NCAA, Final Four, and Pizza Hut logos on them for $2.19 each. I suggested that Pizza Hut sell the balls for $2.99 with every pizza order of $10 or more. Pizza Hut could also purchase NCAA Final Four tickets to incorporate into the promotion. Novak looked at me and said, "That is a hell of an idea because it is a self-liquidator." I agreed. If Pizza Hut sold four million mini-basketballs, it could use the revenue to purchase television and radio advertising.

Novak needed to take the idea to his boss at Pizza Hut, Steve Reinemund, for approval. He called me a few days later and said that Reinemund thought it was a huge risk to spend millions of dollars on mini-basketballs without a clear plan of execution. I said, "David, if this is properly promoted, millions of kids will want these basketballs and drag their parents to Pizza Hut to get a pizza and a basketball. It will be a success!" Then I added, "I will get a warehouse in Memphis [the hub of FedEx]. We will ship all the basketballs there, and then we can distribute them to every Pizza Hut location in the country, along with pumps to blow them up." Pizza Hut eventually signed the deal but purchased only two million balls. It also wanted to ship the balls to its own warehouses because the logistics and the supply lines to franchises were already established. So we signed the contract, ordered the basketballs, and waited to see what would happen.

At that time, the NCAA conducted the Selection Show at the Hyatt in Kansas City near its headquarters. As usual, the selection committee allowed me to wait outside the room so that I could relay the brackets to our printing operation in Lexington. I was sitting outside the committee's conference room when a bellman ran up and asked, "Does anyone know who Mr. Host is?" I said, "I'm right here." He said, "I have an emergency call from Pizza Hut!" I followed the bellman to a phone, and David Novak was on the line. He said, "Jim, I have a problem. We need to stop all the promotional ads on the mini-basketballs." I asked, "Why in the world would you do that?" David replied, "We have already run out of basketballs!" It was the most successful sports promotion anyone had ever done. It was crazy: Pizza Hut ran out of basketballs before the tournament brackets even reached the public! The next year, Pizza Hut doubled the number of basketballs to four million and sold every one of them. That successful promotion made Novak look like a genius, which he was. When KFC, Pizza Hut, and Taco Bell spun off from PepsiCo and eventually became the Yum! Brands, David became the CEO. My friendship with David would play another important role in my life many years later. Marc Kidd, however, deserved most of the credit for spearheading the deal.[5]

For years, Pizza Hut sold out of those basketballs. The promotion worked like a charm. It would be difficult to overstate how important that promotional effort was in expanding the brand of the NCAA and the Final Four. It also revealed to other companies that supporting the NCAA men's basketball tournament had enormous commercial potential. By the late 1980s, the secret was out. Corporations realized the value of and return on an NCAA sponsorship, so we raised the fees but kept adding new accounts. One of the most rewarding corporate sponsorships we ever negotiated came in 1990 with Sara Lee.

My tie to that story developed after Congress passed Title IX in 1972. Originally intended to ensure equality for women in higher education and the workplace, its reach quickly expanded to include athletics. At nearly the same time, the Association for Intercollegiate Athletics for Women (AIAW) began governing women's athletics and hosting a basketball tournament for women's teams. The AIAW operated as a parallel organization to the NCAA, but as the implications of Title IX grew, Walter Byers began to consider how he could incorporate women's athletics into the NCAA. I remember attending meetings in the 1970s where the athletic directors (all of them men) fretted that women's sports would take resources away from the men.

The other group that was opposed to the NCAA incorporating women's sports was the AIAW. Universities all over the country had hired women to administer their women's sports programs, and the AIAW governed those sports—primarily basketball. Many women did not want the NCAA involved because it would essentially end their ability to control their own sports. In fact, the AIAW sued the NCAA in 1981, claiming that the NCAA engaged in predatory pricing by sponsoring women's intercollegiate sports championships without raising the flat fees it charged universities to participate in the NCAA. The AIAW claimed this was a violation of the Sherman Anti-Trust Act, but it lost the case (and the appeal).[6]

Before that case had been settled, Byers convinced the NCAA's executive committee to operate a women's basketball tournament in 1982. He then informed me that HCI needed to set up a radio network and publish all the women's Final Four programs. When I looked at the projected numbers and the lack of publicity, I said, "Walter, I don't know how to make this work." He just looked at me and said, "You'll figure it out just like you have everything else." I did figure it out, but doing work for the women's tournament was a financial burden. Thankfully, that has changed, and women's basketball has developed a successful brand of its own. In the early 1980s, however, trying to sell commercial spots on the radio for the women's tournament was an uphill battle. We lost a lot of money on the women's tournaments in the early 1980s, but I gained a large number of friends who understood the importance of promoting women's sports.

By the late 1980s, I was looking for a separate corporate sponsor for the

NCAA women's tournament. Walter Byers had retired as executive director of the NCAA in 1986. Dick Schultz, a prominent member of the NCAA Division I Men's Basketball Committee and AD at Cornell and the University of Virginia, succeeded Byers. One of Schultz's primary concerns as the new executive director was improving the status of women's athletics. He was continually discussing the need for greater promotion. At one NCAA meeting, I suggested that we find a primary sponsor for the women's tournament. Schultz agreed and suggested that the women's sponsor promote an "NCAA Woman of the Year." Everyone loved the idea.

Unsure of where to turn, I asked Gordon Wade's opinion about choosing the right company. Gordon was good friends with Sara Lee's CEO Paul Fulton, and he thought that would be a good fit. As Gordon had done with Gillette, he helped get me in the door. As an interesting aside, Tom Jernstedt, Dick Schultz, and I traveled to Chicago to make the deal. We were all in a cab strategizing when Tom said, "You know, I have never loved the term 'corporate sponsor.' What do you think about changing it to 'corporate partner'?" He thought "partner" more accurately described what we were actually doing: partnering with companies to promote intercollegiate athletics. We all agreed, and today, almost all sports teams call their corporate sponsors "partners."

We arrived at Sara Lee headquarters in downtown Chicago and made our pitch. It ended up being an easy sell because we presented the partnership strategy as a way to bring greater attention to women's sports and women as student athletes. Sara Lee agreed to a three-year sponsorship for $6 million. Paul Fulton, who was genuinely committed to promoting women in all facets of life, saw the marketing value because Sara Lee also owned Hanes Her Way and its many products for women. Fulton believed in the value of the college experience and would later return to his alma mater, the University of North Carolina, as dean of the Kenan-Flagler Business School. He agreed to a deal that day, and we had our first exclusive partner for the NCAA women's basketball tournament and a sponsor for NCAA Woman of the Year. I called Marc Kidd with the good news. He and I met that weekend and established the criteria for the Woman of the Year award.[7]

It is hard to overstate Sara Lee's role in the growth of women's collegiate athletics. Its partnership clearly boosted interest in the women's tournament. As promised, it also sponsored (and promoted) the NCAA Woman of the Year award, bringing more recognition and revenue to women's sports. Held in Chicago, the first NCAA Woman of Year event was an unbelievable success. Clearly, Sara Lee proved to be the best possible sponsor to bring about positive change for women's sports. Of all the corporate partnership deals we negotiated over the years, Sara Lee's had the greatest positive social impact.[8]

Judy Sweet's election as the first female president of the NCAA coincided with Sara Lee's corporate partnership and marked another seminal moment for women's athletics. Judy had served at the University of California–San Diego as one of the first female athletic directors to lead both men's and women's athletic programs. When she accepted the post as NCAA president (at the time, a volunteer position), a number of critics falsely labeled her a "token" president. She proved her detractors wrong. Securing a corporate sponsor just as she took over as NCAA president provided the financial foundation and momentum she needed to successfully promote women's athletics.

By any standard, the development of corporate partners was a resounding success. The plan worked exactly as intended: companies provided much-needed revenue to run the NCAA's increasingly complex organization. At the same time, corporate advertising helped build the brand and popularity of the tournament. When I started broadcasting on the radio in the 1970s, the NCAA tournament was relatively unknown outside of a few basketball-crazy states. When I first asked Walter Byers about corporate sponsors in 1981 at the Union League in Philadelphia, one would never have known that the NCAA championship was being played there. By the early 1990s, the entire tournament had become a national phenomenon, with millions of brackets being filled out across the country.

NCAA corporate partnerships also changed the complexion of my company. By the early 1990s, we had the following corporate partners: American Airlines, Coca-Cola (and later Pepsi), Gatorade, Gillette, Hyatt, Kodak, National Car Rental, Oldsmobile, Pizza Hut, Rawlings, Sara Lee, and U.S. Sprint. We kept raising the cost of sponsorships, but the list continued to grow as we moved forward. We now had key individuals such as Marc Kidd and Devron Edwards working at HCI to develop stronger relationships with our partners, and we hired many more employees to ensure that our work was serving both the NCAA and its sponsoring companies.

By 1990, a lot had changed at the NCAA. Walter Byers had retired, women's sports were growing, and the NCAA men's basketball tournament had become a national cultural event. Most important, corporate partners had created a revenue stream that helped the NCAA expand its reach over college athletics. Early in the 1980s, it looked as if the CFA might replace the NCAA in many respects. Corporate sponsors, which had been nonexistent at the college level until the Gillette deal, stemmed the tide and kept the NCAA in control of intercollegiate athletics. Of course, the growth in revenue created new challenges as coaching salaries went through the roof, universities undertook massive expansions of their athletic facilities, and television began to dictate scheduling. Funding from national companies made the NCAA much more businesslike, yet the organization tried to maintain and promote the idea of the student athlete. It is a challenge that remains with the NCAA today. Despite the challenges, corporate sponsorships certainly brought the "madness" to March.

9

Back to Kentucky and Bundled Rights

My work with the SWC and the NCAA's corporate sponsors had allowed me to go national. At the same time, my work at UK had taught me how to market and develop individual university athletic programs, so I kept my eyes open for opportunities in that field as well. Managing the NCAA Radio Network gave me the opportunity to form friendships with university presidents, athletic directors, sports information directors, and coaches all over the country.

One of the first schools to reach out to me was Purdue. I knew basketball coach Fred Schaus from the NCAA Men's Basketball Committee, and Fred had become AD at Purdue. Purdue was simply getting crushed by Indiana University and Notre Dame in terms of broadcasting. It had tried an "in-house" radio network, which wasn't working, so Fred invited me to West Lafayette to discuss a partnership. He immediately asked me to run Purdue's network, and I agreed.

First, we found someone who understood the radio industry map of Indiana and negotiated deals for broadcasts covering the state. We brought in a new football announcer and sold more advertising. In 1982 I traveled up to watch Purdue play Stanford, and the latter's senior quarterback, John Elway, throttled the Boilermakers. Despite that loss, we had grown the fan base for Purdue. In addition, the university had just hired Gene Keady, and his success made it easier to market Boilermaker basketball in the Hoosier State. At Purdue, however, I learned that building a college network that already had a flagship university (in this case, Indiana University) made for uphill sledding. At the same time, I learned that if I could find the right schools around the country, my company could be at the forefront of college sports marketing.

While I was working with Purdue, Jackie Sherrill at Texas A&M set in motion the SWC's slow dissolution. Both A&M and the University of Texas (UT) jockeyed for HCI's services, but I could contract with only one of the rivals. I loved the campus and culture at Texas A&M, but I had a close relationship with AD DeLoss Dodds, so I cast my lot with Texas.

I met with DeLoss in Austin multiple times to develop a marketing strategy. It was clear that UT–Austin had the resources and the fan base, but it was woefully behind in terms of corporate advertising. During one visit, I sat in on a meeting where DeLoss was literally negotiating syrup prices with Coca-Cola. He said, "If you can come down on the cost of syrup, I will give you some more signage in the stadium." The company already had its logo on the scoreboard, and DeLoss was willing to give it a few more signs in return for cheaper syrup! Afterward I said, "DeLoss, you're losing money! I bet you left $250,000 on the table!" Although he was an amazing AD, he had not yet grasped the concept of Coca-Cola paying to sell its drinks exclusively *while* promoting the University of Texas. I suggested that he ask Pepsi to make a bid to be the exclusive drink provider of Longhorn athletics. He said he couldn't do that because the university had a policy against exclusive sponsorships. I asked him to arrange a meeting with his friend and Texas booster Mike Myers to plan a pitch to UT board members. After I shared my thoughts, Myers said, "We need this revenue, and if you can show us how to do it without prostituting everything, then I'm for it." I did just that, and he set up a meeting with the UT Board of Trustees. I knew I had at least one ally.

That board meeting changed the trajectory of Texas athletics. I explained how UT could generate revenue for the Longhorns and have corporations promote the university's athletic programs at the same time. We discussed the various sponsorship product categories and the advertising the sponsors would receive in programs, on the radio, and on signs. The board agreed to move forward, and Dodds grudgingly followed, even though he feared too much commercialism.

We slowly developed corporate sponsors for Texas sports programs, primarily through game-day program advertisements and radio advertising (to appease Dodds). HCI actually lost money the first five years we worked for Texas. I loved DeLoss, but he remained a traditionalist and a skeptic when it came to corporate sponsors. In addition, Texas had boosted its academic standards in an attempt to become an elite university. The administration held a hard line on academic requirements for athletes, making it difficult for Texas to compete with schools adhering to less stringent standards.

Once the death of the SWC became imminent in the 1990s, I participated in numerous discussions regarding UT's future conference "home." Former UT president William Cunningham, who had become chancellor of the University of Texas system, and current UT–Austin president Bob Berdahl both favored a move to the PAC-10, but that never materialized. Dodds seriously considered becoming independent and had me develop a strategy and a schedule of the teams Texas would need to play if it ended up outside of any conference.

Ultimately, Texas became a founding member of the Big 12, and the popularity of Longhorn athletics continued to grow. Each year, Dodds became more amenable to my desire to provide additional perks for corporate sponsors. To placate the purists, we allowed minimal advertising at the stadium, but I persuaded DeLoss to approve hospitality tents for the sponsors. He prohibited any signage, but we sold ten tickets to each sponsor and allowed individuals to tailgate under the tents and enjoy the game. Eventually, Dodds came to me and said, "You've slowly crept in with corporate sponsors. Just go ahead and do it all!" By replicating our NCAA corporate sponsorship program as closely as possible, we generated incredible revenue for Texas while expanding the fan base. This created a foundation that benefited both the university and its athletics department. That powerful sponsorship plan, coupled with the large population in Texas, gave the university unprecedented negotiating power within the Big 12 and eventually led to the creation of the Longhorn Network operated by ESPN.

Other athletic directors took note of our marketing strategy. Florida State's AD Hootie Ingram approached me about developing FSU athletics, which had remained independent. I visited Tallahassee to study FSU's gameday programs, radio network, sponsorships, and so forth. After Hootie left FSU for Alabama, Bob Goin became AD at Florida State, and he requested our assistance as well. Competing outside of a conference created a unique set of challenges, but we agreed to operate FSU's sports radio network, publish its programs, and sell corporate sponsorships. Within a few years, we had expanded FSU's income and market reach. With the network in place and Bobby Bowden's football success, FSU's popularity grew exponentially.

Our company's success with a few select schools in the mid-1980s created a foundation for rapid growth in the late 1980s and 1990s. That expansion stemmed from two clear factors. First, the company genuinely helped the schools it served. Second, my connections with athletic directors and sports information directors around the country continued to grow.

Many of these relationships developed because of one fortuitous event: NBC's failure to invite Dave Cawood and his team of volunteer public relations administrators to its corporate party at the 1980 championship weekend in Indianapolis. I knew that NBC usually threw a party on the Sunday evening before the championship game. Coming off the elevator at the hotel that Sunday night, I saw Dave and asked, "Why aren't you at the NBC party?" He replied, "We weren't invited." I told him, "I'm going to start a party that you all will always be invited to." That night, we went to a restaurant and a bar, and I picked up the tab. From that night forward, my company always threw a top-flight party for Dave Cawood and his team of sports information directors and athletic directors working the Final Four, as well as representatives of the corporate sponsors. This afforded me the opportunity to meet even more people interested in sports marketing contracts.

That party took on a new level of importance when the NCAA Final Four came to Lexington in 1985. We had just started the corporate sponsors program the year before in Seattle, but we had laid the groundwork to bring the Final Four to Lexington years earlier when we built Rupp Arena. Lexington mayor Jim Amato, Kentucky AD Cliff Hagan, and I made a presentation to the NCAA Basketball Committee, chaired by Big 10 commissioner Wayne Duke. We explained that Rupp Arena had cable wire running through the structure, so television trucks simply had to "plug in" from outside the convention hall, which connected directly to the arena. Rupp Arena had television platforms at the base of the upper level to provide the best angles. The convention center had plenty of space for the press corps' conferences, reporting, and socializing. I was confident that we had earned the bid, but as we were leaving, Duke said, "Jim, would you stick around for a few minutes? We have a couple of questions we'd like to ask you." He, Dave Cawood, and Tom Jernstedt told me that they would award the Final Four to Lexington if I agreed to help organize and run it. I said, "I'll make sure the mayor forms an organizing committee with the right members who can do the job. I'll work behind the scenes and make sure that it runs smoothly." They agreed, and the 1985 Final Four came to Lexington.

The irony of helping to host the Final Four on UK's behalf in 1985 was that I had been outbid and had lost the rights to the UK Radio Network. Regardless, I wanted to have the most successful Final Four ever. Seattle's hosting model a year earlier gave the organizing committee the idea to create an amazing fan experience all around downtown Lexington. Everything went off without a hitch, and America got to witness one of the few Cinderella champions when Rollie Massamino's Villanova Wildcats defeated John Thompson, Patrick Ewing, and the Georgetown Hoyas.

That weekend, HCI hosted its corporate party at the fabled Calumet Farm. The farm's owner, Bertha Wright, let us use the mansion, and we planned a party like no other. Walter Byers called me and said, "Jim, may I combine my Sunday night party with yours? Everyone wants to go to Calumet." I agreed, and we had a couple hundred guests. The opulent event helped us meet even more athletic directors, sports information directors, and media executives from around the country. Even CBS executives wanted to attend.

Each year, the party grew larger. At the 1986 Final Four in Dallas, we rented the mansion used in the hit television series *Dallas*. We hosted nearly 400 guests, many of whom I had not met before. That weekend, John Scovell from the Woodbine Development Corporation, as well as other sports investors, expressed an interest in my company. However, they wanted HCI to move to Dallas permanently. They offered some unbelievable perks, but in the end, I decided that Kentucky was home and the company would stay in the Bluegrass.

The next year, we were back in New Orleans, and in 1989 the Final Four returned to Seattle. Each year, the host cities tried to "one up" their predecessors. CBS kept plugging the event on television, and the Final Four was growing into the culturally iconic event it is today. The parties we threw in each city were amazing social events, but they also led to important business ventures. In each city I relied on my National Tour Association contacts for catering, restaurants, rental spaces, and the like.

During one Final Four, Roger Valdiserri, an associate AD at Notre Dame, came up to me and said, "Jim, we have some serious problems with the programs for our football games, but I think you can help us." I said, "You should have great programs. Everyone who goes to a Fighting Irish game wants a program!" He responded, "We do have great programs, but we have other issues." Selling game programs was a cash business, and Notre Dame's administration was worried about who ended up with the money and how it was used. I said,

"Well, do you want me to start tomorrow?" I didn't get the job that quickly, but Roger invited me to South Bend to tour the operation. Dick Rosenthal was Notre Dame's new AD. He, Roger, and the Reverend William Beauchamp (who had been President Hesburgh's right-hand man) wanted me to create the best football programs in the country while remaining "pure" and avoiding any commercial symbols on campus. I agreed, but it made promoting the school and generating revenue more challenging. Once we made a little money on the football programs, we developed the radio network for Irish basketball. I had hoped to eventually operate Notre Dame's football radio network, but that never happened.

I knew that corporate sponsorships were the future of big-time college sports, but Notre Dame's tradition kept it rather conservative. Despite my inability to convince Notre Dame to adopt corporate sponsors, it was one of my best clients for nearly two decades. I loved visiting the campus because of the wonderful people there. AD Kevin White eventually decided to take the rights in-house after Notre Dame signed an exclusive TV deal with NBC.

As my company's reach expanded nationally, I hoped to regain the rights to my alma mater, which I had lost in 1980 by a few thousand dollars. However, HCI had retained the publishing of game-day programs for UK football and basketball. Back in 1980, the bidding had been so close that I wondered whether there was some kind of funny business going on, but I was too busy growing my business to appeal the decision.

As time passed, UK's AD Cliff Hagan kept asking me to get involved with the radio network. Fans were constantly bombarding him with complaints because they could no longer pick up a radio signal. The American Network Group (called the Kentucky Network Group in the Bluegrass) had given up its clear-channel stations in Louisville and Cincinnati in order to get more revenue from smaller stations that were willing to pay a fee to broadcast the games. Although Cliff was primarily concerned about angry fans in Kentucky, I knew that UK had lost its broadcast powerhouses and, with them, the ability to market UK athletics across much of the country. Even worse for UK, the University of Louisville had assumed the primary spot on WHAS, which greatly increased the Cardinals' exposure. I had taken an absolute beating in the media when I protested the loss of the UK contract in 1980. My critics said I was a money-hungry sore loser. Although I intended to turn a profit, I knew that accepting ANG's bid would wind up hurting UK, and it had. That is why so many people were begging me to bid again in 1986.

HCI won back the rights to UK sports in 1986 and never lost them again. In the meantime, I had learned a great deal about marketing strategy while working for other schools. My first goal was to rebuild the radio network and sell as many "bundled rights" packages as possible. This involved combining print media, radio, and television for sponsorships. Cable TV and ESPN had revolutionized college sports media. Radio remained a key component, but television would be the future growth market. I envisioned sponsors' fees covering advertisements on radio, in programs, and on locally televised games.

This goal became imperative after an exchange I had with representatives of Coca-Cola while hosting them at a UK Wildcats football game. Coke had just purchased a key UK sponsorship, and during the game one of the executives asked, "Why are there Pepsi cups on UK's sideline?" The question embarrassed me, but the answer was simple: Coach Jerry Claiborne had negotiated his own deal with Pepsi, which included cups with the Pepsi logo on the sideline. This practice was commonplace. Businesses also paid coaches directly for advertising on coaches' shows. The coaches then distributed game tickets to those businesses or to boosters.

This arrangement created confusion and cost universities serious revenue. To remedy the problem, I worked with the UK Athletics Department, Ralph Gabbard at Lexington's CBS affiliate WKYT, and Ralph Hacker at the Lexington radio station WVLK. We hammered out deals that would "bundle" sponsorships on radio and local television. Hacker had coaches' shows on the radio, while Gabbard had them on television. Then I went to UK's administrators and convinced them to agree to exclusive sponsorships across all media platforms. What I originally called "full meal deals" became known as "bundled rights" packages. By creating a single marketing and media rights package, UK generated substantially more revenue for athletics. This model was adopted across the country.

Not long after getting bundled rights in place at UK, the university's basketball recruiting violations made national headlines. In April 1988 a package sent to the father of prized recruit Chris Mills had come open in transit, exposing the contents: $1,000 cash. The NCAA investigation uncovered an avalanche of violations. Before the end of the year, Cliff Hagan resigned as AD.

President David Roselle wanted CM Newton to replace Hagan and asked me to help lure him back to UK. CM had played basketball for Coach Rupp in the 1950s. He then coached at Transylvania in Lexington and later at Alabama. After a short stint working for the SEC, he returned to coaching at Vanderbilt, where he was in 1989. I told Roselle that Newton loved UK and wanted to return, but he was making far more money coaching than he would as AD. Roselle asked me to help pay Newton with the revenue from radio rights and media marketing, and I agreed. Meanwhile, Newton kept asking me, "If I come, can you help me hire a basketball coach?" (Facing eighteen NCAA infractions, UK's embattled basketball coach Eddie Sutton had resigned.) CM understood the finances and wanted to know if, as media rights holder, HCI would be willing to pay a hefty portion of the salary needed to hire a big-name coach. I told him we would, and Newton agreed to become UK's AD early in 1989. CM became the first AD we ever paid from a bundled rights package.

At universities where HCI owned media rights, I often played a role in the hiring of new coaches. I never dictated who would be hired, but ADs almost always asked me to meet with potential coaches because much of their salary would be generated through commercials organized by HCI. I had a special relationship with UK and Newton, so CM and I collaborated on a short list of names. I thought PJ Carlesimo was the best basketball coach available. He had played for Digger Phelps at Fordham and had enjoyed some success coaching at a few small schools before leading Seton Hall to its first-ever tournament appearance and then to the Final Four the next year. I called PJ, and he was interested, so I gave his number to CM, and they scheduled an interview. I picked PJ up at the airport, and we met CM at my office. President Roselle interviewed him too, and we all had lunch at the Campbell House with former governor John Y. Brown Jr. and members of the Athletic Department. We showed PJ around campus, and everything seemed promising.

After a long day of interviews, I was taking Carlesimo to the airport when he asked, "How late do the restaurants stay open?" I said, "PJ, this isn't New York. I know you're a night owl, but there isn't anything open at 2:00 a.m. that's worth visiting." Then he said, "Jim, I don't know how I'll sell in eastern Kentucky." I said, "I'm from eastern Kentucky, and I know you're a perfect fit. As long as you win, the whole state will love you." Then I added, "But if you're going to be uncomfortable in a small city like Lexington or you're afraid you might not connect with rural Kentucky fans, you should probably just use this as an opportunity to get more money from Larry Keating." (Keating was Carlesimo's AD at Seton Hall.) I said that if I didn't hear from him the following day, I would assume he wasn't going to take the job. The next day came and went, so I called PJ and left a voice mail thanking him for his consideration, wishing him the best of luck, and telling him that we would be moving on with the search. PJ's father, Peter, who had been AD at Fordham and ran the National Invitational Tournament (NIT), did call me. He told me that he wanted his son to take the job at UK in the worst way, but PJ just didn't have the heart to do it.

A few days later, CM called me around midnight with a lead. Big East commissioner Dave Gavitt, the former Providence coach and AD, thought that Rick Pitino might be interested. Pitino had left Providence to coach the New York Knicks, but according to Gavitt, Pitino and Knicks general manager Al Bianchi didn't get along. CM flew to New York and talked to Pitino. Rick was interested, but he wanted to wait until the end of the season to consider the matter. By this time, fans in Kentucky were on edge, so CM announced that he would serve as interim coach until the right coach could be found.

When the Knicks' season ended, Pitino flew into Lexington. Nobody knew he was in town. Pitino met with President Roselle, and then CM and I met with Rick. When we sat down, CM asked, "Now Rick, it's not about the money, is it?" Rick looked at CM and said, "No, CM, it's never about the money." CM grinned, leaned in, and said, "I've been in coaching. It's always about the money." Then Rick asked a bunch of insightful questions about the university, UK's probation after the NCAA violations, and the business side of things. He had done his homework.

When we got around to discussing the contract, CM said, "Rick, UK can pay you a little more than $100,000 plus insurance and retirement benefits." Pitino would be able to keep the money he made from his basketball camps and at least $100,000 from the UK shoe contract. Then CM said, "Jim can talk to you about coaches' shows and other revenue." Rick asked, "What's involved in that?" I looked him in the eye and said, "I want to own everything you do. That means books, endorsements, pre- and postgame shows, and weekly call-in shows. You will be restricted to two minutes on any other interviews. That way, we own your exclusivity. The most I have ever paid a coach for this is $100,000, and that's what I'm offering you." Rick laughed and said, "I'm not going to do it for that." I asked, "Then how much?" He countered with $450,000. I thought I was going to wet myself. I said, "We are on probation, we have no live TV, and coaches' shows don't bring in that kind of money." Rick explained his position: "CM started this by saying that, to some degree, it's about the money. I've looked at the finances, and if I understand everything CM has talked about, then I need $450,000 to make this work. And I need the book rights because I already agreed to a deal with Billy Reynolds." Then he added, "I'll give you my local speaking rights, but I'll keep my national speaking rights." He thought he could get $25,000 for speaking engagements and demanded that he keep that money. He said, "I'm sorry, I'm not coming unless I get $450,000 and those exceptions." CM said, "That's right. It's not about the money." We all chuckled, but CM and Rick laughed a bit more than I did because I had no idea how I was going to generate that much revenue.

I invited CM to step outside to discuss Pitino's demands. We walked into another office and CM said, "Jim, I'm begging you. You've got to do this." I replied, "CM, I don't see how to make it work." He said, "Jim, I'll do anything. We can try to do other things with your contract. I'm convinced Rick can get it done, and he will be your hottest seller for commercials and endorsements." So I agreed. We walked back in, and CM told Rick, "We've got a deal." Just to confirm, I asked, "You are agreeing to do whatever endorsements and commercials we need you to do?" He said, "Yep. I'm very difficult to work with during the season, but I'll agree to do it if you're willing to work around my schedule." We shook hands, and Rick reiterated that he was committed to the deal.

A couple days later, I got a call from Pitino's financial agent, Mitch Dukov. He said, "I understand you and Rick Pitino have an agreement for endorsements and commercials, is that right?" I said, "That's right." He asked, "How much did you agree on?" I told him $450,000, to which he replied, "It's actually $600,000, or he's not coming." I said, "You have got to be kidding!" He repeated, "I'm not kidding. It's $600,000 or he's not coming." I asked, "Have you told CM Newton?" Dukov said, "If you don't agree, Rick will tell him the deal is off." I let my emotions get to me and shouted, "We had a deal! You can go to hell!" Then I hung up.

Within fifteen minutes, CM called in a panic: "We already announced that Pitino is coming, but he's gonna back out unless you pay him $600,000!" I reminded him, "CM, you were in the meeting! He agreed to $450,000!" Desperate, he kept on: "I know, but you've got to help me make this work. I'm begging you!" I told him I would have to think about it, and I hung up and drove home. I hadn't been there ten minutes when CM called and asked, "Jim, have you made up your mind? I talked to Rick again, and he wants to set up a press conference." I asked CM how I was going to make the money back, and he said, "Nobody is more innovative. I know you can figure it out!" I said, "Okay, I'll do it." When I told Gabbard and Hacker, they both thought I was out of my mind.

CM announced the press conference, and then I got a call from an attorney in Lexington who said, "We have the contract ready to be signed. It's for $650,000." I said, "What in the hell are you talking about!? We agreed to $450,000, then it went up to $600,000, and now this!" He replied, "Pitino won't do the press conference unless you sign this contract." At that point, I had no choice. I called CM, just to let him know what he was getting into from a business perspective. As I hung up the phone, I kept thinking, "Why didn't I convince PJ to take the job?"

Pitino finally signed the contract with UK. HCI's bundled rights program required that coaching salaries be paid through the university, rather than coaches getting a portion from the university and a percentage from HCI. We paid the rights fees directly to the universities to provide them institutional control. Rick put this setup to the ultimate test. We were paying UK hundreds of thousands of dollars annually so that it could hire Pitino. I needed to find new ways for our partnership with radio and television to generate enough revenue just to break even. Unfortunately, UK's probation included a live television ban, so we couldn't include local TV rights, as we had always done in the past.

By the beginning of basketball season, Pitino was already Kentucky's biggest celebrity. To capitalize on that, I convinced Cawood Ledford to conduct Pitino's postgame radio shows courtside, where fans could stay and listen. UK was the first institution to do this. The state was enamored with Pitino's hard-pressing, three-point-shooting, in-your-face basketball. They tuned in and hung on his every word. The courtside interviews took longer to set up, so I had some additional time to fill with radio commercials. We also extended the coaches' show a few minutes and added advertising time to generate more revenue.

In the meantime, I found as many advertising spots for Pitino as possible. However, HCI's general manager at UK, Kim Ramsey, informed me that Pitino was sometimes an hour or two late for his commercial takes, or he might not show up at all. Paying onsite crews to film commercials cost a lot of money. I must have been the only UK fan who wasn't happy with Pitino. All he had to do was abide by his contract, but he often refused to do so.

The situation continued to get worse, so I called CM and said, "I love you like a brother, but I'm not going to pay you [UK] for the rights because you're not helping me enforce Pitino's contract." I retraced the whole story of how difficult it was to work with Pitino and said, "I can't run a business like this.

I'm going to show you every cost we've assumed and explain how this cannot continue. We need to get in a room with him to straighten this out. Until that happens, I am not paying you."

CM didn't set up a meeting until the Final Four in Denver. In the meantime, I wasn't paying UK the rights fee because Pitino continued to violate his contract. CM was afraid to challenge the coach who had brought so much excitement to UK basketball. CM reserved a room at the NCAA's hotel where we could all meet, but he didn't stay. He just hated confrontation. So Rick and I sat across the table from each other. He admitted that he had been difficult but said he was going to make it right. I countered, "I don't know how you can make this right, but I've decided to form a partnership with you." He interrupted and said, "Well, I already get my $650,000." I responded, "I know. We're going to take all the costs off the top, including the money I pay you. From the first dollar of profit, I'm going to give you 15 percent." He asked, "Why would you do that?" I replied, "It's just what I'm going to do." He said, "Well, I'll never know if you make a profit." I said, "You will know, because I'm going to show you."

Pitino's postgame shows had incredible ratings because he had a brilliant basketball mind, and the shows captured that. Pitino would explain his strategies and in-game adjustments. Basketball-hungry fans around the commonwealth, who had an impressive basketball IQ, just ate it up. I couldn't run the show on live TV because of UK's probation restrictions, so I decided to air it as soon as it was allowed, which was after midnight of game day. I called Ralph Gabbard at WKYT, and he agreed to put it on at 1:00 a.m. WAVE in Louisville did the same, and I secured smaller television stations as well. The stations retained 50 percent of the advertising time, and we kept the other half. We mixed Pitino's comments with game highlights. The show ended up being a huge success. Of the 3 million TVs in the state, more than 20 percent of them were turned on at 1:00 a.m., and 99 percent of them were tuned in to Pitino's taped postgame show. One in five Kentuckians wanted to stay up past midnight to watch game highlights and hear Pitino's analysis of the game. We had to take an overnight rating to verify it, but this allowed us to sell more advertising at a much better rate.

At the conclusion of Pitino's second year, we actually turned a profit. It took a lot of innovation and even a slew of commercials highlighting Pitino's northern accent as he promoted everything from Kroger grocery stores to Ford trucks, but it worked. His larger-than-life personality, along with his basketball acumen, not only brought UK's program back from the verge of death but also covered the $650,000 we were paying him. One day, I walked into his office and gave him a check for more than $27,000—his share of the profits. I had the entire financial statement for him to read, listing the expenses and the revenue. He said, "You could have made this money, and I never would have known!" I said, "Rick, don't ever discount my integrity. I told you this was what I was going to do, so I did it." Rick later sent me a kind note, complimenting my honesty. He tended to be agreeable most of the time, but there were times when he remained as obstinate as ever.

In December 1991, while attending the National Football Foundation's annual meeting in New York, I got a call from Jerry Tipton at the *Lexington Herald-Leader*. He asked, "Did you hear what Coach Pitino said on his postgame show?" I said, "No. What was it?" Jerry read the quote to me. Basically, Pitino said that someone at channel 27 had upset him, so he was going to change the television station that aired his weekly show. Jerry asked me for a comment, and I replied, "He has no right to say where the show goes. We dictate where the show goes. Period." Then CM called me and said, "Rick is really upset with you, so he isn't going to show up for any commercials." My reply: "Then don't pay him!" We eventually worked it all out, but those kind of charades frustrated me no end.[1]

Rick had put my bundled rights plan to the test, but it worked because he won basketball games. He was the best preparation coach I had ever seen, and I believe he saved UK basketball from decades of mediocrity. However, trying to survive financially while dealing with his antics was no easy task. Thankfully, his payments came from the University of Kentucky rather than my company. Had we not made this change to a bundled rights program, it would have placed an incredible financial strain on HCI's partnership with WKYT and WVLK.

Pitino's success in taking a UK program that was on probation and turning it into a perennial powerhouse was unprecedented. After losing to Arizona in overtime in the 1997 championship game, Rick decided to leave Kentucky for the Boston Celtics. CM Newton had no shortage of high-profile coaches who were interested in the position, but he wanted Tubby Smith. I had met Tubby when he was on Pitino's staff at Kentucky. Smith had then gone on to success at both Tulsa and Georgia. When Coach Smith returned to Lexington, he was the perfect fit. The first African American coach at UK, Smith broke the color barrier with dignity and class.

In his first season at UK, Smith won the national championship. I am still convinced that the single greatest coaching adjustment I ever witnessed came when Tubby called a time-out in the second half after falling behind Duke by seventeen points in the regional final. I had a courtside seat with the NCAA Radio Network, and I could hear every word he said to the team. "All right now," he said. "We are going to win this game. Here is how we are going to do it." He went on to explain that UK would spread the floor on offense, and point guard Wayne Turner would isolate Duke's Steve Wojciechowski and drive the lane. Smith instructed Turner to dish the ball to his open perimeter players whenever he was double-teamed on the drive. When play resumed, Turner did just that, and Scott Padgett, Cameron Mills, and Heshimu Evans each buried key perimeter shots down the stretch to beat Duke in an instant classic.

More important than his coaching acumen, Tubby Smith was an individual of the highest character—something UK desperately needed. On the business side, Tubby was simply a delight to work with during his decade at UK. Although he never won another national championship, Coach Smith's positive influence on the university and the community was evident. I have never met a college basketball coach who was a greater human being than Coach Smith.

In the span of a decade, my company had lost UK's rights, revamped its business strategy, expanded outside of Kentucky, developed the NCAA corporate partnership program and replicated it at other universities, and then returned home. Had we retained the UK rights heading into the 1980s, I don't think we would have pursued national opportunities. Financially, the bundled rights strategy survived Pitino's demands. Because of his unbelievable coaching acumen and personality, he turned UK's program around in a way that nobody could have imagined. Everyone benefited, and I was ready to expand this new sports marketing strategy to universities around the country. To use a cliché, heading into the 1990s, my company now had roots and wings.

10

The Solid South

Expanding in the SEC

With corporate partnerships established at the NCAA and a growing portfolio of bundled rights programs at individual universities, I sought to expand HCI. In 1979 the Southeastern Conference reinstituted its men's basketball tournament and contracted with HCI to provide the tournament programs. Football was king in the SEC, but in the early 1980s a number of excellent SEC basketball coaches drew attention to the game, including Don DeVoe at Tennessee, CM Newton at Vanderbilt, and Hugh Durham at Georgia. The most prominent coaches at the time were Joe B. Hall at Kentucky, Dale Brown at Louisiana State University (LSU), and Wimp Sanderson at Alabama. Brown and Sanderson had big personalities and brought basketball excitement to "football schools." Although limited to one week a year, the SEC tournament broadcasts gained some ground across the region.

When Dr. Harvey Schiller succeeded Boyd McWhorter as commissioner of the SEC in 1986, he made it known that he was willing to take risks to improve the status of the conference. I requested a meeting with Schiller to discuss growth opportunities. I suggested that the SEC should be the first conference with a radio network for conference championships, as well as corporate sponsors. Schiller responded, "We would be in conflict with our member institutions." I said, "Not any more than the NCAA is with its schools." Then I explained that the SEC Radio Network would black out broadcasts in an individual school's radio network coverage area if its team was playing. If that team wasn't playing or it had already lost, we would use those channels to broadcast other SEC games. He said, "Well, that makes sense. Could you come talk with the conference's ADs about it?"

When I met with the ADs, they expressed concern about losing revenue from their own sponsors. I said the SEC would sell sponsorships to businesses that wanted to cover the entire Southeast. I used one of Kentucky's sponsors as an example: Kentucky Farm Bureau Insurance would not be interested in an SEC sponsorship, but regional banks or other multistate businesses would see the value in such a program. After further discussion, they voted in favor of my plan.

HCI opened a Birmingham office to sell sponsorships for the SEC. The first sponsors were Pepsi, Golden Flake Potato Chips, Regions Bank, and Chick-Fil-A. Long underfunded compared with rival conferences like the Big 10 and the PAC-10, the SEC used corporate sponsorships to help level the playing field. It took time for the corporate sponsorship model to mature, but at the collegiate conference level, it all began when Harvey Schiller agreed to let HCI get the ball rolling.[1]

Two years into his work with the SEC, Schiller announced his decision to become the executive director of the US Olympic Committee (USOC). The SEC held a going-away party for him at the Opryland Hotel in Nashville. All the conference ADs attended, and a few were campaigning for Schiller's job, even if they would not admit it. After an evening of speeches and accolades highlighting Schiller's accomplishments in two short years, Harvey asked me to have dinner with him. I agreed, and we went to the Jack Daniel's Restaurant at the hotel. As we started talking, Harvey admitted, "Jim, I want to stay with the SEC." I said, "Harvey, this would have been good to know yesterday! Haven't you already signed with the USOC?" He told me he had, but after a couple weeks transitioning, he had some reservations about the timing of the move. Harvey asked whether I thought there was any possibility of his staying and whether I would be willing to help make that happen. Dr. Wilford Bailey from Auburn, who was serving a term as president of the NCAA and had been the SEC's longtime secretary, held great influence in the conference. I knew Bailey walked every morning at around 6:00 a.m. because we often crossed paths, so I told Schiller I would talk to Bailey. Harvey thanked me for trying to make it work.

The next morning, I went to the lobby at around 5:30 and waited for Bailey. When I spotted him, I walked over and said, "Dr. Bailey, I need to talk to you about something." He said, "Yes sir, young man." (He always called me young man.) We sat down and I said, "I'll get right to the point. Harvey wants to stay on as commissioner." Bailey looked stunned. I asked, "Have you offered the job to anyone yet?" Bailey told me that they had formed a committee but had not named a replacement. Bailey asked me to arrange a meeting with Schiller. They met later that day, and Harvey kept his job.

The next two years were critical to the SEC. In the wake of the *Regents* case, conferences were trying to figure out how to negotiate new television contracts for football and generate the most revenue. Schiller understood the implications and worked tirelessly to keep the member institutions on the same page. At the same time, he was trying to grow the popularity of the SEC basketball tournament, add corporate sponsorships, and develop new revenue sources for the conference. A stickler for detail, he had read the NCAA bylaws and learned that conferences with twelve or more teams could host championships. Schiller discussed an expansion to twelve teams and the creation of two divisions, leading to an SEC football championship game between divisional winners. Schiller's proposal did not gain immediate traction, and it would take another commissioner to see it through to completion.[2]

Less than two years later, Schiller finally took the USOC job. The SEC then formed a committee of university presidents to recommend a new commissioner. Through my work with the SEC basketball tournament, I had developed relationships with all the conference's ADs. There were some bright and ambitious leaders, but none of them matched Vanderbilt's Roy Kramer. Originally from eastern Tennessee, Kramer had left to coach football at Central Michigan for a decade. He then returned to Tennessee in 1977 as Vanderbilt's AD. Kramer was the most understated genius I had ever met. Soft-spoken and amiable, Roy possessed strategic brilliance. As great as he was, his wife, Sara Jo, was clearly his better half. Hospitable and welcoming, she was the life of any party.

I knew that Kramer was the top "inside" candidate, but the committee was conducting a national search. A number of us had learned that Andy Geiger was the other finalist. Geiger was Stanford's AD, and he had previously held the same position at Brown and Penn. His résumé impressed university presidents, but I was worried about his ability to function in the SEC's unique environment. I knew the search committee was nearing a decision, and while attending an NCAA convention in Dallas, I just happened to walk into the hotel restaurant where presidents Don Zacharias from Mississippi State and Lamar Alexander from Tennessee and chancellor Gerald Turner from Ole

Miss were having a serious conversation. Unsure if I was making the right move, I walked up to Zacharias and said, "Don, I really apologize, but may I interrupt?" He said, "Sure," but Alexander's glare was far less inviting. Regardless, I continued: "Look, I work with more ADs than anyone. I've got nothing to gain here, but you will be making a horrible mistake if you don't hire Roy Kramer." One of them asked, "Why do you think that?" So I spoke for a couple of minutes about his organizational efficiency and his willingness to listen to the SEC presidents' concerns. Roy understood the importance of academics, I told them, and he loved the SEC. Zacharias nodded his head the entire time, while the others just listened. They thanked me for sharing my perspective, I thanked them for listening, and then I walked off.

I have no idea if my impromptu stumping for Roy played any role in his hiring as the next SEC commissioner, but I do know that he became arguably the best conference commissioner in the country. I worked all over the United States, and I had never seen such a rapid rise in the prominence of a conference. Despite Roy's success, he remained just as humble and kind as ever, while becoming a leading figure in collegiate athletics administration.

Few fans knew that the impetus behind conference realignment in the early 1990s was the *Regents* decision. The NCAA no longer controlled televised football, but it took years for existing contracts to expire and for conferences to develop their own television plans. ESPN was looking to expand, and Kramer understood that the key to negotiating larger contracts was to add more television sets by expanding the conference. When he took over as SEC commissioner in 1990, Kramer's first priority was to grow the conference from ten to twelve members. The four leading contenders were Arkansas, Florida State (FSU), Miami, and South Carolina. The first invite was obvious: the SEC wanted Arkansas, and the Razorbacks wanted the SEC. The second choice was much more difficult. Most SEC presidents favored Florida State, but an invitation required a unanimous decision. University of Florida president John Lombardi finally agreed to invite his in-state rival, FSU, into the SEC. Florida State was also under consideration by the Atlantic Coast Conference (ACC). Since HCI owned FSU's media rights, Kramer asked me to be part of the conversation.

Once Kramer had the conference presidents' support, he asked me to call AD Bob Goin and find out if he would support the move. Goin loved the idea, but he needed to talk with other FSU officials. He suggested that I come down to Tallahassee for a visit. Once I arrived, I met with Goin and other key

FSU administrators and board members, including Sandy D'Alemberte. He was dean of the Law School, had been appointed president of the American Bar Association, and would soon be named president of FSU. Everyone was in favor of joining the SEC except for one person: Coach Bobby Bowden. When the time came for his comment, Bowden simply said, "I am not in favor of the move." When someone asked him why, he explained that FSU could dominate in the ACC, but joining the SEC would create a much more difficult path to national championships. While he never explicitly said so, he insinuated that if FSU joined the SEC, he might leave. Coach Bowden had the last word, and that was it. I called Kramer and told him the news. He immediately offered South Carolina membership in the conference, and it agreed without delay. The SEC had its twelve teams.

With Arkansas and South Carolina joining the SEC, the conference created east and west divisions. Kramer pushed to implement an SEC championship game in football, but the ADs and coaches feared that a conference championship game might knock an SEC school out of contention for the national title. An undefeated team would almost certainly play for the national championship, but a conference championship loss would likely change that. Kramer eventually won over his critics, and the first SEC football championship was held at the close of the 1992 season.

The SEC asked HCI to organize the radio network and publish the game programs. I told Roy, "This is our chance to show our corporate sponsors how valuable their investment in the conference is." He was so busy that he gave me permission to plan the sponsorship event. Legion Field in Birmingham hosted the first SEC football championship, so we worked with Robbie Robertson's company, Colonnade, to set up hospitality tents for the corporate sponsors. I wanted to follow the blueprint at our Final Four parties and make the event special.

The weekend went off without a hitch. The sponsors loved it. They witnessed SEC passion at its finest and saw how their sponsorships were paying off. The undefeated Crimson Tide played a Florida team coached by the young and talented Steve Spurrier. Alabama beat Florida in an incredible game, avoiding the disaster some had predicted if an undefeated SEC team lost. The event was such a success that we expanded it the next year. After that, the SEC moved the game to the Georgia Dome, and other conferences attempted to replicate the event.

While FSU turned down an invitation to join the SEC, my alma mater declined an offer from the ACC. Tom Butters, a former Pittsburgh Pirates pitcher, had been Duke's AD since 1977. He and I loved baseball, and we had developed a special relationship while working together on the NCAA Division I men's basketball tournament. One year, I invited Tom and his wife, Lynn, to stay at our home when he came to Lexington to play in the Senior PGA Pro-Am golf tournament with me. Before the next year's Pro-Am, he called me and asked, "Can you arrange a private meeting with CM Newton? I want you there too, but I don't want anyone else to know about it." So I set up the meeting.

Before the start of the Pro-Am, the three of us met in the back of a corporate sponsor's tent at Kearney Hills Golf Course in Lexington. Tom said, "Here is why I wanted this meeting: I have been empowered by the ACC to extend an invitation for UK to join the ACC. This is the first time Duke has ever agreed to an expansion, and every other conference institution has agreed as well, including North Carolina." He explained that the conference wanted Kentucky because of its geographic location and its academics. He went on to say that it would cost a lot less for Kentucky to travel to ACC schools than SEC schools. Then he said, "I have driven the bus on this. I am committed, and I want you to think about it." Duke had always been opposed to ACC expansion, but Tom and CM had become good friends, and Tom had convinced Duke to agree to the UK addition.

CM looked at me and asked, "Jim, what do you think?" I replied, "If you want to win in football, it's a great move. And I think we'll stay competitive in basketball." CM asked, "What do you think [UK president] Dr. Wethington will say?" I said I didn't know, but I would be happy to talk to him. CM agreed. We shook hands with Tom Butters and told him we would be in touch. CM called me a week later and said, "We are barking up the wrong tree." He and Wethington had determined that UK had too much history with the SEC to move. UK was a founding member of the SEC, and the first president of the conference had been Kentucky's Frank McVey. I never pursued the issue any further.

Regardless, I loved working with the SEC. My time spent with Harvey Schiller and Roy Kramer created new opportunities to work with other SEC schools. One of HCI's first expansions in the SEC came with UK's rival, the University of Tennessee (UT). It started with a phone call from AD Doug Dickey, whom I had known for years. He said, "Jim, I've got a real problem with our radio network, and I'm not sure what to do. We had been working with Edwin Huster on our radio network, but we gave those rights to John Ward. He's a great announcer, but I don't think we're getting our money's worth." Then Doug added, "I just can't let anyone know I'm talking with you because Kentucky and Tennessee are like oil and water. I don't know if fans would accept UT working with someone from UK." I said, "Look, I did the SWC Radio Network and worked with Texas and Texas A&M. I don't see why we can't work together." He agreed but said, "We need to talk about it confidentially."

We met in the back of a restaurant at the Holiday Inn in Corbin, Kentucky. Doug sat down and told me that UT was getting $100,000 for its radio network rights from John Ward, who ran the network. Without researching a thing, I said, "Doug, I will give you $300,000." He countered, "If you give me $600,000, I'll agree to it right now." I probably could have negotiated and saved $100,000, but instead I said, "You have a deal." We shook on it, and the whole meeting took about ten minutes.

Early on, I struggled to convince John Ward, the legendary voice of the UT Volunteers, that this was a good thing. He was fantastic on the radio, but he was less adept at selling advertising and expanding the network. I needed to win him over to be successful, so I offered to pay him $100,000 just to announce games. He could make more money doing coaches' shows and other work. Once he realized that we were going to treat him well, he was on board.

I put one of HCI's most talented employees, Mark Dyer, on the Tennessee account because he was a UT alum. I knew he would enjoy working with UT, and he understood the dynamics of its culture. Every month, Mark and I visited Doug Dickey and showed him our expenses and revenue. Early on, Mark pulled me aside and said, "You are paying the rights fee. Why are you showing them what we're making?" I told him, "That's how you build credibility and trust." Mark immediately understood, and he did an amazing job for both Tennessee and HCI. In fact, Mark helped organize the first ever pay-per-view college football game, named Video Seat, which proved to be a huge success. Eventually, we ended up paying UT a rights fee and created a model in which 55 percent of the adjusted gross revenue went back to Tennessee. We kept the other 45 percent. That model was a huge success, and we partnered with UT for the rest of my time with HCI.

After contracting with Tennessee, HCI entered negotiations with its rival, Alabama. Hootie Ingram had left Florida State to become AD at Alabama, and he invited me to Tuscaloosa to discuss a marketing, licensing, and partnership program for the Crimson Tide. Hootie introduced me to Dr. Finus Gaston, who was involved with Alabama athletics and very interested in collegiate licensing. He was bright, hardworking, and honest. He and I created a model in which we introduced "Tide" drink cups at games and sold them at gas stations across Alabama. We brought in more corporate sponsors and rapidly expanded the Crimson Tide Network. Our corporate sponsorship model worked like a charm, and even though HCI and Alabama eventually parted ways, Gaston kept growing the plan we devised, and Alabama remains an absolute powerhouse.

While I was trying to survive Rick Pitino's first year at Kentucky, Hootie Ingram pushed me into a coaching "matchmaker" role. I hadn't been working with Alabama for long when Ingram called and asked for a favor: "Do you think you could get CM [Newton] to hire Bill Curry?" This made no sense to me because Alabama's coach had lost only one game all year. Ingram explained: "Yeah, Jim, but Curry can't beat Auburn. It would look crazy to fire someone with his record, but they will run me off if I don't get rid of him." Many 'Bama boosters couldn't handle Auburn winning the SEC championship in 1987, 1988, and 1989. To make matters worse, Curry had played under Bear Bryant's archnemesis Bobby Dodd at Georgia Tech and had later coached the Yellow Jackets. Ingram liked Curry, but he wanted me to put a bug in CM's ear that Bill might be interested in coaching at UK. He asked me not to mention that he was orchestrating the move.

I called CM and suggested that if he put together a good offer, Curry might be interested. CM said, "What? Hire away Alabama's coach to UK?" I said, "I think you can do it." CM called Curry's agent, Robert Fraley, who said the coach wasn't interested. Instead, CM decided to go after Mike Shanahan, an assistant coach with the Broncos. That fell through, but in the meantime, Ingram offered Curry a less-than-generous contract extension. Curry was so upset that he decided to talk with CM, and the two of them met before the Sugar Bowl. After the game, Curry visited UK and accepted Kentucky's offer. It seemed like the greatest coaching coup ever: Kentucky had wooed a football coach away from Alabama. Bill Curry was one of the finest human beings I ever met, but he failed to turn UK football around.[3]

Once Curry was gone, I helped negotiate the contract and media obligations for new Alabama coach Gene Stallings. Stallings beat Auburn in his first season. In his second year, the Crimson Tide went 11–1. During the 1992 campaign, Stallings's team was undefeated and won a national championship.

That made the Crimson Tide extremely marketable, and its corporate sponsorships continued to grow.

As the tide was rising at Alabama, the Auburn Tigers' dominance waned. Auburn's longtime sports information director and assistant AD David Housel contacted me about operating the Auburn Sports Network. Housel had been a key member of Dave Cawood's NCAA Final Four committee, and the two of us had become good friends. I said, "I would love to help you, but I'm working with Alabama. Do you really think I could do both?" Housel said, "If Hootie and I can agree that you can do something mutually beneficial for both schools, I don't think it will be a problem." So in the early 1990s, we started handling the media rights for both Alabama *and* Auburn.

Auburn had an incredible run during the late 1980s, but it was a distant second in the state when it came to media coverage and team branding. Shortly after HCI secured Auburn's media rights, the school's football coach and AD Pat Dye resigned in the midst of an NCAA investigation. The NCAA ended up giving Auburn two years of probation, including a one-year television ban. Auburn hired longtime University of Washington AD Mike Lude, who had recently retired, to guide it through its probation. When I visited Mike at Auburn, he suggested that I meet with Bobby Lowder, a multimillionaire businessman and booster who had been appointed to Auburn's Board of Trustees by Governor George Wallace in 1985. Lowder owned some radio stations in Alabama, including an important one in Montgomery.

I followed Lude's advice and met with Lowder at his Montgomery office. He started off by saying, "I want you to understand something: I control Auburn." I said, "Really?" and he replied, "Yep." Then he laid out some rules for organizing the Auburn Network. I said, "Mr. Lowder, I own Auburn's rights, and I'm going to build the best network possible, but you are getting killed by Alabama." Although the meeting wasn't confrontational, it certainly wasn't comfortable. I tried to make it productive, so I explained my plan to traverse the state and sign up stations in areas where Auburn didn't have good coverage. In places where Alabama had two stations in the same market, I would try to flip one to the Auburn Network. Then we worked out a deal concerning the number of commercial spots Lowder's stations would get.

Even after I explained my strategy to develop Auburn's media presence in the state, Lowder's key concern was that I knew he was the boss at Auburn. History would eventually prove him right. At this point, though, I attempted to deflect by explaining that I needed an ambitious HCI liaison for the Auburn account, and I thought Mike Hubbard was the right person. Lowder didn't know Mike at that point, but he liked the idea of having an Auburn man working with HCI.

Shortly after I shared my plans with Lowder, Housel called and said, "I know you are considering hiring Mike Hubbard as your general manager. He is extremely talented, but be careful." I asked him to elaborate, but he wouldn't. Despite the warning, I hired Hubbard because he was such a smart and aggressive guy.

In an amazing "small world" story, I also got to know Jim Fyffe, the voice of Auburn football. Jim's brother Paul had managed a radio station in Paintsville, Kentucky, and I had worked with him while organizing the Kentucky Central Network. This was the same Paul Fyffe that Bill Hazelrigg had tried to get Governor Nunn to replace me with when I worked in state government. Anyway, Jim was a wonderful play-by-play announcer, and I trusted him immediately. When I told him that I was hiring Hubbard, he said nothing but raised his eyebrows. Once again, I didn't take the hint.

Auburn hired Terry Bowden as its football coach, and I immediately developed a good rapport with Terry because I had worked with his father, Bobby, at FSU. In 1993, his inaugural season, Terry kept winning games, while I kept losing money. Auburn had fallen behind in sports marketing, and Alabama's success made it difficult to break into new markets. Because of the NCAA sanctions, we couldn't do anything on live TV. The Tigers were undefeated but were disqualified from playing in a postseason bowl game. I had lost around $300,000 that first year, and I was desperately trying to figure out how to balance the books. I met with the Auburn Alumni Association and pitched the idea of making a highlight video of the Tigers' undefeated season. I offered to produce the video at no cost if the association would pay to mail the videos to alumni who purchased them. We agreed to split the revenue on the project, and it worked like magic. We made $400,000 on the video, and HCI was out of the red on the Auburn account.

After the spectacular video sales, Terry Bowden requested a meeting, so I went to Auburn. When I walked into his office, he pulled out a copy of the video and asked, "Jim, where is my share?" I said, "What do you mean?" Terry wanted a cut of the video proceeds. I explained that HCI owned Auburn's rights, and I showed him how much the company had lost outside of that video. I explained that under HCI's bundled rights contract with Auburn, he was to be paid by the university, and I didn't make side deals with coaches. Terry looked at me and said, "No, no. I own the rights to my likeness." I responded, "Not under the contract I have with Auburn." He said, "Jim, you don't get it. Unless you give me half of that money, I'm going to make sure you don't stay here." He added, "We are undefeated, I am sitting on top of the world, and I am going to get that money, or you won't be here." I reiterated that his salary came from the rights fees HCI had already paid Auburn, and he wasn't getting any money from the video. Then he said, "Okay. This meeting is over. You've made up your mind, and I've made up mine." We didn't even shake hands. I just got up and left.

Only a few years earlier, it would have been standard practice for a coach to have a side deal on a highlight tape. However, those days were gone. HCI had signed a bundled rights deal with Auburn. The single-system package was something Terry didn't want to accept, but with the money we paid Auburn (or any program), the media rights were the only way for HCI to turn a profit. Side deals for coaches were history.

Before leaving campus, I visited Mike Lude and shared what had transpired. He had a pained expression on his face but thanked me for letting him know. A few weeks later, I got a call from David Housel at around 11:00 p.m. that woke me up. He said, "Jim, I hate to tell you this, but Auburn is going to terminate your contract and go in a different direction." I said, "You have got to be kidding!" He responded, "No, I'm sorry. This is devastating to me, but I have to be loyal to my university." I said, "That's too bad, but I don't want to be somewhere I'm not wanted." Auburn was HCI's shortest stint at any institution.

As it turned out, Bobby Lowder helped Mike Hubbard secure the Auburn Network, which assumed the rights HCI once held. Lowder's radio stations, coupled with Hubbard's talent and ambition, led to the development of a powerful football media machine at Auburn. However, the operation eventually caught up with them. The Southern Association of Colleges and Schools (SACS) placed Auburn on probation for undue influence by members of the Board of Trustees. SACS did not list names, but I presume Lowder was one of them, given his earlier assertion that he ran Auburn.[4] In time, Hubbard became Speaker of the Alabama House of Representatives, where he was later convicted of multiple felony ethics charges. To this day, Auburn has a number of talented and wonderful employees, and David Housel was chief among them. The university has a passionate fan base and an exceptional alumni association. However, the institution has faced challenges because of the undue influence of a small group of wealthy and powerful boosters who, more than anything, want to beat Alabama. It was a lesson I learned the hard way.[5]

Across the state in Tuscaloosa, things seemed to be progressing well. Then, Hootie Ingram asked me to hire Kirk Wood as HCI's university liaison. I didn't know it at the time, but Kirk was Hootie's son-in-law. This wasn't necessarily a deal-breaker, but it created a lot of potential problems with regard to nepotism. Over time, it became apparent that Kirk reported to Hootie rather than to Mark Dyer, who oversaw the collegiate marketing part of HCI, so Mark and I kept a close eye on the financials. At one point, we noticed that Wood had negotiated a trade deal between HCI and the Sheraton Hotel on the Alabama campus, across from Coleman Coliseum. The deal looked shady, so I paid for an external audit. Kirk was using the deal to provide rooms for people who weren't associated with HCI, and I feared he was doing some sort of business on his own as well. The whole situation felt wrong. Wood was an HCI employee, and I wasn't going to be involved in anything unethical, so I pulled HCI out of the deal with Alabama. We lost a very lucrative contract because I didn't want to endanger the Crimson Tide athletics program. Maintaining the integrity of our company and the University of Alabama was worth it.

We also expanded our work in the SEC with Mississippi State University (MSU). Larry Templeton had been sports information director at Mississippi State for years before becoming AD in 1987. Like so many other ADs, he wanted to discuss his institution's radio network deal. I met him in Starkville, and it didn't take long to strike a deal with MSU. Mississippi had a small and largely rural population with a divided fan base between Ole Miss and MSU. I told Templeton that I couldn't pay a guaranteed rights fee, but HCI would share a percentage of the revenue we generated as MSU's media rights holder.

Templeton wanted to discuss my proposal with MSU president Don Zacharias. I knew Zacharias quite well because of his Kentucky background. He had attended Georgetown College and eventually became president of Western Kentucky University (WKU). While he was at WKU, Zacharias and I had attended multiple meetings concerning the budgets and state appropriations for regional universities in Kentucky. Zacharias fooled people with his "aw shucks" demeanor, but he knew how to run a university. He agreed to work with HCI, beginning a very successful partnership that also led to close friendships with both Templeton and Zacharias.

MSU basketball coach Richard Williams was building a solid program, but MSU football was struggling. After releasing football coach Rockey Felker at the conclusion of the 1990 season, both Templeton and Zacharias contacted me about potential replacements. One day while I was golfing with my brother in Tallahassee, Zacharias kept calling. I finally excused myself and called him back. "Jim," he said, "I've got a real issue and I think you might be able to help me. I have a choice of hiring two coaches—either Jackie Sherrill or Bobby Collins. Who would you pick?" Sherrill had been at Texas A&M, and Collins had been at SMU. Both had left their schools amidst scandal, so I said, "Dr. Zacharias, I wouldn't hire either one of them." He said, "That isn't going to work. I could lose my job if I don't pick one of them." In that case, I said, "Jackie Sherrill is the better coach by a landslide."

Both Templeton and Zacharias were under a lot of pressure, and they thought they could protect each other by working together. I asked Zacharias for Sherrill's number and said, "Let me call him." When Jackie answered, I said, "Coach, this is Jim Host." He thanked me for calling and sort of apologized for his role in ending our business with the SWC. Then he said, "I really want that MSU job. I know how much Don Zacharias and Larry Templeton think of you and your opinion. Would you recommend me?" I replied, "Jackie, you are a helluva coach, so you don't need to cheat. Larry and Don are two of the best people you could ever work for, and if you hurt their school by cheating, I'll kill you." He chuckled at first and then said, "You're serious, aren't you?!" Of course, I had no intention of harming him, but I told him in no uncertain terms: "Jackie, DO NOT CHEAT!" He responded, "Jim, if you do this for me, I guarantee that I know what to do and how to do it, and I won't cheat." So I recommended him.

I called Zacharias and told him that I had threatened Sherrill's life if he cheated at Mississippi State, but I thought he could coach. Zacharias said, "Jim, I really appreciate that. God bless you." He just kept saying "God bless you" over and over. Sherrill got the job, and in the second game of his first season at MSU, he faced his old rival Texas. Mississippi State beat the ranked Longhorns and finished the regular season 7–4, beating in-state rival Ole Miss in the Egg Bowl. Sherrill turned the program around in a single season. He was that good of a coach. Coach Sherrill stayed in Starkville for more than a decade and has one of the most successful records in the school's history. After the 2003 season, however, the NCAA was investigating MSU, and Coach Sherrill resigned. The Bulldogs were placed on probation for NCAA violations, but allegations against Sherrill were dropped. He brought a defamation suit against the NCAA in 2004, maintaining his innocence and claiming that the NCAA had damaged his ability to coach. After fifteen years, the NCAA finally reached a settlement with Sherrill, the terms of which were not disclosed.[6] Larry Templeton then made history by hiring Sylvester Croom, the first African American head football coach in the SEC. We continued to work with MSU because of the leadership in its Athletic Department.[7]

In the 1990s HCI continued to contract with universities in the South and in the Midwest as well. At our zenith, we were working with close to thirty institutions. Some of the other high-profile institutions included Michigan, LSU, and the University of Southern California (USC). The Southern California partnership lasted only briefly. I was working there with AD Mike McGee and contemplating an expansion into the PAC-10. It was not feasible for HCI to handle the media rights for just one university out west. We needed multiple schools as well as an office in the area to make it profitable. I knew that McGee and Ced Dempsey at Arizona were planning to introduce me to the athletic administration at UCLA. Then, just before I made a decision about the PAC-10, McGee decided to leave one USC for the other USC—South Carolina. He had been a great football player at Duke and wanted to move closer to home. When he made that move, I decided not to expand into the PAC-10. Instead, HCI started a long relationship with South Carolina athletics and focused on the eastern half of the country.

I made plenty of mistakes while expanding HCI's university networks and growing that side of the business. I also learned a number of important lessons. By 1990, I knew that the bundled rights packages we put together would be the sports marketing blueprint of the future. Bundled rights provided a new and efficient mechanism for universities to promote their sports programs and generate substantially more revenue. These booming university programs gained greater exposure with the advent of ESPN.

With this broad view in mind, HCI's allegiance remained with the individual institutions it served. I always worked closely with ADs, but I learned that if I could develop a relationship with a university's president, our partnership was far more likely to be successful. It is easy for writers to lump all "big-time" athletic programs together, but every school has a unique character, and college presidents are the best navigators of these individual cultures. Some presidents love sports, and others see athletics as a distraction from the academic enterprise. These are important things to know.

To assist individual universities, we placed at least one HCI liaison at every institution. Placing the right individual at the right school was essential to our success. Whenever possible, we assigned alumni to work at their alma maters. These individuals were fans, they knew the university culture, and they understood our company. When we had proven liaisons working on campus, it was easier to learn which ADs were the best ones to work with.

I never envisioned a career involving higher education. However, the bundled rights programs we developed with individual schools, along with the corporate sponsorship programs at both the NCAA and the SEC, fundamentally changed the trajectory of "big-time" athletics. Media exposure and revenue for universities grew exponentially. This led to an unbelievable rise in the salaries of college football and basketball coaches. It also created new opportunities for student athletes with regard to facilities, training, travel, and academic support. Unfortunately, these changes created an even greater temptation to cheat and gain a greater share of the spoils. I watched it happen at several universities, and HCI gave up substantial profits to remove itself from unethical situations. However, it is essential to note that in nearly all instances of cheating at universities, usually only one individual or a very small group of people was acting with impunity. Rarely did I see a "culture" of unethical behavior within an athletics program.

HCI continued to grow during the late 1980s and early 1990s. However, numerous challenges lay ahead in the revolutionized world of college sports marketing.

11

Surviving an Era of Crisis

After burning both ends of the candle for my entire career, in early 1989 my wife Carolyn and I separated and began the process of divorce. I had always been a highly motivated workaholic seeking to accomplish as much as I possibly could professionally. Carolyn had always desired a much slower pace for me. At the same time, I couldn't provide the standard of living Carolyn had grown accustomed to as a child. I also knew that the type of work I felt called to perform required extensive time away from home.

This occurred during an extremely busy growth period for my company, and I wanted to stay on top of it all. I would wake up at 4:00 a.m., make a list of the most important tasks to accomplish, and spend the day making sure that happened. I worked late hours, and when I got back to my apartment, I would lay my head down, fall asleep, and then start all over the next day. I was determined to make the business even stronger, and that remained my constant mission.

Then, in May 1989, HCI board members Dick Furst and DeWitt Hisle asked to meet with me. They encouraged me to consider hiring Pat Brown. She called HCI, and we set up a time for an interview. When she arrived, we talked for about thirty minutes, and I showed her around the office. It was clear she would be an asset to the business. However, I ended up not hiring her because I asked her out for dinner instead. Our first date was on May 26, 1989, and exactly one year later, we got married. With each passing day, Pat became a more important part of the business. She never held a position in the company, but I now had a companion with whom I could share all my concerns, strategies, personnel decisions, and so forth. As I shared, Pat offered her own perspective—usually affirming, but occasionally providing a different viewpoint. Whenever she said, "Jim, you might want to consider a different approach," I needed to listen, because her gut feeling was almost always correct. She displayed incredible skill at analyzing situations. It was not long before she started to positively impact the culture of the company. She possessed incredible instincts when it came to people and their motives. She immediately knew which individuals I should do business with and the ones I needed to avoid. All the while, she never forced her will on any of the business decisions I made. In addition, she had amazing event-planning acumen, which was on full display when she organized our annual Kentucky Derby celebration. This entailed a long weekend during which we brought in clients from around the country to participate in Derby-related festivities.

We did not have a single harsh word or argument while we dated, and three decades later, we still have not had one. Pat was (and is) a strong personality, but our union brought together like minds, and we have an amazing ability to understand each other's approach to any solution or outcome. I had found my true companion in Pat, which I needed for the challenges that lay ahead for the business.

As HCI expanded, we needed more capital for up-front costs. Each university we contracted with required a local office and funds for hiring a liaison and a sales representative. This investment debt actually improved our long-term financial outlook. At the same time, I poured as much money back into the company as possible. I strategically offered many of the employees stock in the company rather than cash, so that we could reinvest our revenue and become more profitable. As HCI's number of employees, revenue, and investment debt grew, I decided we needed a board of directors to provide accountability and insight that would protect both me and my employees. I wanted a board comprising individuals I could trust to support a long-term vision for HCI. I first asked DeWitt Hisle and Don Harkins to join the board, and shortly thereafter, we added Dick Furst, Dave Gavitt, and eventually others. As HCI grew, these individuals suggested that I find an equity partner to raise capital. After some exploring, I ended up selling a 13 percent stake in the company to a group called Atlantic Venture Partners. That move gave HCI $1 million of additional capital to pay down debt. With Atlantic Venture, we added additional board members, including Ed Crawford and Jim Heavner. Jim owned a radio station in Chapel Hill, North Carolina, and one in Lexington. I hoped he could help secure a contract with the University of North Carolina and make inroads into the ACC.

Our bundled rights contracts now included television advertising, along with traditional print media and radio broadcasts. At that time, the rights to conference games in football and basketball were controlled by the conferences, but the rights to nonconference games were owned by the individual universities. So HCI partnered with television stations to build statewide networks. HCI owned and controlled the content fans were interested in seeing, and TV stations possessed the delivery mechanism. We produced nonconference games, coaches' shows, and the like and partnered with local television affiliates to build networks. To make our bundled rights contracts more profitable, we partnered with TV outlets across the state of the home university, and we included advertising for the games for which we owned the content. Many will remember watching these games in the 1990s with local or regional announcers shown only on local affiliate stations.

With these developments, Marc Kidd, HCI's key salesperson, encouraged me to add a television component to the company. He was correct; television rights were key to moving forward in sports marketing. After shopping around, Marc met Bray Cary, who owned a Charlotte-based television syndication company called Creative Sports Marketing, and our two businesses seemed to complement each other well. We scheduled a meeting in Lexington with Cary to discuss a merger. He said all the right things, so Pat flew with me to Charlotte to study Cary's operation. Afterward, Pat said she had a bad feeling about both him and the merger. I asked, "What is it that you don't like?" She said, "I can't put my finger on it. I just feel like you are jumping into this too fast."

Because of Pat's concerns, I contacted Jim Delany, commissioner of the Ohio Valley Conference, and asked whether I should be concerned. He said, "Jim, I think it will be a great marriage. I know both of you, and you each bring things to the table the other doesn't have." That made me feel better about moving forward, but I still wanted another opinion, so I called Vic Bubas, the former Duke basketball coach and administrator who became the first commissioner of the Sun Belt Conference. Bray had worked for Bubas in the early years of the Sun Belt Conference, so I thought he would have a good perspective. However, Vic never returned my calls. He apparently had a family situation that required his full attention for a number of months.

I decided to move forward with the merger in 1991. We exchanged audits and financial data. We also developed plans for working together in complementary ways. In June, Cary merged his company's assets with ours. We kept 70 percent ownership of the merged companies. The board would consist of ten people, three of whom would come from Cary's company. We named the new company Host Creative.

Board member Ed Crawford suggested that I take a new role in the newly merged company, so Cary became the president and chief operating officer (COO), while I served as chairman and CEO. Cary ran the day-to-day operations of the company, and I went out to develop new deals. He continued to live in Charlotte but traveled back and forth quite a bit. I asked him to keep our communications open, but I left him alone and allowed him to run the company.

The first few board meetings seemed okay. Cary took over the accounting and said he was focused on cutting costs. He even removed the water coolers from the offices to save money. I thought this was silly, but I tried to adjust to my new role and stay out of the way. He managed to broker a deal with the Great Midwest Conference and its commissioner Mike Slive, which seemed like a positive move.

Despite this, I had always been hands-on and felt uncomfortable in my new role. A couple of months into the merge, I realized that Cary had cut me out of the loop when I showed up at the office and found that a large mainframe computer (which took up most of the second floor) was gone. I asked someone, "Where are all the computers?" I was told, "Bray moved everything to Charlotte." I called Cary, who explained, "I have a better chief financial officer here to help run things for the combined company, so I wanted the data here in Charlotte." Then I learned that he had spent an obscene amount of money to refurbish his offices in Charlotte. In all these instances, I was eager to know more details, but I never demanded anything because I wanted to stay true to my new role.

About a month later, Florida State's AD Dave Hart called and said, "Jim, your check for the rights fee is late. You have never been late. Is something wrong?" I responded, "I don't know, but I'll find out." When I asked Cary about it, he replied, "He shouldn't have called you. He should have called me." I said, "It doesn't matter. Are we late?" He said, "Yes, but there's a reason for it. I'll give you the details soon."

A few weeks later, SEC associate commissioner Mark Womack called and said, "Jim, we were supposed to have your rights fee check last month, but it isn't here yet. I was just curious to see if we have an issue." He added, "If there are any problems, we'll be glad to work with you." I appreciated this and told Mark, "I don't know if there's a problem, but I have a responsibility to find out. I'll be in touch soon." About this time, Vic Bubas called me and said, "Jim, what have you done? I can't believe you went into business with Bray Cary!" Vic went on to describe how disappointed he had been with Cary's work for the Sun Belt Conference. Then he asked, "Why didn't you talk to me?" I said, "Vic, I tried! Look at your records." He replied, "I know. I'm sorry we didn't connect." I said, "So am I."

I immediately called Cary and told him, "I need to see you." Although he was based in Charlotte, he still had an office next to mine in Lexington. When he walked into the office, his first words were, "Well, I think I have successfully broken you." I said, "What!?" He repeated, "I think I have successfully bankrupted you." In disbelief, I asked, "What have you done?" In a very matter-of-fact way, he stated, "You and the board gave me the authority to run the company, which I have done." He then went through the various steps he had taken to put the company in jeopardy. It was a calculated plan to get me out of the picture. Then he said, "Ed Crawford and I want to have a conversation with you." I agreed, so Cary called Crawford and put him on speakerphone. They talked about how little cash I had personally because I had put most of my earnings back into the company. Then Bray said, "I have a plan, and you are going to agree to some stipulations. If you don't agree, then you will be out of business." I said, "What do you mean I will be out of business?!" He replied, "If you don't accept my plan, then I will take over the company. I have already spoken to a few board members about the condition of the company. You are on your way out one way or the other." Then he made his proposition: "I want you to go out on top. You deserve it for the role you have played in college sports marketing. You will stay as chairman of the company to maintain and cultivate the NCAA contract." He said I would continue to make the same salary, and he would pay me $3 million for my share of the company. His one stipulation was that I could not share information about this deal with anyone. I never raised my voice and did not let my anger show. I just said, "Bray, I need a few days to think about it." He agreed but warned me again that if I didn't accept the offer, he would take the company into bankruptcy and I would lose everything.

As I left the office and got into my car, I could feel the rage. In our conversation, Cary made it clear that he had characterized me as inept to certain board members and employees. He had taken the great reputation my company had built through years of diligence and hard work and used it for his own gain. Finally, he had abused the trust I had placed in him. I wanted a fight, but I needed to devise a plan.

I immediately drove home and shared the crisis with Pat. She asked, "What are you going to do?" I said I needed to devise a strategy. I called board members Dick Furst and DeWitt Hisle and asked them to join me for an urgent and confidential lunch meeting. When I shared my story, DeWitt suggested that I contact attorney Joe Terry for legal advice. Terry was legal counsel for the Lexington Center Corporation and was well known for his expertise in corporate governance. I knew Terry from his involvement in Democratic Party politics, but he had never worked for me or the company, so I knew he could examine the situation from a totally unbiased perspective and tell me my options.

I spoke with Terry and asked him to come to my office to discuss a "corporate matter." We met on a Saturday morning. I relayed the whole story, including the board's structure and my conversations with Cary. Terry asked numerous questions during our lengthy discussion. At the conclusion of the meeting, I said, "I want to hire you. I will be personally responsible for paying you. You will have total access to all the records, but I need this done in a week." I continued, "I need you to look at all the evidence and determine if I am at fault or if Bray Cary is at fault for the state of the business. I don't want you to tell me anything but the truth." Then I asked him to determine whether I could keep the company, and if so, how to do it in a manner that would stand up in court. He agreed to take the job. Terry was going to review the documents and conduct an investigation.

After the initial discussion with Terry, I went home, took a cold shower, and mapped out a plan on a pad of paper. Then I invited several key HCI officers to my house for a confidential meeting. Marc Kidd, Mark Dyer, Joe Freeman, Rick Ford, Tim Campbell, and Hank Phillips came over, and we assembled on the back porch. I told them exactly what had happened. I shared my game plan to take back the company, but then I stated, "If we are going to survive this, I need your commitment. If you are not with me, I understand that, but I want each of you to look me in the eye and tell me you will stand with me." They pledged their support. I thanked them and told them not to do anything until they heard from me.

The next morning, I met with Bill Guthrie at Citizens Union Bank in Lexington. The company owed the bank a substantial sum of money that it had borrowed as investment capital. I shared my story and said, "You are the key to all of this. If you determine that you want to put me out of business, then you can do that." Bill said, "I don't want to do that. You have always done what you have said. I trust you." He said he would stand by me, but he advised me that I needed to get more capital into the business. To get the line of credit we needed, Pat offered her assets and life savings as collateral. She put up nearly a million dollars—everything she had—to help save the company I had spent my entire professional life trying to build.

I managed to buy a few extra days by calling an emergency board meeting. It was difficult for some of the members to attend, especially Dave Gavitt, who was in the middle of his own struggles with the Boston Celtics. Despite the short notice, everyone agreed to come. Without offering any indication of resistance, I called Cary and told him, "We need to have a board meeting to lay out all the facts. If the board determines that it's the right thing to do, then I will step aside and accept your offer."

Those extra days gave Joe Terry enough time to review matters. Terry was of the opinion that Cary had pushed the company to the point of bankruptcy in an attempt to gain control of Host Creative. He believed that Cary may have disparaged me to certain board members and senior employees. In preparation for the board meeting, Terry developed a multipoint plan to firmly regain control of the company. He detailed Cary's accusations and actions taken, my response, and a series of recommended actions for the board. He advised a settlement that included returning to Cary everything Creative Sports Marketing had owned when the companies merged.

Armed with Terry's report, I was ready for the board meeting. Cary and Crawford entered the room confidently. I was cordial until I called the meeting to order by saying, "The purpose of this board meeting is to send Mr. Cary back to Charlotte." I explained Terry's plan to separate the company, returning it to its two original parts. To be fair, the plan gave Cary his portion of the company and enumerated all the various divestments the company would give to Cary. He would also keep the contracts he had executed that year with the Great Midwest Conference and the University of Kansas. I added that I had obtained temporary financing from the bank and my wife Pat, so staying solvent would not be an issue.

The board voted six to three in my favor, with an abstention from Jim

Heavner. My friend David Granger was concerned about the finances but voted with me. If Heavner had voted against me, I think Granger might have followed suit, and I would have lost the company. Thankfully, that did not happen. Cary looked at me across the table and said, "You can't do this!" I simply responded, "I just did." That ended my relationship with Bray Cary, which lasted for eight months in 1991.

Fighting through that crisis cost us money, but we won. I still controlled the company that so many people had helped build. Our employees kept their jobs. We learned who our true friends were. My next order of business was making sure we maintained our good name with the companies we served.[1] I made the rounds, explaining the situation to our clients. I let everyone know that we were going to make it, but my payments might be a little late during the next few months.

I also spoke with my friend Chuck Jarvie about finding additional capital. I had first met Chuck in the 1960s at P&G. A brilliant Cornell alum, he had become CEO of Dr. Pepper. Chuck had also invested in a three-on-three basketball enterprise called Streetball Partners. I asked him for suggestions about a potential equity partner for HCI. After visiting our operation, Chuck said he had a good friend at GE Capital (the investment equity arm of General Electric) who might be interested in an ownership stake in HCI. Separately, he told me that his son, Doug, was working for Streetball Partners, which had a television deal with NBC. He hoped to find some way for HCI and Streetball Partners to work together.

Chuck and I traveled to Stamford, Connecticut, and met with Bob Thompson at GE Capital. After a couple of months of negotiations, GE Capital agreed to pay $8 million for 49 percent ownership in HCI. GE Capital held a preferred position at 8 percent interest and warrants on the exchange of preferred capital stock if we sold HCI. The $8 million infused into HCI paid off all its existing debt, and our new partners were actually interested in improving the company's value.

During the next few years, I worked closely with Bob Thompson as well as Dave Kelsey at GE Capital. They were absolutely wonderful. They occasionally sent consultants to advise us on restructuring and organizational efficiency. In fact, Kelsey eventually became HCI's chief administrative officer. John Flannery, who would go on to head General Electric, also assisted on the project. GE worked to grow its investment by making us better. With GE's assistance and my newfound drive to make the company succeed, we experienced healthy growth during the 1990s. In addition, Chuck Jarvie became president and COO of HCI. As a new business partner, he was instrumental in HCI's rebound to success.

The growing value of HCI caught the eye of J. Mack Robinson, a billionaire from Atlanta who had made his initial money in finance, banking, and Delta Life Insurance. One of his key advisers, Bob Prather, had convinced him to purchase Bull Run, a dormant public company that had been in the mining business. In 1992 Robinson also purchased Gray Communications, a company from Albany, Georgia, that owned some local newspapers and a few television affiliates.

Our UK television partners, CBS affiliates WKYT in Lexington and WYMT in eastern Kentucky, were indirectly owned by Kentucky Central Insurance. Following the death of Garvice Kincaid, Kentucky Central was placed in liquidation, which included the sale of its television and radio properties. The TV stations were operated by Ralph Gabbard. Ralph Hacker owned WVLK radio. The two of them helped me put together a bundled rights package with UK. Gabbard attempted to purchase WKYT and WYMT, but Gray Communications outbid him. Upon purchasing the stations, however, Bob Prather and Mack Robinson, the COO and CEO of Gray Communications, respectively, realized that Gabbard played an integral role in the rights deal for UK athletics. Without Gabbard, UK's television rights would revert back to HCI, and Gray had purchased WKYT specifically to share in those rights.

Robinson and Prather came to Lexington to discuss this dilemma with me. When they arrived, I gave them a tour of the office and showed them a promotional video we used to impress potential new clients. Collegiate sports marketing had a "glamorous" side, and they loved it. Robinson said, "When we bought the television stations, we didn't realize that you controlled our destiny. So we want to buy your company." I said I wasn't interested in selling, but I thought it could be mutually beneficial if they bought out GE Capital's ownership interest in the company. We held marketing rights to universities in the South and the Midwest, and they were expanding their television ownership in those areas, so it seemed like a logical fit. For example, they had purchased a TV station in Knoxville, and we owned the University of Tennessee's media rights. Likewise, HCI controlled Florida State's media rights, and they owned a television station in Tallahassee.

When Bull Run bought out GE Capital, all parties won. GE Capital made approximately 35 percent on its investment in two years. Bull Run gained a share of HCI, which would help make its television ownership and expansion more profitable. Finally, whereas GE Capital had owned 49 percent of HCI, we valued Bull Run's shares at 33 percent of the company.

During the mid-1990s our business made great strides. With the exception of CBS's television contract, we owned all the NCAA basketball tournament rights (to programs, corporate sponsorships, and radio). Every corporate partnership deal we signed for the basketball tournament made our NCAA deal more profitable. More universities wanted us to create bundled rights packages for them. The partnership with Gray Communications and Bull Run made negotiating these bundled rights packages much easier, and in markets where we had the rights, it made their TV stations much more profitable.

GE Capital's investment in HCI played a large role in our expansion, and I felt indebted to Chuck Jarvie for facilitating that association. To express my gratitude, I gave him some of my personal shares in the company and made him a business partner. He was hoping to find a way for HCI to work more closely with Streetball Partners, where his son was president and CEO. Streetball Partners held three-on-three basketball tournaments all over the country, and the company was growing, so we agreed to invest in it. With the blessing of Bob Prather at Bull Run, we formed Universal Sports America (USA) and proceeded to merge part of Streetball Partners, which would be operated through USA. This was considered a "grassroots" sports and marketing venture, and hundreds of thousands of amateurs signed up to play in Streetball Partners' tournaments across the country. Corporate sponsors paid for advertising at the local events, and NBC televised the finals of the tournaments. Streetball Partners had developed a model to combine local and national sponsorships.

Business was so good that one day, out of the blue, I received a call from Texas Rangers owner Tom Hicks. Tom was a Texas Longhorns booster, and we shared a mutual friend in DeLoss Dodds. Despite the connection, I was surprised when he said, "I have a real interest in buying your company." After telling him I wasn't interested in selling, Tom said, "I know you're a baseball fan. We're playing the Yankees. Why don't I send a plane to Lexington tomorrow and have you go to the game with me?" I said, "I'm not going to turn that down!" So the next day I flew down to Dallas on Tom Hicks's jet.

Tom escorted me onto the field, where I met the players and the manager. Then he took me to his skybox for dinner. He had the CEOs of the companies he had acquired join us. Each one told me what a great guy Tom was and how much they enjoyed working with him. People slowly started leaving, and by the seventh inning, we were the only two left in the box. We were talking baseball when Tom said, "Well, what do you think?" I asked, "About what?" He answered, "I would like to buy your company." I said, "We haven't talked about the numbers." He responded, "We think your company is worth between $75 and $80 million." I thought that was low, considering our current profitability and growth forecasts. Before long, we were talking about figures in excess of $100 million.

By the end of the evening, I was ready to begin serious negotiations. Tom said, "We've got a room for you at a hotel downtown near my office. Let's meet tomorrow and hammer out the details." The next morning, Chuck Jarvie and I met with Tom and his chief negotiator. We landed on a $117 million price tag for HCI, Streetball Partners, and USA. I called Bob Prather and told him that Hicks wanted to buy the companies. Bob wasn't sure about Hicks and thought it was a bad idea. When I told him the offer stood at $117 million and Bull Run would keep a third of that amount, he literally dropped the phone. When he picked it up, he said, "Take the money and run!"[2]

I called every HCI board member, shared the news, and scheduled a board meeting, where they approved the sale of the company. Over the next few months, I worked closely with Tom Hicks's finance team on the due diligence for the acquisition. We went through every piece of paperwork, and I thought things were going well. Then, one of Hicks's representatives asked if we could meet at the Lexington Country Club. Once we sat down, he said, "I'm not sure we can close the deal." I asked why, and he responded, "If we could just buy your company, we would do it in a minute. Everything is clean and profitable. The problem is USA and Streetball." When I asked him to elaborate, he said, "We can't put our finger on it, but their numbers just aren't right." I said, "How could that be? We have a certified audit from Ernst and Young." He replied, "It doesn't make a difference. Something is wrong there, and we don't want to be part of it." The following day, they officially canceled the acquisition. Then Tom Hicks called and said he still wanted to buy HCI. Pat and I spoke at length about the offer, and Tom was relentless about moving forward. Although it was a difficult decision, I opted not to sell HCI and leave my friend Chuck Jarvie, who had helped save us after the Bray Cary fiasco, out in the cold.[3]

When I called Bob Prather, he said, "I always thought something was going to go wrong, but I want Bull Run to purchase the companies instead." I said, "You're kidding!" He replied, "No, I'm not. Meet me in Lincoln, Nebraska, and we can talk about the details." I asked if Mack Robinson was okay with it, and he responded, "He will be." So I flew out to Nebraska in anticipation of an offer. While I was there, Bob also wanted me to negotiate a deal with the University of Nebraska. Bull Run owned a Lincoln TV station, and controlling the Cornhuskers' media rights would boost the station's revenue. Once I arrived, Bob and I sat down in a restaurant with a piece of paper and worked out all the details of the purchase. My only concern was Bull Run's $50 million debt. For two decades, I had channeled profits back into the business to build a foundation for long-term success. Bob assured me, "Mack is committed to paying down the debt so your company can grow."

Bob Prather, Mack Robinson, and Mack's son-in-law, Hilton Howell, met Chuck Jarvie and me at the Atlanta Piedmont Driving Club, one of the most luxurious country clubs in the nation. Robinson basically said that he wanted our companies to grow, and this acquisition would make that happen. After that meeting, we made an official announcement of the sale of HCI and USA to Bull Run for $93 million. After the acquisition, we planned to merge the two companies into one and call it Host USA. I would receive more than $11 million in Bull Run stock and more than $3 million in cash. HCI shareholders, most of whom were employees, would obtain Bull Run stock, which they could sell after a few months. The same was true of USA employees and the stock they received. My stock, however, needed to remain with the company and would be locked up for a lengthy period of time. It appeared that our hard work had finally come to fruition.[4]

Then, two days before the official closing of the deal, Prather called me and said, "The banks are saying there is something wrong with USA. The financial numbers aren't correct." I asked again if the official audit was accurate. Once again, I was told that the official audit looked fine, but something was amiss with USA. I still remember Bob's analogy: "We're pregnant and going into delivery, so we want to finish the deal. In order to close, Mack Robinson put up some of his own cash, and he wants you to do the same so you have skin in the game." I agreed to put more than $3 million back into a separate account that I couldn't access until the funds were released by Bull Run. This served as collateral against USA so the deal could be completed. When I called Jarvie and told him the plan, he said, "You can't do that! You might lose your money!" I responded, "I already have."

We moved forward with the sale in 1999. More than eighty individuals who had worked for or been associated with HCI received stock or cash. Bull Run also provided stock to a number of USA employees. Meanwhile, I had promised not to sell my Bull Run stock and to keep my $3 million cash in a separate account as collateral. That certainly motivated me to run the company well. It was also used as an incentive to keep me there.

After Bull Run's acquisition of HCI and USA, Prather sent me, along with Bull Run's financial officer Fred Erickson, to Dallas to figure out what the problems were with Streetball Partners and USA. I sat down with Streetball's chief financial officer and simply started asking questions and requesting documents. Although I was no accountant, I knew how read profit-and-loss statements and look for the revenue coming in and the expenses going out. The more questions I asked, the worse things appeared. Before long, I knew that Streetball Partners was operating without much cash and had very little future revenue coming in. It had taken multiyear sponsorship deals with companies like Gatorade and listed the total revenue over a five-year period in a single year. That wasn't a problem as long as you kept adding sponsors every year, but the second it stopped—and it had—the well ran dry, and there was no cash left.

In that first week, I fired more than sixty people at Streetball Partners. It was an absolute nightmare. I would call Pat every night, and one evening she said, "How can you live with this?" I said, "I hate this, but it's the only option." In addition to the layoffs, I canceled leases all over the country and took advantage of every other opportunity to cut spending. Then I had to address Streetball Partners' top management. I never will forget what Terry Murphy, who had founded Streetball and still worked with USA, said to me: "I can't believe that you have completely ruined our company!" I said, "Terry, I'm doing everything I can to save your company." The same thing happened with Tad Brown, head of sales at USA. He came into my temporary office, pounded his fist on the desk, and exclaimed, "You are destroying everything we have built!" I said, "Tad, I'm trying to save everything you have built." Both of them were very bitter for a while, but I believe they eventually understood that I was trying to do the right thing.

The most difficult moment was when I had to inform my friend Chuck Jarvie what I had learned and what I needed to do. I went into his office and started, "Chuck, this is what I have found. . . ." I detailed the complete financial situation of the company. Then I said, "I'm going to have to fire your son." Not knowing what to expect, I waited for Chuck's reply. He looked up and said, "God bless you. Do what you have to do." We never discussed it again, but I believe Chuck knew that's what needed to happen.

When Bull Run acquired HCI, USA, and Streetball Partners, it already carried more than $50 million in debt. My discoveries more than doubled that amount. Bull Run was a publicly traded company, and almost overnight I lost my investment in it. The $11 million in stock I had received became almost worthless. If there was a silver lining, it was that by keeping my funds locked up in Bull Run, my other employees and board members were able to cash out their own investments and obtain some financial benefit for their hard work.

Near the beginning of the decade, Bray Cary almost destroyed my company. By 1998, we had found a good investor with Bull Run and Mack Robinson. HCI's traditional work continued to expand, and USA served as the umbrella company for Streetball Partners. When Bull Run offered to buy the company, it appeared that all our hard work was going to pay great dividends. We had hundreds of employees working in offices in New York, Dallas, Birmingham, and Lexington. We also had much smaller offices at each university where HCI held the athletic rights. We had excellent managers at every location. TJ Nelligan in New York and Marc Kidd in Dallas did a great job building the national scope of our business.

Those were challenging days as I watched the financial rewards of my professional work dissolve. It was emotionally draining and painful. However, I took satisfaction in knowing that in both the Bray Cary situation and the USA debacle, we managed to keep our company safe and strong—protecting people's jobs and our integrity. Difficult experiences are life's best teachers, and I learned a great deal. This episode affirmed the importance of hard work, the value of telling the truth, and the fact that decisions, good and bad, have an impact beyond yourself. Through it all, I was thankful and humbled to have a soul mate in Pat, who stood by me through each high and low.

With so many life lessons learned, my next task involved figuring out how to keep HCI growing despite Bull Run's lack of capital. Thankfully, I still had at least one big pitch to make and one big deal to seal.

12

My Last Great Pitch for the NCAA

HCI continued to expand its clientele, while I was constantly renegotiating NCAA contracts related to the men's basketball tournament. Historically, corporate partnerships had generated large sums of operating revenue for the NCAA. Over time, the contracts CBS negotiated with the NCAA outpaced the sums generated from the corporate partnerships because the network made its money from the sale of commercials during the tournament. CBS held all its financials close to the vest, but I saw the details in the corporate partner contracts my company negotiated. I encouraged all NCAA corporate partners to purchase TV advertising from CBS. Many of them did, and I estimated that almost 30 percent of CBS's revenue from the NCAA tournament came from companies with corporate partnerships brokered by HCI. In short, my company was helping to generate a third of CBS's revenue from tournament advertising, and I believed the corporations spending this money had been "brought to the table" through HCI's sponsorship program with the NCAA.

At the same time, the NCAA Radio Network established in the 1970s was not nearly as lucrative as the booming television industry. We held the rights to the NCAA tournament website, but this was well before the days of streaming games online. The future of corporate revenue had to be tied to television advertising, which HCI could accomplish by selling bundled rights packages at the national level. I did not want HCI or our partnership program to be outmoded, so I decided to make a new pitch for the future of the men's basketball tournament and the NCAA at large.

It seemed like perfect timing for a bundled rights proposal, because CBS's tournament contract would soon be renegotiated. In addition, UK president Charles Wethington was serving as president of the NCAA, while my friend and UK's athletic director CM Newton chaired the Division I Men's Basketball Committee. Executive vice president of the NCAA Tom Jernstedt worked with the committee as well and was another close friend of mine. I also had good relationships with NCAA executive director Ced Dempsey, chief financial officer Jim Isch, and public relations executive Wally Renfro, all of whom served on (or advised) the Division I Committee.

I spent days developing a proposal because I knew how much a bundled rights model would mean to the NCAA and HCI. I wrote multiple drafts until I had the perfect "white paper" on the future of NCAA sports marketing. Then I traveled to the NCAA's new home city, Indianapolis, to make my presentation. I told the committee that the NCAA had been losing out on revenue by signing individual contracts with different companies for the basketball tournament as well as other sports. I argued that if the NCAA bundled corporate sponsorships into a single package that included radio, publishing, and television for a broad array of sports, it could command substantially more revenue. A key part of the proposal was the establishment of an NCAA Network on cable television that would be funded by corporate partners. The NCAA would own the network but would partner with a cable television network (such as ESPN) to broadcast even more sporting events. If the NCAA adopted this model, it would control all the revenue coming in from corporate partners and gain greater negotiating power in choosing a network partner.

I sensed that the committee members were on board. They expressed numerous concerns, but my responses showed them just how much promise this model offered. Each question they asked gave me an opportunity to show just how valuable it could be. The NCAA could usher in a new era of unprecedented revenue that would support the association, its member institutions, and multiple sports, giving more students television exposure.

I had hoped the committee would adopt the proposal that day. Instead, Ced Dempsey wanted to ask various television network executives their opinion on the reforms. CBS held the current tournament TV contract, and it had an exclusive window of time to renegotiate with the NCAA. Therefore, Dempsey could not officially negotiate with other networks; he simply let the competitors know that the NCAA was considering a new formula and format for its basketball tournament and other sports.

I had no idea Ced had shared my proposal until the president of CBS Sports, Sean McManus, called and said, "Jim, I want to talk with you about bundling rights for the NCAA." He asked whether I would be interested in partnering with CBS on the NCAA bid. I called Tom Jernstedt to confirm my suspicions, and he told me that Dempsey had shared parts of the proposal, but the NCAA was not interested in creating a separate cable network. I found that perplexing. The network initiative, in my opinion, was the most lucrative part of my proposal and would have allowed the NCAA to control more of its own content rather than contracting out to various networks. Years later, the "power conferences," such as the Big 10 and the SEC, would adopt this idea.

I respected Ced and understood that he was protecting the NCAA's interests, but I was frustrated that he had shared the plan to see how it might be received by the other networks. It put me in a precarious position because HCI had no guarantee that it would be involved in any new bundled rights deal. With this in mind, I accepted Sean McManus's offer to partner on CBS's upcoming NCAA bid. I agreed to meet with Sean at CBS headquarters in Manhattan to develop a bidding strategy. He wanted HCI to cover the radio, publishing, and corporate partnerships, while CBS would handle the television rights. Sean also wanted me to make the presentation with him, presumably because of my previous work with the NCAA and my friends on the Division I Committee. I agreed and left New York as CBS's "partner."

Over the next few weeks, McManus and I discussed the value of the bid, and CBS decided to offer $5.3 billion to televise the NCAA men's basketball tournament for eleven years. HCI would provide the print programs, organize the radio network, and secure corporate sponsors. We set up a meeting with the NCAA in Indianapolis. At the time, I was suffering from a terrible inner ear problem. The pain and dizziness could be so crippling that my doctor prohibited flying. I had an employee, Terry Johnson, drive me to Indianapolis, where I joined HCI's recently named president Marc Kidd, along with Sean McManus and his associate Mike Aresco.

When we entered the room for our presentation, we saw the four individuals who had already heard my proposal: Ced Dempsey, Tom Jernstedt, Charles Wethington, and CM Newton. They were joined by three conference commissioners: Carolyn Schlie Femovich (Patriot League), Mike Tranghese (Big East), and Jim Delany (Big 10). Memphis president Lane Rawlins, who had just accepted the same position at Washington State, also served on the committee.

McManus started by announcing that CBS's new bid—$5.3 billion over eleven years—would triple the amount of revenue for the NCAA. I then detailed the bundled rights proposal, explaining the new revenue streams and how corporate sponsorships would span the marketing spectrum to include advertising in print publications, on the NCAA Radio Network, and on television, including ESPN. In short, corporate partners would help promote all NCAA sports (except for Division I football) in all media formats. I could tell that the committee was stunned by the offer. Dempsey then excused us from the room so the committee members could discuss the bid.

As we left the room, we all thought the presentation was a home run. Sean asked me, "What are you going to pay us for the radio, publishing, and corporate partnerships?" I had already worked out the numbers with Marc Kidd, so I said, "We'll pay you $200 million for the radio network and publishing. We'll take a commission on each corporate sponsorship we sell, but you'll keep all the revenue from those sales." Sean looked at me and said, "That sounds fair. You'll help sell the corporate sponsorships, right?" I agreed, and we shook hands.

When the committee invited us back into the conference room, Charles Wethington asked about acquiring ESPN's rights to the women's basketball tournament and other sports. Everyone knew we were making a bundled rights offer, but nobody had checked on the implications for existing ESPN contracts. We all figured that a buyout would cost approximately $200 million, so McManus said that if CBS had to buy out ESPN, the contract with the NCAA would be reduced to $5.1 billion. At that point, Lane Rawlins chimed in and said, "I'm not sure if this is enough money. I think we should have 6 percent revenue increases at various points over the next eleven years." I responded, "This is $3 billion more than the NCAA has been getting! This is not going to be negotiated further." I looked at Marc Kidd and said, "We've made our offer. Let's go." Jim Delany spoke up: "This is more money than we ever anticipated. We understand what you're saying." Gesturing toward Rawlins, I asked, "Does he understand?" Then Delany said, "We appreciate your offer. We just need to talk about it." I said, "That's fine," and started to leave.[1]

As I walked out, I told McManus, "I'm going back to Lexington." When I got halfway down the escalator, Dempsey leaned over the balcony rail and yelled, "Don't leave, Jim!" I said, "We've made our proposal and I feel terrible." My inner ear problem had flared up, and it was excruciating. He said, "It's going to work out! You're going to have a deal!" I said, "Okay," and kept going. Then Terry Johnson drove me home.

That meeting took place on a Monday in August 1999. On Tuesday, Sean McManus called and said, "Jim, we need to resolve this because the clock is now ticking on our exclusive negotiation window." I said I would call Jernstedt and Dempsey to see where we stood. They were both noncommittal. Then Mike Tranghese called me and reported that the committee was on board, so I needed get my agreement with CBS signed.

As I tried to seal the deal, an employee at HCI named Rita Rowady informed me that her cousin, John Rowady, was involved in sports marketing and had mentioned something about working with International Sport and Leisure (ISL) and CBS to broker a deal with the NCAA. She had no details, but ISL was a Swiss company that had done a lot of work with FIFA (the international soccer federation) and the Olympics. I had heard of ISL only because it was trying to break into US markets and had made some halfhearted overtures aimed at purchasing my company.

As the weekend approached, I grew concerned. That Friday, Ced Dempsey told me the NCAA was on board with the proposal and I needed close my deal with CBS over the weekend. I spent Friday and Saturday as an intermediary between CBS and the NCAA. Sean McManus was at the PGA tournament, so Mike Aresco was my CBS contact. I faxed him a memorandum of understanding (MOU) between HCI and CBS, but he never replied. Saturday night, Dempsey called to say he had spoken with McManus. An NCAA delegation was going to New York on Monday because CBS was ready to sign an MOU. After the signing, they planned a celebration dinner and then a press conference on Tuesday morning to announce the deal. Ced told me, "You need to get your agreement inked. We're worried CBS is planning to cut you out of the deal." I said I had heard the same rumor, but I added, "Sean and I shook hands on my offer to CBS." Ced replied, "That's fine, but you need something signed before we arrive at CBS Monday afternoon."

I immediately called Mike Aresco, who agreed to meet with me Monday morning at CBS headquarters in Manhattan. I still couldn't fly because of my inner ear problem, so I got Terry Johnson to drive me there on Sunday. Marc Kidd flew in, and we had dinner together on Sunday night and mapped out our strategy for the next morning. When we met with Aresco at 10:00 a.m., I pulled out a contract and said, "We're ready. Let's get this done." He said, "Jim,

I can't do this right now." I asked, "Why not?" He responded, "We have some other details to work out." He ushered us into a conference room and said he would be back in an hour. Almost two hours later, I went looking for him. When I finally found him, he had a pained look on his face and said, "It's going to be a bit longer." I demanded to see Sean, but Mike said he wasn't available. I asked, "Do you want me to tell the NCAA delegation not to come?" He responded, "No, they should still come." Tom Jernstedt called to find out what was going on, and I said, "I don't have a clue." He informed me, "McManus just called us and told us to come on, so we'll be there at 4:00."

CBS stonewalled all day, and by 4:00, everyone had left, including the receptionists. At about that time, the elevator door opened and out walked Ced Dempsey, Tom Jernstedt, Jim Isch, and Wally Renfro. I apologized because Marc and I were the only ones there. I shared the day's story with the group and then took them to a conference room. At first, it was somewhat funny. They teased me about being the head of CBS. After an hour, however, the mood started to change. Ced took a more serious tone and asked, "Jim, what's going on?" I told them I had no clue. Ced pointed out that CBS was my partner, but I said, "They haven't treated me like a partner. It's been total isolation. I'm sorry that I don't have any answers, but my guess is that they're trying to get [CBS CEO] Mel Karmazin's approval."

When 5:30 rolled around, we contemplated leaving, but then McManus showed up and apologized, saying there had been some crucial developments that had to be addressed. Then he asked to speak with Dempsey privately. They left the room, and we all waited for another half an hour. When they returned, I looked at Ced's notepad. It was upside down, but I could see a bunch of scribbled numbers and something that I thought looked like "ISL" and "No Host." McManus then asked Marc and me to leave the room briefly, which we did. After an hour I walked back in and said, "Guys, we were supposed to sign a deal this morning. We're going back to the hotel." McManus said, "Jim, I understand you're upset. Will you be in your room around nine? I want to call you." I said I would be, and then I left with Marc. As we got on the elevator, I looked at him and said, "I've been screwed before, but never like this." Marc said, "I can't believe what they did!" Then he asked how we would survive without the NCAA, and I said, "By doing more individual universities and conferences, we'll find a way to succeed." We discussed options over dinner before going back to the hotel.

McManus called me that night and said, "We've got a deal with the

NCAA. If you can come back early in the morning, we'll work out your agreement." So Marc and I showed up about 7:45 a.m., but nobody was in the office. About 8:15 I saw McManus, Tony Petitti (CBS senior vice president), and Aresco walking down the hall. As they passed the door, I jumped up and got their attention. Sean said, "There you are! Have a seat in the conference room." McManus then asked some questions about collegiate licensing rights, and I informed him we had already subcontracted with Bill Battle (owner of the Collegiate Licensing Company), and HCI's contract included licensing rights. My head was spinning (literally and figuratively), as once again we were left alone, waiting to see what would happen next.

Marc and I had been waiting about two hours when Tony Petitti entered the room yelling, "This whole thing is BS, and it has blown up in our faces!" I asked Tony to explain what had happened, but he just said, "The whole thing has blown up! I need your help!" He then ushered me into Sean's office. Sean was standing at a table away from his desk, yelling at some attorneys, who were screaming back at him. Everyone was blaming everyone else and shouting something like, "You messed this up," but using much more colorful language.

As I sat and listened, I learned that Mel Karmazin had agreed to the NCAA deal but wanted a signed contract rather than an MOU before publicizing it. CBS had drawn up a contract the night before and placed it under Ced Dempsey's hotel-room door early in the morning. While Marc and I were waiting in the conference room, Dempsey had called CBS and reminded the network executives that he had flown to New York to sign a simple MOU. Ced refused to sign a contract unless the NCAA's attorneys had read it first. Unprepared to sign a full contract, he and the others had flown back to Indianapolis.

While the men in the room accused one another for the debacle, I took a seat in Sean's chair and beat my hand against his desk. Once they had quieted down, I said, "You all have really screwed this up. Do you want to save this deal?" They half nodded in silence, so I said, "Mike, you have a good relationship with Jernstedt, so you need to call him. Sean, you have a good relationship with Dempsey, so you need to call him." I recommended that they fly to Indianapolis and try to restore the relationship with the NCAA that they had nearly destroyed. I finished, "That is the best advice I can give you. I'm heading back to Kentucky. Keep me updated on your progress."

Marc Kidd flew home, and Terry Johnson chauffeured me back to Lexington. I spent nearly the entire ride on the phone. I called Dempsey and said,

"Whatever you decide to do, I want to be your partner and will do whatever you need me to do. I don't care which network you sign with, I would just like to be involved if I'm still wanted." Then I called CBS and ended up speaking to Aresco. He told me they were flying to Indianapolis. I said, "Good, but you all screwed this up. CBS had control, but now the NCAA has the leverage."

Nobody from CBS called to tell me how the meeting went, but Dempsey invited me to talk about the arrangements while playing a round of golf. I agreed, so Pat drove us to Indianapolis. We had a nice dinner with our spouses that evening, and the next morning, Ced and I played at the Brickyard Golf Course. Because the CBS team had traveled to Indianapolis to make amends, Tom and Ced were still inclined to go with them. However, they believed the NCAA now had the right to negotiate with other networks too. Then Ced told me, "I think we're going to try to work this out with CBS, but I want you to get your deal worked out with them. I'm going to be up there at the beginning of next week, but I am not bringing a bunch of people like we did last time."

When I got home, McManus called me for an update. I told him the NCAA was inclined to stay with CBS, but there were no guarantees. Finally able to fly again, I left for Birmingham to renegotiate HCI's media rights contract with the SEC. We signed the deal, and as I was leaving SEC headquarters, commissioner Roy Kramer said, "I've spoken with [Big 10 commissioner] Jim Delany and some others. We need you to get this deal done." I informed him that I was leaving for New York to try to make that happen.

During my layover in Atlanta, an angry McManus called and said, "This damn deal is over! They sent us a crap contract, and now they are out negotiating with another network!" He asked, "Have you seen this contract?" I told him I had not, and he shouted, "Did you know anything about this?" I denied it again, but I don't think he believed me. In fact, if Sean was correct, this was bad news for me, because it meant that the NCAA was not going to work with HCI either.

I landed in New York and, at Aresco's request, visited CBS the next morning. When I showed up, they ushered me into McManus's office, and he threw the NCAA contract in my face. He said, "Can you believe this? The whole NCAA committee is here, and they're meeting with ESPN!" He was looking at me like I had orchestrated it all, so I said, "I have no idea what's going on, so I'm going back to Lexington. I hope we can work out a deal."

Apparently, Len DeLuca, who had once been at CBS but now worked for ESPN, had contacted the NCAA and made an offer. The NCAA sent CBS a far less favorable contract than the network had been expecting, and then the NCAA committee met with ESPN rather than CBS. The rumor was that ESPN had offered the NCAA $7 billion, but nobody told me, presumably because I was CBS's "partner." I tried to call CM, Tom, and Ced. Nobody would answer or return my calls. They had clearly chosen to keep me in the dark.

A few days later, on Labor Day weekend, UK hosted Louisville in the newly renovated Commonwealth Stadium, replete with luxury skyboxes. Newton visited the HCI box to thank us for supporting UK athletics. CM was one of my closest friends, but all he said was, "Jim, I'm sorry." He didn't elaborate, but I knew he was talking about the NCAA-CBS deal, and it felt like bad news.

The following week, Jernstedt called and said, "Jim, I want to apologize. We haven't treated you fairly. Ced wanted to let you know the ESPN deal is off." I had been told that ESPN chairman and CEO Steve Bornstein (who I thought was brilliant) and Michael Eisner (head of Disney, the parent company of ABC and ESPN) disagreed on the price. However, I have no proof that this was the problem. Either way, Jernstedt confirmed that they had decided not to tell me anything because I was a "partner" with CBS. Once the ESPN deal fell apart, the NCAA decided to issue a new RFP for bids, and it was going to entertain the top three offers. The NCAA would encourage the winning network to contract with me, but it would not be required.

Amidst the drama, attorney Joe Terry had reviewed HCI's NCAA contract and said, "Jim, you can stop this whole thing dead in its tracks. The NCAA is issuing an RFP for bundled rights bids, but you actually have contracted for two years beyond the RFP they are currently advertising." Sure enough, my contract extended two years beyond CBS's current deal, and it gave me rights to the NCAA Radio Network, all the print programs and advertising, and a percentage of the revenue from corporate partnerships and rights fees. Without these, there would be no bundled rights for the NCAA. I had an ace in the hole, so to speak, so I waited to see how things unfolded.

During the next week, every network that was interested in making a bid contacted us. Sean McManus called and said, "It's an open game! Tell me what's going on." I said, "I have no idea." Then Len DeLuca from ESPN took me out to dinner and asked what we were willing to pay for our portion of the media rights. I told him I couldn't divulge that because it was proprietary information I had provided to CBS. President of Fox Sports Enterprises, Rick Welts, asked Marc Kidd for the same information. I told Marc not to share it, and he asked, "Why are you doing this? CBS screwed you! They won't even sign a contract." I replied, "I know they did, but we are going to do the right thing." McManus called back and asked to renegotiate our deal. I said, "Sean, if you get the bid, then I will work with you. If someone else gets the bid, I will try to work with them." I added, "I want you to know that even though I haven't been treated right, I've refused to share the amount I offered to pay you with the other networks." Sean responded, "That sounds fair," and that was the end of our conversation.

The NCAA invited me to the Hyatt in Indianapolis in case I was needed to answer questions as Fox, ESPN, and CBS presented their bids. At one point during a break, Jernstedt stepped out and said, "Fox made the best presentation. They understand what we want to accomplish, but I'm not sure they offered enough money." A little while later, I saw Aresco scurrying around the floor. I told Marc Kidd, "CBS must have won it. They're all excited." Shortly thereafter, the NCAA officially accepted CBS's bid.

I got a call on my cell phone asking me to come down to the basement, where some members of the NCAA committee wanted to speak with me privately. When I arrived, Tom Jernstedt, Ced Dempsey, and Charles Wethington were all grinning. I asked, "What's going on?" They said CBS had upped its original $5.3 billion bid to $6 billion. All the shenanigans had cost CBS $700 million. Then they told me that CBS had stated in its presentation that the network planned to work with HCI, but we still needed to negotiate our part of the deal and sign a contract.[2]

I found Sean McManus at a little celebration party, and he said he would call me shortly and we would get together that evening. I returned to my room and waited, but Sean never called. When I eventually called his room, someone else answered. I heard that person say, "Jim Host is on the phone." Another person shouted back, "Tell him to come up here." So I went to McManus's suite, where he and Tony Petitti were smoking cigars. Sean said he wanted to sign a deal, but after such a hard negotiation, he needed a vacation. He suggested that when he returned, I could fly to New York and hammer out the details. I agreed.

So Marc Kidd and I made another trip to Manhattan. McManus and Petitti started the meeting by saying that they had already negotiated with Westwood One for NCAA radio broadcasts, so that was off the table. Then Sean said, "Jim, $200 million isn't enough." I retorted, "So, did you get a better deal from ISL?" Looking stunned, he asked, "How did you know that?" I simply said, "You can take your ISL deal and stick it up your ass." I turned to Marc and said, "Let's go."[3] When we were out on the street, Marc exclaimed, "You have just thrown your life's work away! Why would you do that?" I responded, "Marc, you don't want to get into bed with a dog that has fleas." We could not do business with a company that refused to take us seriously. I believed CBS had been jerking us around, and I was unwilling to be bullied for more money. Some of my bold behavior, however, was a result of Joe Terry's discovery that although CBS had one year left on its current contract with the NCAA, HCI had two. This meant that I controlled the radio network, print programs, and, most important, the right to negotiate the NCAA's corporate sponsors for the first year of any new contract with any new network. HCI had control. Now we waited.

About a week later, Ced Dempsey called and said, "Jim, we have got to do something about your contract. Our attorneys are telling us we can't close on any deals unless you release your rights." At that point, I basically asked Ced, "What's in it for my company?" He didn't give me an answer. He just asked to meet me at a Holiday Inn off I-65 in Scottsburg, Indiana, to talk about it. Pat accompanied me, and Ced brought his wife, June. We exchanged greetings, and then Ced and I found a table in the corner of the restaurant while our wives went off to talk somewhere else. Ced got straight to the point: "Jim, you really need to give up your rights for the NCAA to move forward." I said, "Ced, this has been one of the worst sagas I've ever been through. You've watched it all. How can I be assured that this is going to work out for us if I give up the rights?" Ced spoke honestly and replied, "I can't guarantee anything." He went on to say that the NCAA would strongly recommend me to whatever network won the rights, but he couldn't promise that HCI would still be involved.

That day in Scottsburg was one of the defining moments for me both professionally and personally. On the one hand, I had a chance to be the proverbial "fly in the ointment" and stick it to everyone who had mistreated me. Joe Terry had been pleading with me to protect the company's rights. On the other hand, if I refused to help Ced, I would make enemies of a lot of people I considered friends. I would make money off the NCAA for two more years, but then that part of my business would be finished. I had worked hard all my life to promote college athletics and provide resources to universities, which I believe truly changed people's lives for the better. At the end of the day, that was how I wanted to be remembered. So I looked at Ced and told him, "Okay, I'll give up my rights." That was an interesting phrase. I was giving up commercial rights, but I was also giving up my own personal right to get even. Ced had a letter drawn up stating that I relinquished my rights, which I signed. I received no compensation, but I retained my integrity.

CBS and the NCAA continued negotiations with ISL. News reports suggested that ISL would pay around $850 million for the rights. I simply didn't see how ISL could make a profit paying that kind of money to CBS. In a nearly unreal turn of events, a few months later I got a call from Sean McManus. He said, "Jim, I've got to see you." I asked, "About what?" He admitted, "Our agreement with ISL hasn't worked out, and we're stuck. We need someone who has experience with all this stuff." So I agreed that Marc Kidd and I would return to New York once again and try to work out a deal.[4]

Negotiations were tough, but we finally had some leverage. With Westwood One running the radio network, we still had the print programs and the corporate sponsorships. We paid CBS a $600 million rights fee, but in return, HCI received much larger commissions on the corporate sponsorships we sold. In addition, once the sponsorship revenue crossed a certain monetary threshold, we entered a revenue-sharing agreement with CBS. Before signing the deal, I told everyone in the room, "I want to make one thing clear. If we do this, you can't sell a corporate partner without my approval, and I can't sell one without your approval. Otherwise, I won't agree to the deal. That is how we solidify this partnership." They agreed, and we signed the deal. I was finally a partner with CBS in selling corporate sponsorships. It appeared that the drama had finally settled, and we were back in the game.[5]

CBS and the NCAA actually began the eleven-year contract with the 2003 basketball tournament, giving us time to develop much larger bundled rights packages. To accomplish this, we announced the creation of NCAA "corporate champions," an idea developed by HCI executive Rob Temple. These sponsorship packages would cost companies far more than they had paid in the past, but they would also provide the bundled advertising I had pitched to the NCAA. In essence, when we signed a "corporate champion," that company would gain advertising access to all the media formats involved with March Madness, as well as a wider array of collegiate sports.

One of the first sponsorships up for renewal was the soft-drink sponsor: Pepsi. Coca-Cola had once been an NCAA corporate partner, but it had lost those rights to Pepsi years earlier. Just recently, it had lost its NFL sponsorship when it was outbid by Pepsi at the last minute. Looking for redemption, Coca-Cola wanted a sport sponsorship for its advertising dollars.

In past years, I had worked closely with Rick Rock, a vice president at Pepsi. Pepsi was now using OMD, a large advertising firm owned by the Omnicom Group. OMD represented multiple corporations and negotiated package deals for all kinds of program advertising on CBS.[6] OMD and CBS proposed a contract for more than $75 million for Pepsi and the NCAA. I believed the relatively low offer was part of a larger marketing deal that would primarily benefit CBS, not the NCAA. In essence, it seemed to me that CBS was trying to bundle advertising not with the NCAA but with its other television shows.[7]

My partnership with CBS required me to negotiate and approve deals for the NCAA, so it did not sit well with me when *Sports Business Journal* obtained a leaked document stating that CBS and HCI had agreed to a three-year Pepsi deal and that only NCAA approval was needed. We had not given our approval to that contract. Then, Rick Rock called and asked me about some of the new contract details. I told him nothing had been finalized, and I had the right to refuse the deal. He asked, "Are you telling me CBS can't negotiate without you?" I replied, "That's correct. You're a good guy, Rick, but this is going to be done the right way or I'll block it."[8]

I immediately told the NCAA that both it and CBS could secure more money from Coca-Cola on a single sponsorship deal. I told Jernstedt that I thought OMD had offered a "low-ball" Pepsi sponsorship in return for larger advertising contracts on CBS shows that would allow the network to keep all the money. I also let the NCAA know that its contract with CBS gave the NCAA the right to approve (or not) any corporate partnership.

Well before CBS made its $6 billion deal with the NCAA, a series of events brought Coca-Cola back into the picture as a potential sponsor. Bob Prather at Bull Run regularly flew on a private jet from Atlanta to New York with Don Keough, longtime president and COO of Coca-Cola. Keough had become chairman of the board of Allen & Company in New York. This family-owned business was involved in highly lucrative investment banking and corporate acquisitions. Allen & Company was one of Coca-Cola's largest shareholders and was therefore deeply interested in its success. Prather started talking with Keough about Coca-Cola becoming involved with the NCAA again. Keough requested a meeting with me in Manhattan to explain HCI's operations. While there, I let him know that we would be pleased to entertain a sponsorship bid from Allen & Company. Keough introduced me to Herbert Allen III, who was in the process of becoming CEO and president of the family business. Allen, in turn, asked whether he could visit HCI in Kentucky.

When Allen visited Kentucky, I met him at the airport and gave him a personal tour of Lexington's horse farms, Keeneland, and a few historic landmarks before taking him back to my office. When we arrived, I offered him a soft drink and showed him our selection of beverages. He was displeased that we had only Pepsi products, so I said, "Pepsi sponsors the NCAA. If Coke did, that would be full of your drinks." Then we discussed HCI's operations.

The next day, I got a call from Coca-Cola CEO Doug Daft, who wanted to know how the company had lost its sponsorship with the NCAA. I told Daft that I had worked with Walter Dunn and Coca-Cola back in the 1980s, but Pepsi had outbid Coke in the 1990s, and the NCAA had stayed with Pepsi-Co ever since. About a month later, Daft came to see me in Lexington with the head of Coca-Cola's international marketing, Scott McCune. I gave them the Lexington tour and discussed the possibility of an NCAA sponsorship. When they left, I knew they were serious about obtaining the soft-drink rights.

Not long after negotiations with Coca-Cola began, I met with the company's senior vice president Chuck Fruit, who brought Peggy Ann West with him. I knew that after losing its NFL sponsorship, Coca-Cola wanted to redeem itself by taking the NCAA from Pepsi. I talked with Bob Prather at Bull Run about it, and he contacted Don Keough. Bob advised Don, "Unless you make an aggressive move now, you won't get the contract. CBS is already negotiating with OMD and Pepsi." Chuck Fruit then made some serious overtures to CBS, but he thought CBS wasn't even considering the deal because the network favored Pepsi. Marc Kidd and I informed CBS that Coca-Cola seemed intent on making a competitive bid, but CBS showed little interest in seriously pursuing it.

Despite this, we moved forward. Keough told me that Coca-Cola was going to prepare a substantial offer for the NCAA sponsorship, and he wanted me to meet with the company's new COO and president Steve Heyer. So I flew to New York, where Steve and I met at a little diner in Manhattan for breakfast. Steve was the person responsible for the contract, and he wanted my advice. We agreed to meet again the following week in Atlanta at Coca-Cola headquarters, where the two of us sat down and I suggested what a good deal for the NCAA and CBS would look like. I made a few trips to Atlanta while working with Steve Heyer, Chuck Fruit, and Peggy Ann West.

I advised the NCAA that it needed to look at the bid from Pepsi very closely and wait to hear from Coca-Cola. Shortly thereafter, I was attending the Final Four, and Tom Jernstedt asked me, "How can CBS be telling us to go with Pepsi even though I hear Coke is going to offer more money?" I said, "Tom, CBS is my partner, but I want to work with them in the right way. The NCAA and HCI have to agree on the deal before anything is final." Then I told him I couldn't say anything else but begged him to have the NCAA's attorneys read the contract with CBS. I added, "You have every right to make sure you get the best deal."

I then told Heyer that the NCAA had the right to approve sponsors, and it wanted companies that showed interest in collegiate sports across the board. I continued to travel to Atlanta and work with the Coke team. After the Final Four, Coke CEO Daft met with Ced Dempsey and informed him that Coke was going to make a formal offer to the NCAA and CBS. The initial offer consisted of a four-year, $135 million deal.

Pepsi decided to match Coke's offer. At that point, Pepsi president Steve Reinemund called to find out what was going on. "Jim, what are you doing to me?" he asked. "When did this go off track! How do we keep our deal?" I said, "Steve, I'm in a partnership with CBS to negotiate corporate sponsorships for the NCAA." I explained how I handled negotiations and how CBS handled negotiations. Then I said, "I wish we had been negotiating with Pepsi directly rather than OMD. I don't think OMD has Pepsi's best interests in mind." I explained that OMD was looking to find the best price for its entire advertising deal with CBS. I concluded, "The negotiations aren't over, so you can raise your bid."

That began a bidding war. The month of May was full of intrigue as each soft-drink company tried to outdo the other. Some said I wanted Coca-Cola to get the deal, which was untrue. I simply wanted the NCAA to get the best deal possible. As it turned out, that deal came from Coca-Cola, which eventually offered more than $500 million for an eleven-year deal that would last the entire term of CBS's NCAA contract. Coke had taken HCI's advice to offer more money that could be used to promote multiple "minor" sports championships, so it truly benefited the NCAA across the board.

Pepsi then matched Coke's offer, so the NCAA leadership held a cloistered meeting to determine which contract to accept. Making reference to the Catholic Church's method of announcing papal decisions, Tom Jernstedt called me and said, "Jim, the smoke is red!" I knew this meant that Coca-Cola had won the bid. While the contract was a huge boon for CBS's contract with the NCAA, it also brought more funding to ESPN, which held the rights to many of the other college sports championships. CBS executives publicly praised the deal, but privately they were upset with me because I had negotiated outside the umbrella negotiations with OMD.[9]

That sweet victory was the last great sale I helped orchestrate with the NCAA. It reminded me of my early work with the NCAA and my promise to Walter Byers to spend my professional life promoting college sports and college athletes. The Coke deal did just that. It included media rights for more than twenty different NCAA sports. Over the next decade, Coke's contract provided funding to help other "minor" sports grow exponentially. Sports that had previously received little money from university athletic departments began to attract public attention and generate revenue. It literally altered the landscape of college sports marketing.

13

A Time of Transition

The half-billion-dollar deal we negotiated with Coca-Cola was the largest of its kind in the history of sports marketing. Despite this, it seemed to me that some at CBS were upset because they had been outmaneuvered by a Kentucky boy. The Coke deal made our already strained relationship even more challenging. Despite our "partnership," some individuals at CBS disliked working with someone who took a different approach to sales, sports marketing, and client relations. As tensions between HCI and CBS continued, CBS announced that it would forgo the remainder of our contract. All at once, my work with the NCAA came to an end.

Throughout the saga, Mack Robinson's son-in-law Hilton Howell had been encouraging me to find a young executive to mentor—someone who could eventually assume the day-to-day operations of HCI. Hilton recommended Gordon Whitener. Gordon had attended the University of Tennessee before becoming a graduate assistant for the football program at Oklahoma State. I believe Gordon began his foray into sports marketing by creating the United States Cowboy Tour in the late 1990s.

I first met Gordon when he invited me to his ranch in northern Georgia, where he made a solid first impression. I agreed to make him COO of the company while I continued as CEO and trained him to take my place. He moved into the office Bray Cary had occupied years earlier in Lexington. I taught him the business while introducing him to key employees and crucial business acquaintances around the country. Our partnership worked well during the first couple of months. Gordon was a bright individual and an excellent salesman.

After a few months, Gordon wanted to host a professional development retreat for employees. He paid an exorbitant amount of money to bring in a motivational speaker he knew. The event was a type of mental-training, self-cleansing retreat where people sat in circles on the floor and performed visualization exercises. I wasn't asked to attend, but I stopped by for a session. While there, I caught the eyes of some of my longtime employees, and they had this worried look like they thought I might lose it. Instead, I just walked out. Gordon followed me and said, "You didn't stay very long." I replied, "No, I can't stand this . . . whatever."

Perplexed as to how these activities were going to improve employee productivity, I learned that Gordon intended to change the highly disciplined culture I had labored so many years to create. He thought my management style was far too rigid, and he wanted to modernize our approach with a much less formal environment. The retreat was the first step.

While the cultural shift made me uncomfortable, it was less alarming than Gordon's business strategy. Whitener had a part-ownership stake in a NASCAR team and car. Although I had never been interested in NASCAR, I was open to Gordon's idea of expanding into that market. His business decisions, however, unsettled me. Whitener had Kevin Bryant, who was responsible for selling SEC sponsorships, devote more of his time to selling sponsorships for Gordon's NASCAR vehicle. In my mind, this was a clear conflict of interest, and I also feared that removing Bryant from the SEC sponsors could jeopardize that relationship.

I met with Whitener and CFO Jerry Felix and read them a paper I had written about the future of the company and the errors I thought were being made. Clearly, Gordon believed that moving into NASCAR would be beneficial for the company. I disagreed with his methods, and I let him know that, as CEO, I wasn't happy with the direction he was taking the company. I said I would take my concerns to Bull Run's leadership if nothing changed. Gordon said he would get back to me, but he never did.

I called Bob Prather at Bull Run to request a meeting. A few days later, we met at a Manhattan restaurant and I handed him the same paper I had read to Gordon. It took him a few minutes to go through it, and when he looked up he said, "You mean he has ownership in a NASCAR car and he is using our employee to sell sponsorships that benefit him?" I said, "Yes, but he says he's giving us a commission." Bob replied, "Regardless of his paying a commission, it's still wrong." Then I added, "I've been mentoring Gordon, but I need to let him go because I brought this to his attention and he did nothing." Additionally, the company culture was changing in ways that I believed would not be profitable. Bob seemed stunned. I offered to step back in and operate the company for a few months while they found a new executive for HCI. He asked whether Marc Kidd would come back, but Marc and his family had decided to stay in Dallas. Bob said he needed to discuss the issue with Mack Robinson and would be back in touch.

A week later, Bob wanted to meet in Lexington. Convinced that he was going to let Whitener go, I had been thinking strategically about ways to move HCI forward. I picked Bob up from the airport, and he proceeded to inform me that they had decided to give Gordon an opportunity to move forward with his plans. Bob's entire demeanor had changed, so I presumed that he had heard a very different story from Gordon. I had agreed to mentor Gordon so that he could take over the company in a productive fashion, but he was being allowed to run it in his own way, regardless of my opinion. Either way, Bob's message was my cue. I let him know that I would be stepping down as CEO. I informed the Bull Run Board of Directors as well. Then, on Friday, June 20, 2003, I sent an email to all Host Communications employees informing them that Whitener would be the new CEO. That weekend, Pat helped me clean out my office downtown, and I moved to my "retirement" office near Harrodsburg Road.[1]

My resignation package included a spot on Bull Run's board and an eight-year consultant's retainer. My administrative assistant Ann Hill remained with me. I had hoped I could still play a role in helping HCI succeed, but within a week, I realized that was not going to happen. Everyone at the HCI offices quit speaking to me. I had been completely shut out. It was extremely painful to be ostracized. Years later, some employees told me that Whitener had instructed them not to communicate with me. During the next few months, I pursued some consulting opportunities with various universities and the NCAA. I also helped the Lexington Center Corporation and started doing fund-raising for charitable organizations.

One year later, I was working in Kentucky state government when Tom Stultz called and said, "Bob Prather has asked me to become CEO of Host Communications, but I told him I wouldn't agree to it unless you were allowed to help me." Of course, I agreed to help and asked, "What happened to Whitener?" Tom replied, "They're going to let him go tomorrow, but he doesn't have a clue." Then he said, "Bob Prather asked me to tell you he wishes he had taken your advice and he's sorry." Gordon's approach had not worked out as they had hoped, so Bob needed to make a change. Tom met me in Lexington that night, and we worked until the early-morning hours developing a strategy to improve HCI. When we were done, Tom asked if he could meet with me once a week to get my advice, and I told him I would be glad to. During the next months, Tom turned the company around and made it profitable again.

That change happened in the summer of 2004, but a lot had transpired in my professional life since stepping down at HCI in June 2003. One day that summer, while sitting in my office, my longtime friend Ralph Hacker stuck his head in the door and said, "I need you to go to Frankfort with me and Ernie. Just come with me to this one event. That's all." I hesitatingly agreed and followed Ralph out to a bus, where I shook hands with Congressman Ernie Fletcher, who was running for Kentucky governor. We were headed to a rally for Fletcher in Frankfort near the Capitol. After we arrived, I was listening to the speeches when Ralph said, "I'd like you to say a few words in support of Ernie." I protested, "I don't have anything planned," but he said, "That's okay, you don't need to talk for a long time." Then Ralph took the stage and said, "We have someone who was here before, and he is here now!" Then he introduced me to the crowd. Without a single word prepared, I gave the best five-minute speech I could come up with.

I finally figured out why they had invited me when Fletcher embraced me and said, "Jim, I need one more favor from you. Governor Nunn has agreed to meet with me and I know you two are close. Would you come with us?" Fletcher feared that Nunn would support Democrat Ben Chandler, whose grandfather Happy had crossed party lines to endorse Nunn in the 1960s. So I hopped back on the bus with Ralph, Fletcher, and Fletcher's wife, Glenna. We drove to the mansion at Pin Oak Farm, which UK now owned and Nunn rented from the university. As we walked up the sidewalk, I noticed that the front door was open but the screen door was closed. Louie Nunn was at the far end of the living room wearing a fancy smoking jacket and had his back turned to us. I had no idea who planned the meeting, but it clearly felt staged. Regardless, the visit was important because Fletcher needed Nunn's support to improve his chances of winning the governor's race.

As we approached the door, I said, "Governor Nunn!" He turned around and said, "Jim, I had no idea you were coming!" He gave me a big hug and proceeded to shake hands with Ernie, Glenna, and Ralph as we walked into the house. As we entered the living room, the former governor motioned for me to come sit with him on a couch. Ernie, Glenna, and Ralph sat on another couch across from us. Louie said, "I'm glad you came to see me even though I'm old and irrelevant now."

I chimed in, "Governor, Congressman Fletcher wants your support. I'm here to make sure that if you have anything on your mind, you have this opportunity to say it." Nunn then proceeded to rip into Fletcher, scolding him for not taking care of some Republicans, not addressing the key issues strategically, and not seeking support in the right manner. In the middle of Nunn's rant, I tried to stop him. He looked up at me and said, "Well, Host, you always did interrupt at the proper time!" I said, "Governor, you know I don't have to be here, but I'm here because I love you. I want you to do the right thing by Ernie and for Kentucky." I spoke for another minute before Nunn interrupted me and asked, "What do you want me to do?" At that point, Fletcher spoke up: "I would like for you to speak on my behalf in London [Kentucky]." Governor Nunn asked who would drive him there, and I said, "I'll drive you myself if I have to!" Ernie interjected, "No, no—I'll have someone pick you up." Louie agreed, and he stayed on board for the remainder of the campaign.

Governor Nunn's support gave Fletcher additional momentum. From then on, Ernie kept talking about my role in his administration. By this time, Pat and I had officially become Florida residents for tax reasons, and we stayed on Jupiter Island for more than half the year. I told Fletcher that I was no longer a Kentucky resident and wouldn't be able to serve. As an interesting aside, we had changed residency before the 2000 presidential election and had voted in Palm Beach County during the Bush-Gore race. Our precinct was at the center of the "hanging chads" saga. That crisis, which went all the way to the Supreme Court, gripped the national headlines.

Back in Kentucky, Fletcher won in 2003 and became the first Republican governor since Louie Nunn more than three decades earlier. The following day, I met with former Louisville mayor Dave Armstrong at the Lexington Country Club to discuss some civic projects. While there, Governor-elect Fletcher walked in with his entourage. He spotted me and walked over to our table. I congratulated him, and he said, "You've got to be a part of the administration." I replied, "Thank you, Governor, but I'm not interested." He responded, "I will be in touch," and he walked away.

That week, various Republicans who were joining Fletcher's administration tried to convince me to serve, but I politely declined. Then Mike Duncan, a well-connected Kentucky Republican and rising star on the national scene, asked me to visit him in Frankfort. At that point, he was serving as general counsel to the Republican National Committee but had accepted the role as head of Fletcher's transition committee. When I arrived, a whole panel of people led by Dick Murgatroyd from Kenton County began to interview me. I said, "Look, I have no desire to be a cabinet secretary. I've already done this." After nearly an hour of questioning, I finally convinced them to stop.

Mike Duncan called me afterward and asked if the two of us could discuss some possibilities. I agreed, and Mike shared his plans for leadership in Frankfort. He said that if I would join the cabinet, he would leave DC to become the governor's chief of staff. He asked me to meet with the governor, just to discuss it, so I acquiesced. Jim Bunning, Mitch McConnell, and Hal Rogers all encouraged me to serve. After Elaine Chao and Mary Bunning talked to Pat, she advised me, "You might enjoy this. You should give it some serious consideration."

Knowing that Fletcher wanted me as a cabinet secretary, I wrote down a list of thirty-five items that I wanted him to agree to before I became a member of his team. Ralph Hacker joined Mike Duncan and Fletcher at our meeting. I checked off items as the governor-elect agreed to them. Most important, I did not want to serve as secretary of tourism again. I desired a new challenge. Fletcher said he wanted me to lead the newly formed commerce cabinet, with the economic development and tourism cabinets reporting to me. The rest of the list focused on letting me run my own show. I wanted to be able to hire and fire my own people, establish my own commissions, and execute my strategic plans to promote business and job growth in Kentucky. The governor-elect agreed to all thirty-five points. That should have been a warning sign.

At a press conference a few days later, Mike Duncan and Governor-elect Fletcher introduced me as the new secretary of the Commerce Department. After the announcement, I met with them and asked, "Governor, where is my office?" He looked at Duncan and asked, "Mike, where is Jim's office?" Mike didn't know either, so I said, "Let me make a few phone calls and I'll figure it out." I discovered that my office was in the Capitol Plaza. I traveled over there to look at it, and it was an absolute disaster.

As I began cleaning the office and getting it organized, Fletcher called and said, "I'm sorry, Jim, but I'm not sure if we can do what we hoped with your position. I'm getting some resistance." He proceeded to tell me I needed to meet with Gene Strong, the secretary of economic development, and persuade him to work with me. I said, "Governor, I'll only do that if I have your complete support," which he offered.

Gene met me at a McDonald's in Versailles and refused to report to me. His cabinet had been created by state statute, and it could not be folded under another one. Gene informed me, "Apparently, they didn't do their homework. You can't touch me." David Williams, president of the Kentucky Senate, agreed with Gene. I reported this news to the governor, and nothing happened.

The next setback came just after Fletcher's inauguration. Duncan called and said, "Jim, I'm really sorry, but I'm not going to be in the administration. Fletcher is appointing Daniel Groves as his chief of staff." I was stunned. Groves was a sharp young man who had organized Fletcher's campaigns and served as his chief of staff in Washington, but choosing him over a seasoned veteran like Duncan, with his political ties and experience, seemed unwise. I shared that opinion with Mike, and he lamented, "Well, that's what's going to happen. I'm really sorry. I know I told you I would be here." I said, "That's right. I wouldn't have taken this job otherwise!" He apologized again, and I thanked him for telling me and wished him the best. Two of the primary reasons I had agreed to become secretary of commerce were now nonexistent. I would not be working with Duncan or with the Department of Economic Development.

Then Fletcher's press secretary Wes Irvin resigned. Duncan, who had not left yet, called me and asked, "Didn't you serve as Nunn's press secretary while you were a cabinet head?" I confirmed that I had, and Mike asked if I could handle both jobs again. I agreed on the condition that I would have total access to the governor and that he would move quickly to find a full-time replacement. The Commerce Department employees disliked it because I moved our daily cabinet meetings to 6:30 a.m. so that I could get to the governor's office by 8:00 a.m. I held both positions for a few months until the governor found a new press secretary.

Early in my tenure, Ro Parra, a Dell executive who owned a horse farm outside of Lexington, called and said, "Jim, I'm so happy you're working in commerce. We were interested in bringing a big Dell operation to Kentucky, but right now we fly over the state." I asked, "What does that mean?" He responded, "Kentucky is not a 'right-to-work state,' so Dell won't come." Kentucky unions possessed great power with the legislature, so it simply turned big corporations away. I told Ro, "I'll ask the governor if there's anything we can do."

I told Gene Strong about Dell. Clearly upset, Gene said, "There is nothing but confusion with you and your new role!" I said, "You've got that right, but it's up to the governor whether he's going to do anything about it or not." When I told the governor about Dell, he said, "How did you get that call? It should have gone to Gene Strong." I replied, "Because I run the commerce cabinet!" I continued, "Ro knows me, and that's why he called. Others will call me too." Sure enough, after more inquiries that could have been handled just as easily by economic development, Fletcher called me into a private meeting and informed me, "Gene is going to retire in April after the legislative session. Then we will merge your offices." As it turned out, Gene didn't retire, and our offices remained separate. It created confusion, overlap, and conflict. Gene and I got along, but too often we were addressing the same issues. In addition, there was no serious push to make Kentucky a right-to-work state, and Dell ended up moving its operation to Nashville. Other companies followed a similar path.

I did develop one special relationship on the governor's cabinet with Robbie Rudolph. Robbie had turned his local tire sales operation in Murray, Kentucky, into a booming international wholesale transportation business. He did excellent work as Fletcher's secretary of finance and administration. We were the only two cabinet secretaries with private business backgrounds, and we thought alike. He regularly came by my office before 8:00 a.m. to talk policy strategy, and we developed a close working relationship.

One of my first priorities as secretary involved applying my knowledge of branding and marketing to state government. After some research, my office determined that state government agencies used fifty-one different "brands" or logos. I told the governor and the cabinet members that Kentucky needed a single brand for the entire state. Most agreed, so we sent out an RFP to private marketing agencies for a new Kentucky logo and slogan. A selection committee reviewed the bid presentations and narrowed them down to four. Some older firms that had done business with the state government for years disliked my approach because they could not benefit from political ties.

We set up an online voting system for the final four slogans: "Where Legends Are Born," "Make History," "Limitless," and "Unbridled Spirit." The last option won, and Kentucky had a new brand and logo. I became the "enforcer," and when I found that state agencies or offices were not using the new brand,

I made them change their stationery. "Unbridled Spirit" became one of the most recognizable state slogans in the nation, and soon several other states centralized their own brands.[2]

We accomplished most of the cabinet's work with little fanfare. However, one attempt at reform created controversy. More than three decades after growing the state park system during Nunn's administration, many of the park grounds and lodges had fallen into disrepair. Understandably, few families chose to spend their vacation time at Kentucky state parks. This led to an annual operating shortfall of nearly $30 million, so the governor asked me to cut the deficits. Looking for a way to make the parks more attractive and less costly, I visited them unannounced. Rooms at the parks' lodges were dark and musty, and some of the grounds were unkempt. We needed to find a strategy to change this.

The controversy started at Lake Cumberland State Park. When I drove up to the front of the lodge there, a nice-looking young family was unpacking their luggage for a stay, but nobody was assisting them. At the same time, three park employees were walking toward the front of the lodge. They all looked dirty and disheveled. One had his hat on backwards; another had his sleeves rolled up, showcasing the tattoos covering his arms; and the other's pants were sagging down below his butt. I walked over to them and asked, "What are your jobs, and what are you doing?" One of them said, "Why do you care?" I responded, "Because I am the cabinet secretary who approves your checks!" They all tried to straighten up, and I warned, "You had better not look like this if you want to walk around these grounds or the lodge."

I went inside and asked to speak with the manager, who was nowhere to be found. I told the clerk, "Tell him the cabinet secretary who approves his paycheck is here." He immediately got on the two-way radio, and within a matter of minutes, the manager came screeching up to the front of the lodge in a golf cart. "Mr. Secretary," he said, "why didn't you tell us you were coming?" I said that wasn't how I operated, and I let him know about the sorry state of the grounds and the hotel. In a sad twist of irony, I could not replace this manager because he was a "merit" employee.

I devised a plan to remedy the situation I had just seen. I instituted a dress code for state park employees and created a policy that no tattoos could be visible while employees were at work. The negative press we received for those measures was unreal. The governor sympathized with my plan but asked me to "tone it down" to lessen the criticism.[3]

On a far more substantive level, my inability to effect real change to the park system during my time in Frankfort frustrated me. For example, I lobbied to close three rarely played golf courses that were sucking resources from the budget, but I was unsuccessful because of political pressure to keep them open. I wanted to close certain state parks in the winter because virtually nobody visited them during the coldest months, but the same political forces—unwilling to take away salaries from employees in the merit system—stopped me. I hoped to outsource some of the maintenance work because it was far less expensive to contract with private companies, but again, I faced resistance for identical reasons.

One of the more successful initiatives my department implemented was the Kentucky Sports Authority. Having spent much of my career in sports marketing, I understood the economic impact of sporting events. Cities from all over the country lobbied the NCAA to host college sports championships, but Kentucky did very little of this. My department developed the Kentucky Sports Authority to coordinate boosters from the state's many regions and attract various sporting events to the commonwealth.

The first area I explored to improve the visibility of Kentucky's sporting events was its most famous industry: horses. Sometime around 2000 I met with *Lexington Herald-Leader* president Tim Kelly and the general manager of Lexington's CBS affiliate WKYT, Wayne Martin. They had put together a proposal to bring the FEI (the International Equestrian Federation in English) World Equestrian Games to Lexington. I told them their sales pitch had little chance of winning without the official backing of the state government, but I suggested they make the presentation anyway to get Kentucky on the FEI's radar for future events. Kentucky did not win the bid to host the 2006 games, which were awarded to Aachen, Germany. However, that bid provided the groundwork for a future opportunity.

Since I was the secretary of commerce, the Kentucky Horse Park (KHP) reported to me. I asked KHP head John Nicholson what we needed to do to bring the FEI World Equestrian Games (WEG) to Kentucky. John suggested that I make a presentation to the FEI's top officials. I knew that before I made a proposal to host the WEG, I needed Fletcher's support. The governor wanted the games to be held in Kentucky, but he remained noncommittal on the financial resources. Finally, as we were on our way to the unveiling of the Man O' War statue at the KHP, I said, "Governor, if you want the World Equestrian Games in Kentucky, you need to announce it today at this unveiling." He didn't say much in the car, but during his address he publicly supported funding for the renovations at the Horse Park needed to bring the WEG to Kentucky.

I solicited support from other key government officials. We devised a financial plan that utilized the 1 percent increase in the statewide hotel room tax. We also estimated that the state would need to supply $38 million to make the necessary upgrades at the KHP. I asked for letters of support from Governor Fletcher and the legislature. We asked Lexington mayor Jim Newberry for police and law enforcement assistance. Finally, Senator Mitch McConnell agreed to write a letter of support, and the US Department of Agriculture agreed to allow expedited quarantine procedures for horses coming from overseas.

At that point, we invited FEI secretary-general Michael Stone and his staff to meet at the KHP with me and executive director John Nicholson. I laid out all the funding strategies and our plans to expand the KHP so that it could host the best games that had ever been held. Horses would fly into the Greater Cincinnati airport, which was located in northern Kentucky, for expedited quarantines.

Finding a title sponsor was essential to make the WEG a financial success. I decided to start with Pearse Lyons and his company Alltech. It did not have the same recognition as UPS or Toyota, but Alltech supplied animal feed infused with additives to horses and other livestock around the world. I had known Lyons for decades. We first met in 1977, when he had recently moved from Ireland. He entered my small office on Main Street and asked, "Is James here?" I greeted him, and he introduced himself: "I am Dr. Pearse Lyons and I've just arrived in America to make my fortune. I'm from Ireland and I don't have a pot to piss in, but I am going to make a fortune, and everyone says you are the guy that can help me do it." I asked, "How can I help you?" He answered, "I need you to put on a seminar, so I can showcase gasohol." I said, "What in the world is gasohol?" He explained, "It is ethanol, and I am an expert on it. I earned my PhD studying yeast, and I worked for Guinness in Ireland. I wanted to start my own business, but Ireland's government is in the toilet, and I can't break through all the politics." He added, "If you can help me put on a successful seminar on gasohol, I can start my company." So I said, "I will run the seminar if you allow us to take the costs off the top. Then, I will keep 25 percent of the revenue, and you can keep 75 percent." Pearse said, "That sounds fair," so we shook hands on it, I typed up a one-page memorandum of understanding, and we both signed it.

The first year, my company made $24,000 on the seminar. The second year, we made more than $50,000. By the third year, our profits exceeded $100,000. Pearse Lyons was well on his way to making his fortune when he said, "I want you to be a partner in my business." I said, "Pearse, I'm not going into business with you. We're too much alike. We would kill each other!" Then I added, "But I will always be your friend, and if you need assistance, I will be glad to help." Pearse eventually expanded Alltech into a wildly successfully global business.

In 2005 I asked Pearse to meet with me to discuss being a sponsor of the WEG. I hadn't planned a presentation. I just hoped that he would consider the offer and we could meet again later to hammer out the details. When I entered his office, Pearse had made himself some tea and had a cup of coffee waiting for me. We sat down and I said, "I'm here because I want you to be a corporate partner of the FEI World Equestrian Games." He knew very little about the event or corporate sponsorships, so I explained how this would help both his company and the WEG. He said, "Only 7 percent of my business comes from horses. Why should I support it?" I explained that wealthy horse owners from around the world would attend. In addition, the European television ratings for the games were second only to soccer events. I concluded, "We can put your logo on all the feed sacks all over the world and spread Alltech's name on television across Europe and the rest of the globe."

Pearse paused and asked, "How much will it cost me?" I said, "It costs $5 million to be a corporate partner." He asked, "What about a presenting sponsor?" Thinking off the top of my head, I responded, "That's $7.5 million, but you don't want the Toyota World Equestrian Games presented by Alltech. For $10 million, we can have the Alltech World Equestrian Games. I promise it will be worth it." Pearse looked at me and said, "Okay. I'll do it." I said, "Wonderful!" At that point, Lyons added, "I want the beer category too." (Alltech brewed Kentucky Bourbon Barrel Ale.) I said, "That's a secondary sponsorship, and you'll have to bid on it separately." Then he backed off and said, "Okay, then I'm not going to take it." I thanked him for his time and got up to leave. At that point, he said, "All right, we'll figure out the beer later." This all transpired within fifteen minutes. He ended up buying the beer sponsorship for an additional $1 million. Pearse often said, "That was the most expensive cup of coffee I ever had."

As we planned to bid for the World Equestrian Games, I spent a great deal of time studying other sports in Kentucky as well. Naturally, my attention turned to basketball. I noticed that Louisville had not hosted an NCAA men's basketball tournament weekend in more than a decade. I asked Tom Jernstedt in Indianapolis why this was, and he said, "Honestly, the tournament won't come to Louisville as long as they play in Freedom Hall." The NCAA generated more revenue, and fans had a much better experience, when the host sites were downtown, within walking distance of hotels and restaurants. Tom actually used the term "walkability." Host cities in relative proximity to Louisville (such as Lexington, Nashville, Indianapolis, St. Louis, and Memphis) would always be selected instead of Louisville because of Freedom Hall's inconvenient location at the Kentucky State Fairgrounds.

I shared this information with the governor, and he informed me that Rick Pitino and the University of Louisville's AD Tom Jurich had been discussing the construction of a new arena. I learned that the governor had never attended a Final Four, so I invited him to join me at the 2005 Final Four in St. Louis. As fate would have it, Louisville's Cardinals made it to the Final Four that year, so I was able to convene a meeting with Tom Jernstedt, Governor Fletcher, and University of Louisville president Jim Ramsey, where Tom explained the NCAA's perspective on the arena's location.

After the meeting, the governor told me, "Jim, I'm going to set up a task force, and [Lieutenant Governor] Steve Pence will chair it, but you need to be the vice chairman and run it. You got Rupp Arena built, and you understand this better than anybody." I said, "Governor, I'm not sure I should do that." I wanted the best for the university and for the city of Louisville because it would help the commonwealth, but I worried about the backlash if I (a Lexington-UK guy) was in charge of the committee studying the construction of a new arena in Louisville. Fletcher said, "You have to do it," so I agreed. We organized a committee in May 2005, with the goal of completing a feasibility report that fall.

As I continued my work in the commerce cabinet, Attorney General Greg Stumbo began a highly politicized investigation into possible violations of the state's "merit system" in hiring government employees. Clearly, some individuals in the administration had engaged in political patronage—an unfortunate but common practice in Kentucky politics. However, most cabinet secretaries, like myself, refused to engage in such practices. Despite this, Stumbo's claims grabbed the headlines nearly every day, and the governor remained on the defensive as his approval ratings declined. These relentless (and often unsubstantiated) attacks made it nearly impossible to accomplish anything of substance. Governor Fletcher was one of the brightest and kindest people I knew, and he was not a political fighter who easily went on the attack. I think he was (and still is) proud of that, but in the rough-and-tumble world of Kentucky state politics, he found it difficult to move his agenda forward.

I too was frustrated with Stumbo's incessant attacks on the governor and his staff. In addition, Pat and I had been experiencing some minor health problems. So I decided to resign my post in the fall of 2005. Both Robbie Rudolph and Governor Fletcher asked me to continue to work on the Louisville arena project and the effort to bring the WEG to Kentucky, and I agreed to do so. Both were full-time jobs in themselves, but I simply volunteered my time and service. The new arena was far from a done deal, but Kentucky was about to be awarded the World Equestrian Games. I served as chair of the WEG 2010 Foundation.[4]

Since Pearse Lyons and Alltech spent $10 million for the WEG title sponsorship, Lyons remained heavily involved in planning. One day, he invited me to Alltech's headquarters, where he showed me a luxurious office that had my name etched in glass outside the door. Pearse said, "This is your office. I want you to run the games from here." I said, "Pearse, I'm not running the games as a paid executive, and I don't want to work for you." He replied, "I don't want you to work for me. I just want you to run the games—make sure they're successful."

Most weeks, I spent three days in Louisville working on arena planning and two days at Alltech working on the WEG. My first priority for the games involved finding the best executive director possible. In 2006 the National Association of Sports Commissions' Event Symposium met in Lexington. I was slated to speak at the event, as was Jack Kelly. I had heard good things about Jack, who had served as CEO of the Goodwill Games for Turner Broadcasting before moving on to chair USA Baseball and serve as executive director of the Space City (Houston) Sports Commission. After listening to Jack's presentation, I asked him to be the CEO of the 2010 World Equestrian Games, pending the approval of the governor and the WEG Board. Both were impressed with Jack, and he accepted the offer to serve as CEO. He immediately had a positive impact on the momentum of the games.

We had a unique governing structure for the WEG. The executive committee for the games consisted of myself, John Long (CEO of the US Equestrian Foundation), and Michael Stone (FEI secretary-general). Jack Kelly helped coordinate and execute our efforts. We developed plans for the Kentucky Horse Park's expansion and renovation and created a detailed outline of the many ceremonies and events that needed to happen. Each event required teams to manage the security, publicity, transportation, and ticketing, as well as the event itself. This was a massive undertaking, and each phase required the assistance of multiple groups. We included at least one Alltech representative in nearly all the event planning, and they were excellent.

I still communicated with the governor and cabinet secretaries about the ongoing work. To help the government officials understand the magnitude of the games, we planned to send a delegation to the 2006 games in Aachen, Germany. Understandably, the delegation's findings were overshadowed by the tragic crash of Comair Flight 5191 as it left Lexington, headed for Atlanta. Pat and I had actually been on that flight the previous week on our way to Germany, and we were devastated to learn that all forty-seven passengers died, including one individual who had worked with HCI. Only one of the pilots survived.

While attending the games in Germany, we spent time with Princess Haya Bint al-Hussein of Jordan and her husband Sheikh Mohammed Bin Rashid al-Maktoum, the vice president and prime minister of the United Arab Emirates and ruler of the emirate of Dubai. The sheikh had purchased Jonabell Farm in Lexington a few years earlier, and Princess Haya had been elected FEI president. Princess Haya was wonderful to work with. Her efforts solidified the FEI's support of the games and the organization's relationship with the title sponsor Alltech.

We learned many lessons from the Aachen games. First, we needed to expand the outdoor event stadium. Second, the KHP needed an indoor arena. Third, the details related to parking and security were complex, and we needed to expand the KHP's facilities and enlist the assistance of nearby farms. I also determined that in the not-too-distant future I would resign as chair of the WEG 2010 Foundation. My work on the Louisville arena had become more than a full-time job, and the WEG had a great leadership team in place, including attorney Joe Terry. I just wanted to be sure that neither project would fail. I let Lyons know that I would no longer be needing my office at Alltech. I waited until the 2007 legislature appropriated the funds required for the KHP, and I helped create a detailed plan and timeline for the tasks to be completed to host the WEG. Then I announced that I would be stepping down from my position.

My time away from the World Equestrian Games lasted about six months. Steve Beshear won the governor's race in 2007. Steve and I had been fraternity brothers from opposite political parties, and Pat and I were friends with Steve and his wife, Jane. After the election, Jane approached me about returning to help with the games. She said, "You don't need to *run* the games, but I need your help making sure that everything goes smoothly." I acquiesced and met with the key players to ensure that everything was on schedule. I also took over planning for the WEG opening ceremony.

During the next couple of years, part of my job involved ascertaining that the WEG sponsorships were executed properly. I continued to work closely with Jack Kelly to ensure that the logistics for the event were in place. By the time the FEI Alltech World Equestrian Games opened in September 2010, the commonwealth was ready. The games provided an incredible financial and public relations boom for Kentucky. More than 500,000 people attended the events, many of them prominent dignitaries and business owners from around the globe. During the games, we had more than 55,000 hotel rooms booked across the state. The weather was near perfect, and the events went off without a hitch. The closing ceremony on October 10, 2010, marked a special day in my life, but much of that had to do with the Louisville arena project, which I had promised the governor I would continue to spearhead.

14

The KFC Yum! Center

In addition to assisting with the World Equestrian Games, I spent most of my time working on the Louisville arena. When I was appointed vice chair of the Louisville Arena Task Force (LATF) in May 2005, our goal was to study the feasibility of constructing a new arena for University of Louisville basketball that would serve as an economic engine for both the city of Louisville and the state of Kentucky.

The task force's first meeting in May 2005 was not the first discussion about building a new arena in Louisville. In 2001 Rick Pitino had left the Boston Celtics to become head coach of the University of Louisville Cardinals, replacing the legendary Denny Crum. With the larger-than-life Pitino returning to the state to work for Louisville's always aggressive AD Tom Jurich, rumors of a new arena surfaced regularly.[1] Louisville's move from Conference USA to the Big East in 2003 added fuel to that discussion. Freedom Hall had been built in the 1950s at the Kentucky State Fairgrounds, and the facility needed renovation. Once Louisville joined the Big East, a task force was formed to study options for renovating Freedom Hall or constructing a new arena. Rosser International presented a plan to build a new arena at the Fairgrounds. But after listening to Tom Jernstedt at the 2005 Final Four, Governor Fletcher really wanted the new arena to be located downtown to spur economic development.[2]

These various perspectives still existed when we held our first task force meeting in 2005. The group consisted of dignitaries, politicians, and business owners. From its first meeting in May until the LATF issued its final report in late September, the strongest personalities on the task force demanded to be heard. They included Senator Mitch McConnell, Louisville mayor Jerry Abramson, Louisville AD Tom Jurich, Louisville state representative Larry Clark, and "Papa" John Schnatter (founder of a worldwide pizza empire). Many other bright and hardworking members participated as well. From the outset, though, Lieutenant Governor Pence (LATF chair) and I made it clear that we needed to determine the feasibility of such a facility and what would be best for both Louisville and Kentucky. And our work needed to be totally transparent.[3]

Early on, LATF member Jim Patterson allowed the group to use his jet, and we spent a day examining new arenas that had been built in the neighboring cities of Indianapolis, Nashville, and Memphis. A few key themes quickly dominated the discussion. First, nearly everyone agreed that Louisville needed a new arena. The primary issues then became location and cost. Many members held very strong opinions about location, and they were not afraid to be "transparent" in sharing their ideas at our public meetings. Jurich mentioned an on-campus arena near the "silos" off I-65. Clark and Schnatter favored the State Fairgrounds, while Abramson and others wanted a downtown arena on the old Water Company site, as it was referred to at the time.[4]

Although I was open to all arguments, the NCAA tournament's requirement of a downtown arena influenced my opinion. Louisville had the strongest college basketball media ratings in the country, so hosting NCAA basketball tournaments seemed essential. To make sure that the task force understood this, I organized a visit to NCAA headquarters to discuss what the association needed in an arena. NCAA representatives emphasized "walkability" and mentioned a number of other important factors, including the size of the floor, which would determine whether the venue could host other NCAA championships such as volleyball and wrestling.[5] That meeting convinced many task force members that a downtown location was essential, but not everyone agreed. Although LATF meetings were open to the public, the individual members privately engaged in posturing, pressure, and political jockeying to influence the group. Those with the most at stake typically wanted to discuss their ideas with me individually.

Mayor Abramson, for example, made no secret of his preference for a downtown location to benefit the city. However, tension existed between the University of Louisville and city leaders. Other key participants opposed a downtown arena as well. Although I favored a downtown location, I told the mayor that the old Water Company site, with less than six acres, was too small for the facility we wanted to build. I pointed out that Conseco Fieldhouse in Indianapolis was a beautiful arena, but building it on less than six acres had created a number of logistical problems, such as access for television trucks.

The challenge was finding a viable alternative. Early that summer, Ed Manassah at the *Louisville Courier-Journal* took me to the Louisville Gas and Electric (LG&E) substation at Third and Main Streets. The northern border of the property along River Road faced the Ohio River. After that first visit, I immediately drove back to the site and walked the property with my assistant, Blake Brickman. Circling the perimeter, I tried to think of any potential problems. In each instance, I believed I had an answer. I left convinced that this site offered the best alternative: it was accessible to downtown hotels and shops, and an arena located along the river would provide a striking landmark for anyone traveling east-west on I-64 or driving south from Indiana on I-65. We needed to determine the cost of demolishing the buildings on the property and relocating LG&E employees, as well as those working in the adjacent old Federal Land Bank building, which was occupied by Humana. That would determine the site's feasibility.

I first checked with LG&E CEO Vic Staffieri to get his opinion on the possibility of moving the LG&E facility to a new location. As we stood on top of the LG&E building and looked down on the property, I turned to Vic and said, "That is where the arena should go." He retorted, "You are out of your [expletive] mind!" I responded, "No, I'm not. I need to know that when this site is considered by the task force, we have your support." Vic agreed to support the idea, probably because he didn't believe it ever had a chance.

After getting Staffieri's approval, I went to lunch with task force members Ron Carmicle and John Schnatter. John asked me a series of questions about the arena's location. He correctly presumed that I thought the riverfront site was best, and he clearly opposed it. He then lectured me, expressing his conviction that the new arena needed to be at the Fairgrounds and emphasizing his concern about the projected costs. Carmicle encouraged him to drop it, but Schnatter continued, finally pointing his finger at me and saying, "I am going to beat your ass." I said, "John, I'm not as successful as you are. I haven't built a company like yours. I don't have your money or a jet like you, but I am going to do what I think is the right thing to do." Unassuaged, he restated his threat, to which I responded, "I can outwork almost anyone, and if this is how you see it, I am going to outwork you." The conversation was not hostile, but Schnatter had drawn a battle line.

University president James Ramsey and AD Tom Jurich held opinions that differed, in many ways, from both the mayor's and Schnatter's. One day, Jurich asked me to join them for a round of golf. As we played, they let me know that they didn't like Mayor Abramson and the city "dictating" where they would play sports. They also let me know, however, that they were not opposed to a downtown arena so long as it was located on Main Street and on the riverfront.

After these private discussions, the task force held a public meeting for citizens to express their opinions and ideas before we developed a final list of site possibilities. Many were naysayers who opposed any new arena. However, the vast majority favored a new downtown arena. When the LATF announced the final options, there were no surprises. They included the Fairgrounds, the University of Louisville campus, the old Water Company site, and the LG&E site. The task force then began to study the funding, financing, and operation costs. Several experts provided insights on methods to generate revenue and manage the facility. Another consulting group warned that the old Water Company site was not large enough, while the riverfront location seemed to be the best choice in terms the committee's priorities.

Mayor Abramson stated that the city of Louisville would pay one-third of the arena's debt service costs if it was located downtown. The LATF site selection subcommittee officially recommended the LG&E riverfront site. Then Schnatter became more vocal in his opposition to that location, accusing me of ramrodding my personal preference through the task force. My response was that someone needed to provide leadership, and I was supporting what I believed to be the best site for the arena. Noting the costs associated with demolishing the existing buildings and moving operations for LG&E and Humana, Schnatter correctly asserted that, because of these expenses, this site would be more costly than the on-campus or Fairgrounds location. Even so, I believed the riverfront site offered the best venue for events and the long-term welfare of the city. When someone suggested that the Fairgrounds had not received due consideration, Abramson said the city would provide financial support only if the arena was downtown. All this disagreement made our meetings rather confrontational.[6]

As we moved forward, the LATF invited two large facilities-management groups to discuss operating and managing the arena. Both presented their operational plans for maintaining the facility and highlighted their ability to bring in top-tier concerts and entertainment. We also invited Harold Workman, CEO of the Kentucky State Fair Board, which managed Freedom Hall, to make a pitch for operating the new arena, regardless of the location. The Fair Board had some entertainment connections, but it lacked the other companies' network with the global entertainment industry. Representative Larry Clark made it clear, however, that for him to fully support the project, the Fair Board would have to manage the new arena. I generally supported private enterprise rather than state government in various operations, but we needed Clark's political influence to secure initial funding from the state to make the arena project a reality.

With the governor's October deadline for the report rapidly approaching, the task force placed the arena location to a vote. The final tally was 16–1 in favor of the riverfront location, with Schnatter providing the lone dissent. He protested, saying that I had manipulated the task force and had chosen a predetermined site without truly considering other locations. Despite all the drama, the task force presented its report and recommendations to Governor Fletcher. Schnatter, who disagreed with those recommendations, announced that he would still be donating $5 million toward the project. The governor then created the Louisville Arena Authority (LAA), a nonprofit corporation responsible for developing a plan to finance the arena and to issue bonds for its construction.[7]

I spoke with both Governor Fletcher and Mayor Abramson regarding the makeup of the LAA. I recommended that it should consist of fifteen members, with ten members and the chair appointed by the governor and five members and the vice chair appointed by the mayor. Fletcher promptly appointed me chair of the Louisville Arena Authority. Consisting of talented and civic-minded citizens, the group was eager to do something special for Louisville and Kentucky.

As it turned out, we desperately needed such a talented, dedicated, and well-connected group. The arena project required a substantial financial commitment from the state. I had done my best to get key legislators on board, and it appeared that the state would provide the initial funding. When rural legislators protested spending money for Louisville, I worked with the governor to publicize my mantra: "As Louisville goes, so goes Kentucky." We highlighted the fact that forty cents of every tax dollar generated in Louisville went to help the rest of the state. My other argument targeted basketball-loving legislators in basketball-crazy Kentucky. I reminded them how much they disliked Duke and North Carolina getting to play NCAA tournament games in their home state. Then I reminded them, "UK isn't allowed to play on its home court, but if we build this arena in Louisville, UK can play NCAA tournament games in Kentucky." I honestly believe this helped garner the necessary state support.

I initially thought the governor would allocate $100 million toward the arena, but that was trimmed to $75 million. Although less than we hoped for, that funding was essential to get the project started. It financed the removal of the LG&E substation and the old Federal Land Bank building. Few people ever knew that demolishing the LG&E substation accomplished more than simply making way for a new arena. First, the LG&E building was an eyesore. The Galt House actually had trouble renting rooms that faced the old facility, which resembled a Cold War–era structure in the Soviet Union. Far more important, studies revealed that the old substation was a terrorist threat. If someone had thrown an explosive into the building, it would have shut down Louisville's power for two to four weeks. Nearly all of Louisville's natural gas and electricity passed through that site, as well as much of western Kentucky's natural gas. So the $75 million the state spent to clear the site made Louisville a much safer city. That fact alone made it a worthwhile investment. Without state funding, relocating the LG&E substation would have drastically increased rates for the company's customers. And architects designed the new LG&E building to be one of the safest facilities in the nation.

Despite Schnatter's $5 million commitment, he continued to fight the arena location. I am not sure how, but Schnatter convinced David Jones, co-founder of Humana and one of Kentucky's great philanthropists, to join the fight against us. Schnatter and Jones initiated their own study to compare the riverfront site and the Water Company site, which our consultants had already determined would be too small. They spent more than $200,000 to hire Dean Bonham (who had worked as a consultant for HCI) and the Bonham Group to analyze and compare the costs of the two sites. Thankfully, Ramsey and Jurich held true to their statements on the golf course: they would oppose any downtown site that wasn't on the riverfront. After Jones and Schnatter announced the results of their study, the University of Louisville board unanimously voted to support the riverfront location.[8]

Undeterred, Jones and Schnatter held a press conference to announce that, according to their study, construction at the Water Company site would save more than $100 million. This, of course, caused a great stir in the middle of the legislative session. I made a public announcement that the LAA would suspend all meetings until the legislature determined whether it would follow the task force's recommendations. The old Water Company site would have been cheaper, but it simply was not large enough for a world-class arena. In addition, it would not address the removal of the old LG&E substation for safety reasons. The Kentucky House of Representatives appropriated $75 million on the condition that the arena be built on the Water Company site. Thankfully, Senate president David Williams successfully removed that stipulation, so the money could be utilized for the LG&E site.[9]

A serious challenge in Louisville was its long history of strained race relations. With the project moving forward, the Reverend Louis "Buster" Coleman, a civil rights activist and director of the Justice Resource Center in Louisville, voiced concerns about the LAA awarding construction contracts to companies that had poor track records when it came to hiring minorities. At that point, I spoke with Junior Bridgeman, William Summers V, and Alice Houston, all African American members of the LAA, about the history of such projects in Louisville. We wanted to ensure that our work served as a model for the fair treatment of all people, regardless of race or creed. I also spoke with my friend PG Peeples, president of the Lexington Urban League, who helped me set up a meeting with Buster.

Buster loved baseball and had collected memorabilia from the old Negro League. Before discussing the arena, we spent hours looking at his collection and developed a close bond over the next few months. I told him I appreciated his concerns regarding fair hiring practices. He shared some of his worries, and then I asked him, "So what would you like to see happen?" Buster wanted a guarantee that a certain percentage of minorities would be hired to construct the arena, and he wanted us to employ local workers. Even if we contracted with national construction companies, we could still set some minimum hiring thresholds that I could fight for.[10]

The LAA also created a subcommittee to address minority hiring. The members worked with the Louisville Metro Council as well as PC Sports out of Texas and determined that at least 20 percent of those hired to work on the arena would be minorities, 75 percent would come from the Louisville region, and 5 percent of the subcontractor companies would be owned by women.[11]

I continually worked to make sure that Mayor Abramson and the Louisville Metro Council were on board with the arrangement. The council members, most of whom were staunchly Democratic, made some concessions with regard to labor agreements and the use of nonunion labor to construct the facility. The council, however, took too much control away from the LAA, so I suspended the authority's work until we could broker a resolution allowing our group to execute its responsibilities without interference. Mayor Abramson then took a political risk by announcing that he would veto any agreement that gave unions negotiating power on the project itself. That gave the LAA the power to do its job, and the Metro Council followed suit. We also kept our promise to hire a minimum of 20 percent minorities, 75 percent local workers, and 5 percent women-owned businesses.

In November 2006 we held a groundbreaking ceremony for the arena. I have never seen so many politicians jockeying to get their picture taken with a shovel. We were finally making progress, but I knew other important political and financial battles lay ahead. The first challenge involved the Metro Council's approval of the tax incremental finance plan (TIF), which we needed to create revenue to pay for the arena debt service. The TIF designated a certain geographic area around the new arena where any increased tax revenue (such as sales tax or state property tax) would be earmarked for the construction debt. Our arrangement was that 20 percent of the increased tax revenue would go to the state, and the other 80 percent would go to the LAA to pay the debt on the facility. Before the council voted on the TIF, I called Buster and said, "I need a favor. We need the council to approve the TIF for the project to survive." Then I asked him to help ensure that the council's African American members would vote for the TIF. He simply replied, "It will happen."

David Jones and John Schnatter, despite claims that they had ceased their opposition to the arena, continued to criticize me and the LAA's work. For example, one day, Francene Cucinello, host of a popular call-in show on WHAS, asked me to listen to her on-air interview of Jones and then respond to his comments. I agreed and listened to David say what a disaster the arena was going to be and how horrible our plan was. He questioned why a UK graduate who lived in Lexington should lead construction of an arena for Louisville. He totally dressed me down with what I felt were personal attacks. However, when Francene put me on the air, I simply said that David Jones was a great Kentuckian and a great Louisville citizen. I said that I admired (and always would) his work as a businessman and a philanthropist, but regarding the arena location, I felt he was wrong. The task force, the governor, the University of Louisville, and the Metro Council all favored the site. Jones's opposition was misguided.

As the public attacks continued, I regularly received calls from reporters or concerned citizens who had heard rumors that I was benefiting personally from my work with the LAA. Apparently, some people did not believe that my objective was simply to benefit Kentucky. In every instance, I informed whoever would listen that my work was voluntary. I paid every penny of my own expenses while driving from Lexington to Louisville. I would not even let anyone buy me a cup of coffee because I did not want to destroy the public's trust in what I wanted to accomplish.

Before the Metro Council voted on TIF, both Jones and Schnatter intended to address the council, so I had been doing some mental homework to figure out how to respond to their criticisms. David Jones took the stage first and assaulted me from every angle. He blasted the LAA and attacked me personally again. Once he was done, John Schnatter stood up and did the same thing. When it was my turn to address the council, I refused to engage in any personal attacks or even defend myself. Instead, I took a little bit of poetic license and said something like this: "When I got up this morning around 4:00 a.m., I got dressed, drank a cup of coffee, and headed to my car. Before I left, my wife said, 'Jim, this is crazy. Why are you doing this? You spend so much time on the road traveling to Louisville at our own expense. Then people attack you simply for trying to help Louisville and Kentucky.'" I looked at the council members and said, "You know, maybe she's right. Maybe I should go back home and let someone else do this. My wife would love that, and maybe I would too." As I started walking back to my seat, someone on the council said, "Mr. Chairman, you can't leave!" Then someone else yelled the same thing. Before long, a number of people were saying, "Don't leave! You can't leave!" Jim King, who was presiding over the council, rapped his gavel and asked, "Is there any other comment?" Councilwoman Ellen Call thanked me for my hard work, dedication, and transparency and concluded, "We support what you are doing." The TIF passed unanimously.

When Schnatter lost that battle, his $5 million pledge went out the window too. One day, Tom Jurich called me and asked, "Jim, would you mind giving up John's five million, so we can use it on something else?" I responded, "Tom, he never gave it to us." He asked, "He never sent the check to you?" I said, "He never sent anything." Then Tom asked, "Will you sign a paper saying you're not going to go after him for the money?" I said, "Tom, I'm not going after him for the money. I don't have a contract, just all the newspaper articles praising him for the gift he never gave." Schnatter never contributed the $5 million for the arena, and I never counted on it.

With the TIF secured, we began planning for construction. I took LAA member Zev Buffman's advice and flew to several different arenas, asking about the mistakes they had made. That provided insight for building the best basketball and concert arena in the country. We named a short list of contractor finalists, and they made presentations. Mortenson Construction Company of Minneapolis won the contract for overseeing the construction, and HOK was selected as the architect. Arena construction had been estimated at $252 million, with a 15 percent contingency ceiling for unexpected expenses. As noted earlier, the state's $75 million covered demolition of the LG&E and Humana buildings on the site.[12]

I spent 2007 coordinating the efforts of the construction firms, city officials, and key players from the University of Louisville. Along the way, many different LAA members were willing to provide their input and advice in their various areas of expertise. I hired an attorney, Laura Chandler, as my full-time assistant. She was amazing and was my right hand during the entire process. We met every day I was in Louisville. She attended virtually every important meeting, and as we determined what needed to be done, she helped me keep individuals and companies on task and on time. She could also strategize about potential problems and worked to avoid as many of them as possible on the front end of the project. Another key member was Dan Ulmer, who was invaluable as chair of the construction committee.

We faced multiple political and financial challenges in 2007, but the LAA navigated all of them with skill. Vice chairman Larry Hayes, Mayor Abramson's chief of staff, provided invaluable guidance along the way. He became a close personal friend and remains one today. By the end of the year, it appeared that we had jumped the most important hurdles. However, they were nothing compared with the challenges we would face in 2008.

The LAA had hired Goldman Sachs for the bond issue to finance the project. Even after breaking ground, the project would not be able to continue without approximately $350 million in bonds. I spent countless hours with LAA member Dan Ulmer, a retired banker who was part owner of Louisville's minor league baseball team. Dan helped me strategize the bond issue, which we wanted to complete by March 2008.

Some of the most difficult negotiations occurred with the Ambac Financial Group, the agency Goldman Sachs had recommended as the bond insurer. We finally agreed on an $11.4 million payment to Ambac, which would then insure repayment of the bonds in the event the LAA defaulted on its bond payments or could not repay its debt. After the first tremors of the nation's economic crisis, Ambac lost its AAA rating, which would have led to higher interest rates on the bonds. I met with Ulmer and other LAA members to study creative ways to package the bonds. Then we reentered the marketplace, looking for another bond insurer. We required the insurance so that the state and the city would not be on the hook if a financial calamity hit the arena.[13]

By May, we had signed a deal with Assured Guaranty for the insurance and planned to execute the bond issue with Goldman Sachs in the summer of 2008. All the while, I was flying back and forth to New York City at my own expense to sit down with representatives from Assured and Goldman Sachs to hammer out the intricate details of the bond issue. The final execution date kept getting delayed, but we eventually set July 23, 2008, as the big day. On July 22 I signed more than 400 documents as chair of the LAA, and we were ready to close the deal. We planned a big press conference the following day with Governor Beshear, Mayor Abramson, and other dignitaries.[14]

I drove home on July 22 thinking that everything was in place. As I pulled into my driveway, Greg Carey at Goldman Sachs called and asked, "Jim, are you sitting down?" Fearing what this introduction might mean, I said, "Yes, I'm just pulling into my garage." Then he told me, "We can't close tomorrow because Assured went on credit watch today." I asked him what that meant, and he responded that the interest rates on the $360 million in bonds (the vast majority of which were variable rate) would jump 200 basis points, dramatically increasing what the LAA would owe on the bonds.[15]

With Assured on credit watch, the total debt service payments (what would be paid in interest and principal on the bonds over their lifetime) now exceeded $700 million. We had projected more than a billion dollars in revenue during the life of the bonds, but Assured refused to insure any bonds above $700 million. I said, "Well, the higher interest rate blows the deal out of the water, doesn't it?" Greg said, "Yes, it does." Then he asked, "Jim, what are you going to do?" I said, "I'm going inside to fix a bourbon and water—maybe two. Then I'm going to bed, getting up early tomorrow, and driving to Louisville and figure this thing out. I'll be in touch."

In Louisville the next morning, I called off the press conference and the celebration party. I met with Dan Ulmer and Laura Chandler and explained the problem. We met with our attorney and started looking for solutions. We determined that we needed far more fixed-rate bonds, which would require a higher interest rate. This, in turn, meant that we needed to cut costs on arena construction. I told John Wood at Mortenson that we needed to meet. He balked at first, but we owed him almost $500,000, and when I said, "We can't pay you unless we reduce costs to get the financing we need," that motivated him to come see us.

Wood flew in, and I explained that we needed to cut $15 million in costs without making any substantive changes to the facility. In an hour's time, we had removed one escalator area and another elevator hub. We scrapped plans for terrazzo tile in all the concourses and switched to stained concrete. We devised some other adjustments and made it work. The contractors disliked the changes, but everyone understood that we had no other options if we wanted to move forward. We worked with Goldman Sachs to find other ways to save money, and we convinced Assured to drastically reduce the premiums on the bond insurance from $18 million to $6 million.

Dan Ulmer and I sat down and started to piece together an incredibly complex financing puzzle. We developed a patchwork of fixed- and variable-rate bonds, taxable and nontaxable bonds, and zero-coupon bonds. Every night, Pat asked me, "What did you work on today?" I would say, "Honey, it's so complicated I don't know how to explain it to you." Thankfully, Dan understood our strategy, and we convinced banks and investors in Louisville to buy the bonds. But even after coming up with every scheme imaginable, we were still short about $30 million, which could be funded only with high-risk ("junk") bonds.

After studying the finances and bond issues, our attorney, Ed Glasscock, suggested that we meet with Hilliard Lyons CEO Jim Allen. We hoped the Louisville-based investment firm would see the value in supporting the local construction and sports markets. Allen brought along Pete Mahurin, a senior vice president and chair of financial services at Hilliard Lyons. Mahurin, a Democrat from Bowling Green, had supported me for lieutenant governor in 1971, so at least we had some connection.

I told Allen and Mahurin that we needed a favor from Hilliard Lyons, and I asked them to purchase high-risk bonds so we could finance the arena project. Pete asked, "How much of this rescue are you asking us to take?" I responded, "$30 million." Pete looked at Jim and then at me and said, "Well, I'm not sure we want to buy uninsured bonds." I replied, "Pete, I'm telling you this is going to work. Those bonds will pay 8.5 percent. You will look like a genius." They remained noncommittal, so I knew I had to sweeten the deal. I added, "If you do this, you get to ride a white horse into Louisville and save the day.

Plus, we'll make you a corporate partner of the arena." Pete asked, "What does that mean?" I explained that it meant free advertising for the company and then said, "Hilliard Lyons will also get a corporate luxury suite at no cost for twenty years." Then I said, "If you do this, I will promote Hilliard Lyons whenever I speak. I'll tell them there wouldn't be an arena without you." I thought that would seal the deal, but Pete and Jim wanted to discuss the matter before making a decision. I spent the rest of the week drumming up demand for the bonds from wealthy investors in Louisville. When Mahurin and Allen agreed to the deal, we finally had a financing package that worked. There is no question that Hilliard Lyons saved the arena.[16]

I called Goldman Sachs vice president Tom Rousakis and said, "We're ready to close." In disbelief, he asked, "How is that possible?" I told him about Hilliard Lyons and local investors' interest in the bonds. Then I said, "We need to get this done in the next week or two." Anyone following the global markets knew that Wall Street was headed for a volatile ride, so I wanted to seal the deal immediately. Rousakis interrupted and said, "We can't. We take off the last two weeks in August and go to the Hamptons." I retorted, "Tom, the title of my book is going to be 'They Went to the Hamptons.'" He half-chuckled and said, "You would do that, wouldn't you?" I said, "I sure would. We've worked too hard to piece this puzzle together. Tell me how we can get this done before the end of August."

Greg Carey and Tom Rousakis agreed to keep a skeleton crew in the office to put the bond issue together. On August 28, 2008, we met with Goldman Sachs representatives, and I again signed more than 400 legal documents on behalf of the LAA. As it turned out, because this was Goldman Sachs' only bond issue at that time, there was additional demand for the bonds. Our $349 million bond issue attracted more than a billion in demand, so we ended up bringing in nearly $5 million more than anticipated. We placed that money in reserve in case we had any unanticipated construction problems.

I still remember sitting in Louisville on a conference call as a woman on the other end of the phone said, "Okay, Mr. Host, the money has been transferred into the account." That moment was one of the happiest in my entire professional career. I had spent more than three years working on the project, and now it was going to happen.

I called Governor Beshear and Mayor Abramson. Both of them were stunned that we had pulled it off in such ominous financial times. Sure enough, the stock market crashed a few weeks later in September 2008. By

March 2009, the Dow had lost approximately half its value. Had we not issued the bonds when we did, I don't think Louisville and Kentucky would have gotten a new arena.

With funds in the bank, construction moved forward. I traveled to Louisville nearly every weekday to make sure things were running smoothly. Laura Chandler kept me apprised of all the details when I wasn't there. The other LAA board members persisted in seeing the task through to completion amidst numerous challenges. For example, as construction crews dug deep into the ground to lay the foundation, they discovered remnants of the old downtown Louisville, including railroad ties, cables, and building foundations. Removing all this debris required additional expenditures, but the contingency fund kept things moving. We had hung a large "countdown clock" to opening day at the site. We hoped it would build public anticipation while reminding construction crews of the tight timeline.[17]

One of the most exciting developments involved utilizing the Kentucky Pipeline Project that Governor Fletcher established and his successor Governor Beshear continued. The Pipeline Project trained individuals previously convicted of nonviolent crimes and eventually placed them in construction jobs. We trained welders, pipe fitters, electricians, and others to work on the arena. We employed more than 140 individuals from the Pipeline Project, and it transformed the lives of many families. Some of the promotional videos showcased children who talked on camera about how proud they were that their parents were out of prison and holding down jobs. It was powerful and particularly meaningful because so many people (especially in the construction business) were losing their jobs as the nation sank deeper into the Great Recession. The project kept hundreds of people at work every day and off the unemployment rolls.

I met with President Ramsey monthly to update him on construction progress and negotiations related to the various financial agreements between the LAA and the University of Louisville. Some of these negotiations were challenging because everyone knew about UK's financial agreement with Rupp Arena at the Lexington Center. When trying to convince then-president Otis Singletary to move UK basketball downtown in the 1970s, we had guaranteed UK all the revenue it would have made at Memorial Coliseum and promised that UK would not pay a dime toward arena construction. Originally, this looked like a sweetheart deal for UK, but the dramatic increase in ticket prices over the years made basketball much more lucrative for the Lexington Center Corporation, and UK complained that it wasn't receiving its fair share of the revenue. President Ramsey and AD Jurich knew this history and pushed for the University of Louisville to keep as much revenue as possible from the new arena. At the same time, I needed to ensure that the LAA kept enough revenue to make its debt service payments. We eventually worked out a complex plan of revenue sharing that both the LAA and the University of Louisville could agree on.

We also needed a naming sponsor for the arena. Originally, we had hoped to secure $40 million for a thirty-year sponsorship, but the recession changed our outlook. We ended up signing KFC Yum! to an arena sponsorship worth $13.5 million over ten years. Louisville-based Yum! Brands Inc. owned (and still owns) the fast-food chains Kentucky Fried Chicken, Pizza Hut, and Taco Bell, among other holdings. Yum! president David Novak had assigned Jonathan Blum from KFC to quietly work on the deal with me. I have always believed that Novak's decision to sponsor the arena may have been due, in part, to the wildly successful Pizza Hut mini-basketball promotion in the 1980s.[18]

We held the ribbon-cutting ceremony for the KFC Yum! Center on October 10, 2010—on budget and on time. I served as emcee at the ceremony and then turned the microphone over to the governor and the mayor. When they announced that the arena's atrium had been named Host Hall, that was a special moment for me. The following week, we held a black-tie opening gala, with the Louisville Orchestra providing the music. The new arena's luxury boxes and its glass walls with panoramic views of the river were spectacular. In all aspects, the arena was arguably the best basketball venue in the nation.

October 10 also held significance for me because it was the day of the closing ceremony of the Alltech World Equestrian Games. I spent the morning at the KFC Yum! Center and then drove to the Kentucky Horse Park. Later that week, the KFC Yum! Center hosted its first concert, featuring the Eagles. I had flown out to Los Angeles months earlier at my own expense and met with Tim Leiweke, hoping to book Paul McCartney. McCartney wouldn't come, I was told, because he was opposed to how KFC handled chickens, so we booked the Eagles instead. When the band arrived, we presented them all with autographed Louisville Slugger bats. I was surprised that Don Henley was a big baseball fan, and he clearly enjoyed the gift. The band played a terrific concert, showing off the arena's acoustics. Then the Cardinals moved into their new home.

The KFC Yum! Center's rave reviews generated great pride for Louisville and Kentucky. It opened in the midst of the Great Recession, when businesses and real estate investments were defaulting and properties were being repossessed. The LAA has never missed a payment. In fact, it never tapped into the debt service reserves set aside for a worst-case scenario. The management of the Kentucky State Fair Board struggled in year one, however, so we used some operational reserves.

After the arena had been in operation for few months, I walked in one day and found Fair Board employees everywhere, just standing around. When I asked what they were doing, they said they had been transferred from the Fairgrounds to the arena for an event. After leaving, I immediately requested an audit of the facility's management and hired an individual who had operated Bridgestone Arena before starting his own business. His report was astounding. It was clear that the KFC Yum! Center needed new management. The LAA bought out the Fair Board's contract and hired AEG to operate the facility. Under the Fair Board's management, which lasted thirty months, the KFC Yum! Center ran at a deficit of approximately $3 million. After AEG's first eighteen months of managing the facility, it reported a profit of more than $3.3 million. AEG continues to operate the Yum! Center in a fiscally responsible manner and now provides a guarantee of operational profit to the arena.[19]

The TIF zone's baseline tax projections were based on 2005, when the economy was booming. When the facility opened in 2010, tax revenues were suffering from the recession. The government downsized the TIF zone, and since that time, the increased revenue has assisted in making debt service payments. The first issue of bonds on the project paid, on average, more than 6 percent annually. Since then, interest rates have dropped considerably. Scott Cox, the current LAA chairman, did a masterful job renegotiating the bond issue with substantially lower interest rates that will save the LAA millions of dollars, vastly improving its financial outlook. The University of Louisville has increased its annual payments to the LAA, and its athletic program remains one of the most valuable in the country. The city of Louisville has guaranteed an annual subsidy to the LAA (the maximum amount in the original bond issue), but the growth in hotels, bars, restaurants, and other businesses has made the city's investment worthwhile. The arena has generated higher property taxes and local occupational taxes that exceed the city's subsidy to the LAA. In short, the KFC Yum! Center is a profitable investment for the city and the commonwealth.

Critics will always claim that the sky is falling, but the fact is that the KFC Yum! Center has been a resounding success and a shot in the arm for Kentucky's economy. It is one of the top concert venues in the world. The Louisville Cardinals—both men's and women's teams—have the finest home court in all of college basketball. The arena is now a regular site for NCAA tournaments and other events. Louisville is better for it, and Kentucky is better for it.

In 2014 the Louisville Visitors and Convention Bureau funded a study conducted by an out-of-state firm to measure the economic impact of the KFC Yum! Center during its first four years of operation. The study found that the arena had generated $346.5 million for the local economy since 2010. More than $100 million of that came from individuals living outside of the Louisville metropolitan area. The arena and its events generated more than $29 million, all but $7 million of which came in the form of state sales tax. If another study were conducted today, it would find that those numbers have increased dramatically.[20]

Despite this success, many critics claim that the arena has fleeced the taxpayers and will cost too much to finance, leaving the state with the burden. Such criticisms are either ignorant or, worse, intentionally dishonest. Such diatribes fail to mention that the arena bonds are insured. If the LAA ever defaults on its debt payments, the insurance would kick in, and all the investors would still earn their money. The insurance company would then take possession of the arena, and the University of Louisville would have the first option to purchase the facility. However, that is never going to happen. The taxpayers are safe. We wrote the contract with that objective in mind.

The real question is what it would cost Kentucky *not* to have the KFC Yum! Center. The state needs a world-class city, and such a city requires a world-class venue for sports and entertainment. Louisville no longer takes a backseat to the neighboring cities of Cincinnati, Nashville, Indianapolis, St. Louis, and Memphis. It has revived the heart of downtown at a time when it is clear that both businesses and young professionals are heading back to city centers across America.

I fell in love with baseball at a young age, but I fell in love with basketball (and college sports in general) as a student at UK. I dedicated years to promoting UK sports, which eventually led me to the opportunity to be a pioneering sports marketer for the NCAA around the country. It was fitting that the last major college sports marketing job of my professional career was as a volunteer to help build a premier venue that would be utilized for college athletics. It gave me an opportunity to focus on what Walter Byers demanded of me when I started promoting college basketball for the NCAA. He wanted me to focus on helping universities and providing student athletes with the best opportunities possible. At the same time, it allowed me to help the commonwealth of Kentucky, my other deeply held passion. Taking on the task of building an arena in Louisville helped me return, in some ways, to where it all began.

Epilogue

Examining the Past and Looking to the Future

I have lived a charmed life for more than eight decades in a country that provides so much opportunity for those willing to work for it. Some days have been more challenging than others, but as I often say, I have never had a bad day in my life. In looking back at my past, I owe so much to the commonwealth of Kentucky and to the University of Kentucky. Because I accepted one of the first two baseball scholarships offered by UK, I eventually found my way into college sports marketing and broadcasting. This gave me the opportunity to spend much of my career on university campuses with coaches, athletic directors, and university presidents, many of whom became my good friends. Even though I never attended graduate school or earned a PhD, I learned a great deal about university operations, especially with regard to intercollegiate athletics.

Despite what some might think, making money never motivated me. If it had, I never would have spent any time in politics or volunteering on nonprofit ventures. Also, I would have run my company much differently. I certainly wanted to turn a profit, but my motivation has always been to do the best I could do with the task in front of me. As an athlete, I loved to win, and this competitive streak transferred into my professional life. For example, when I almost lost my company in the early 1990s, the fight cost lots of money, but the company remained intact, and people kept their jobs. This brought me satisfaction. When I was working on the Louisville arena, some people were convinced that I had some vested monetary interest in the project. Nothing could have been further from the truth. In fact, over the seven years I spent driving back and forth to Louisville and occasionally flying around the country, I spent nearly a million dollars of my own money. In the end, the KFC Yum! Center became a reality, and that was a win for the state. I still like to win, but it has nothing to do with digits in a bank account.

My political appointments in Kentucky also afforded me the opportunity to spend my time devising ways to help improve the future of the commonwealth. My first state service came in the 1960s, and my second opportunity occurred in the twenty-first century. During my time in the Nunn administration, Kentucky resembled other states in the upper South. The 1960 census showed that Kentucky's population was just over 3 million, Tennessee's was 3.5 million, Virginia had under 4 million, and North Carolina boasted a population of 4.5 million. When I returned to state government in the Fletcher administration, other state populations had skyrocketed, but Kentucky's remained stagnant. Today, both Virginia and North Carolina have more than doubled their populations since 1960. Tennessee will hit 7 million residents, doubling its 1960 population, in the next few years. Kentucky, in contrast, is just now striving to eclipse the 4.5 million mark. Essentially, Kentucky has grown at half the rate of its closest neighbors in the South. The growth in these other states has occurred largely in their cities. Unfortunately, Kentucky politics during my lifetime has generally combined a parochial political ideology of rural protectionism and an archaic tax structure. All tax referendums are run through Frankfort, denying local taxing options to communities throughout the state. Kentucky shares its longest border with Tennessee, which has no state income tax. So military employees at Kentucky's Fort Campbell, for example, reside with their families in Tennessee. They work in Kentucky but pay no taxes to the commonwealth. Many older Kentuckians spend half the year in Florida or Texas to avoid an income tax as well.

In addition to these challenges, residents of Kentucky's rural areas have viewed its cities with suspicion and contempt, while a more cooperative approach in neighboring states has allowed metropolitan areas to grow, providing additional funds for poorer regions. These other states have long been "right-to-work" states, while Kentucky has only recently implemented reforms to follow their lead. The commonwealth's archaic tax code remains a hindrance too. Finally, only Texas and Georgia have more counties than Kentucky's 120. This has made government services far more expensive and less efficient.

Despite these historic challenges, the commonwealth is blessed with a number of advantages that must be utilized. Kentucky is a "gateway" state connecting the South with the Midwest and the East Coast. Kentucky needs to find creative ways to bring in more companies that would capitalize on the geographic location. Kentucky politicians need to set aside their prejudices and party politics to attract this growth to the commonwealth. I have spent decades of my life proclaiming that forty cents of every tax dollar generated in Louisville is spent on the rest of the state. I have often said, "As Louisville goes, so goes the commonwealth." Approximately one-quarter of every tax dollar generated in Lexington does the same. If the urban and rural factions were willing to work together, and if Louisville, Lexington, and northern Kentucky would unite their efforts, great things could happen.

Along those lines, I have spent much of my time promoting cooperation within and among Kentucky's cities and regions. Shortly after the KFC Yum! Center opened, the recently elected mayors of Lexington and Louisville (Jim Gray and Greg Fischer, respectively) created the Bluegrass Economic Advancement Movement (BEAM) and asked me to chair it. I agreed, in the hope that this initiative would combine the resources of both cities and make the Bluegrass a superregion like Dallas–Fort Worth. In fact, when I chaired the Lexington Chamber of Commerce in the 1980s, I worked with my counterpart in Louisville, Joe Peden. We tried to halt expansion plans for both Standiford Field in Louisville and Bluegrass Field in Lexington and advocated the building of a mega-airport in Shelby County to serve both cities. However, Lexington mayor Scotty Baesler refused to support the project, and it died. I hoped BEAM would reinvigorate such ideas.[1]

I stepped down as the chair of BEAM (but remained on the board) in 2012 for a couple of reasons. First, I felt it was time to let others lead the charge on key initiatives, while I would continue to be involved in a supporting role. In addition, I believed that BEAM lacked both the proper resources and a strategic plan to bring substantive change to the region. However, I still do whatever I can to promote business in the region and cooperation between Lexington and Louisville.

Shortly after I resigned as chair of BEAM, Governor Steve Beshear and Congressman Hal Rogers asked me to run the Shaping Our Appalachian Region (SOAR) initiative for economic development in eastern Kentucky. I told them I would work behind the scenes and serve on the executive committee, but they needed to be out in front as cochairs of the group. SOAR has collaborated closely with the Kentucky Wired project to bring high-speed broadband to the rural counties in eastern Kentucky. Kentucky Wired's goal is to bring broadband to every county in the commonwealth. I view this initiative as similar to FDR's Tennessee Valley Authority, which brought electricity to the South. Any future economic growth will require high-speed Internet, which will also allow Kentucky's cities to partner with its rural neighbors.

I have volunteered with the Urban Leagues in both Louisville and Lexington to improve the lives of the commonwealth's marginalized citizens. In Louisville, I have worked closely with the Urban League's talented and energetic CEO and president Sadiqa Reynolds, who has developed a visionary plan for an indoor track and field facility in West Louisville's Russell neighborhood. We have met with the NCAA and USA Track and Field to ensure that when the project is completed, they will bring events to the city.

In Lexington, I have assisted my good friend and longtime Urban League CEO PG Peeples. In honor of the Urban League's fiftieth anniversary in Lexington, I suggested that we raise $1 million for affordable housing in the city. We convinced the late philanthropist Don Ball and his wife, Myra, to donate the initial gift for this capital campaign. After the Balls' generous gift, PG and I canvassed the city, asking individuals and companies to contribute to the Urban League's affordable housing initiative and explaining why this was so important. Lexington has strict zoning regulations to protect the fabled horse farms surrounding the city. At the same time, wealthy individuals are moving back into the city center to take advantage of the growing food, arts, and entertainment scenes. With this gentrification of the inner city, property tax rates and rental prices on homes have skyrocketed in many areas, making it difficult for Lexington residents, many of them African American, to remain in their homes. Some of these individuals and families have lived in the same houses for decades, and it is essential that affordable housing options exist to help Lexington residents stay in their neighborhoods if that is where they want to live. In October 2018 we announced that we had collected more than $1.2 million for affordable housing assistance.

I hope this volunteer work will help Kentucky grow in a positive way. I know it is possible. However, the three states I contrasted with Kentucky also possess something else Kentucky lacks: a globally elite university such as the University of Virginia, Duke, the University of North Carolina, and Vanderbilt. Although two of these are private institutions, all have managed to gain a level of financial support (public or private) that Kentucky's flagship university has never matched. I love the University of Kentucky, and I owe much of my success to UK. I cannot imagine receiving a better education anywhere, and I have often said that from a teaching and research perspective, UK is the commonwealth's best-kept secret. That needs to change. UK can hold its own against other prestigious institutions, but until the commonwealth chooses to give UK adequate support, it will not get the recognition and publicity it deserves.

I gained some important insights regarding higher education while working in college sports marketing. Most states have both a state flagship university and a state land-grant university. The University of Kentucky serves as both. It makes no sense that South Carolina can support *both* Clemson and the University of South Carolina with funds comparable to UK's. Alabama does the same with Auburn and the University of Alabama. In Kentucky, many legislators regularly complain about the "favoritism" UK receives compared with the regional universities, failing to acknowledge that UK's mission as a top-tier research university requires more funding that would, in the long term, benefit the state's regional institutions. You will not find a booming state that does not have an elite research university, and Kentucky needs to make this a priority.

UK is doing exceptional work, and the state needs to ensure that its best and brightest have the opportunity to attend that university if they so desire. UK boasts some of the best medical programs and research centers in the country. UK has developed research and outreach to stem the opioid crisis in Kentucky. A $15 million project funded by the National Institutes of Health is seeking to eradicate hepatitis C in eastern Kentucky. UK is home to the state's only National Cancer Institute–designated facility, and the Markey Cancer Center has attracted some of the most talented minds in the world to fight cancer, which plagues Kentucky.

UK is also one of the most powerful economic engines in Kentucky. Agricultural extension programs serve every county in the state, and the Gatton College of Business and Economics has opened a world-class facility. UK's expansion has brought in hundreds of millions of dollars for research. At the same time, UK remains committed to serving undergraduates. Nearly 80 percent of UK graduates remain in the state, and their estimated average income is 25 percent higher than the national average. In short, the institution changes lives for the better, and I am profoundly grateful for the ways UK altered the trajectory of my life. Of all the awards and accolades I have been given, none has meant more to me than the honorary doctorate I received from my alma mater in 2019.

My involvement with UK athletics and my work broadcasting Kentucky sports played a vital role in both my personal life and my professional life. None of my pioneering work in collegiate sports marketing would have happened without UK; nor would it have happened if I hadn't lost the UK radio rights heading into the 1980s. The world of intercollegiate athletics looked entirely different when I got involved with Kentucky and the NCAA in the 1970s. Up to that point, colleges, conferences, and the entire NCAA had failed to tap into college sports marketing and corporate athletic sponsorships.

Looking back over my decades in the college sports marketing business, it is clear that the development of corporate sponsors for the NCAA (and then the SEC), along with the creation of bundled rights packages for individual universities, altered the trajectory of intercollegiate athletics. It has truly changed the game. These innovations, along with the *Regents* case in 1984 and the growth of ESPN, turned college sports into a business. I believe that the business model served colleges and their student athletes well. Athletic Department budgets have ballooned, and teams in the most powerful conferences have spent the money on stadium renovations with luxury boxes, elaborate workout facilities, state-of-the art residence halls, pristine dining halls and "fueling stations" to feed athletes, and academic centers to provide tutoring, as well as hefty salaries for administrators and coaches. Athletic departments have been trailblazers in improving the student experience at their institutions. For example, UK Athletics donated $65 million toward the construction of the Don and Cathy Jacobs Science Building.

Most of the developments in college athletics have been good. The quality of life that athletes are afforded is far superior to what I experienced in my college baseball days in the 1950s. However, the number of games played, the length of various sports seasons, and the timing of games so that they can be covered on television begs an important question: are these student athletes actually amateurs who play simply for the love of the game, as we did in the 1950s? No doubt, virtually all of them love their sport, but everything else has been professionalized. Professionalism, it is important to note, is not a bad thing. For example, universities still offer degrees in the liberal arts, but more diplomas are now being awarded in "professional" areas of study.

In recent years, a new criticism has been directed at me and other college sports marketing companies. Namely, detractors complain that our businesses exploit college athletes, many of whom are poor or African American. There is no denying that the college sports marketing side of the business would not exist without athletes. I am not ashamed to say that my company partnered with institutions, conferences, and the NCAA and created mutually beneficial (and profitable) sports marketing and media rights deals. It is important to note, however, that business deals with athletes were (and still are) prohibited. Had we worked to promote individual student athletes, those students would have been disqualified, and Host Communications would have been barred from working with universities, conferences, and the NCAA.

The current scholarly and public debates regarding revenue sharing should not ignore the context in which college sports marketing developed. The controversial topics surrounding student athletes were much different during the 1980s and 1990s. At that time, outspoken critics of the NCAA were not challenging the entire system of intercollegiate athletics. Instead, they were fighting for greater access to the system. For example, Georgetown basketball coach John Thompson was a vocal civil rights advocate during my time working with the NCAA. He regularly protested any NCAA policy that would limit the number of young black men who could benefit from a college education. In the 1980s he opposed Proposition 48, which introduced higher entrance standards for student athletes. He argued that the new measure would harm young athletes by depriving them of the opportunity to attend a university. In the 1990s Coach Thompson railed against the NCAA when it reduced the number of basketball scholarships from fifteen to thirteen. Once again, Thompson argued that the NCAA was limiting access to higher education, which was the key to a young person's success in modern America.

I did not know Coach Thompson well, but his arguments resonated with me because of my own upbringing in eastern Kentucky and the benefits I received from an athletic scholarship that allowed me to attend a university. However, I was well acquainted with Coach Nolan Richardson at Arkansas because of our work with the SEC and the NCAA. He also pushed for greater access to the system through athletic scholarships. Like me, both of these legendary coaches were born before World War II, and both understood the life-changing opportunities a college education provided. As I have stated often in this memoir, my time at UK meant far more to me than the $25,000 (nearly $250,000 in 2020 dollars, adjusted for inflation) I could have accepted in 1955 to sign with a major league baseball team. The knowledge, understanding, and social capital I gained as a college student are difficult to quantify, but I am certain that any success I have had is due, in large measure, to my time as a student at UK.

Despite my belief in the value of athletic scholarships, my perspective on revenue sharing with college athletes has evolved over the last two decades. When I played baseball for UK, the $15 monthly "laundry allowance" meant everything to me. Not long after I left college, the NCAA did away with that allowance for college athletes. Since that time, the budgets of major college sports programs have grown by tens of millions of dollars. Under pressure to let students reap some of the rewards of their talent, the NCAA now allows universities with big-time athletic programs to give students a "full cost of attendance" stipend that generally falls between $2,000 and $5,000. This permits students to pay their cell phone bills, attend social events, and travel home over the holidays. Many other students receive federal Pell grants. This is a good start, but it is not enough for those athletes who bring in millions of dollars to their schools.

The NCAA's unwillingness to adapt to the changes brought about by college sports marketing could lead to its downfall. As this book goes to press, California governor Gavin Newsom just signed legislation that will allow student athletes to earn money from the use of their names and likenesses. Starting in 2023, athletes at universities in California that generate in excess of $10 million in revenue will be permitted to keep the rights to their own names and images. In short, they will be able to endorse products and share in the revenue from jersey sales and the like. Other states have introduced similar legislation, and Ohio congressman Anthony Gonzalez plans to do the same at the federal level. If the NCAA wants to continue to be the primary governing body of intercollegiate athletics, it is going to have to address the situation before legislative bodies do so without it.

Few people understand exactly what the NCAA is, even if they understand some of what it does. Many fans claim to dislike the NCAA leadership but love their own university and its leadership, not realizing that university presidents play a role in governing the NCAA. The NCAA is not an "outside" enforcement agency. Rather, it is a voluntary, "nonprofit" group of universities that creates the rules for organized intercollegiate athletics. The Board of Governors, for example, is composed primarily of university presidents. The Division I presidents are chief executives of institutions that benefit from high-profile athletic competitions. Because of the *Regents* case, the presidents of the "power five" conferences largely control college football, the conference television channels, and the football bowl games—including the college football playoff. This financial setup circumvents the NCAA. Because of this, more than 80 percent of the NCAA's revenue comes from the NCAA basketball tournament. This revenue pattern developed when Walter Byers replaced NBC with CBS in the early 1980s. CBS did a much better job marketing the tournament. At nearly the same time, the NCAA trademarked the term "Final Four," and Byers granted me permission to recruit corporate partners to promote the tournament.[2]

Presidents, by the nature of their job requirements, desperately want to avoid any controversy or negative publicity. Historically, the presidential leadership at the NCAA has been unwilling to address problems related to men's college basketball, the sport that provides the vast majority of the money needed to run the organization. Because of this, the FBI has become involved in investigating abuses surrounding the sport. Further inaction by the NCAA may create a problem that is nearly impossible to solve. I hope this is not the case, but substantive changes need to be made. When certain media personalities preach "pay the players," they rarely mention that, for the vast majority of the thousands of student athletes who participate every year, scholarships providing tuition, room and board, books, and living expenses are worth far more than the athletes' "market value" (the revenue they generate). However, there are usually a few star athletes who are the exceptions to this rule.

It is my hope that coaches, athletic directors, conferences, and NCAA presidents will spend less energy trying to preserve the status quo and make it their mission to keep talented athletes (in all sports) in college until they graduate. That is, after all, the goal of higher education across the country. The best strategy to accomplish this goal is to give student athletes the right to their own likenesses and the ability to endorse products. Universities could regulate specific windows of time when students could promote car dealerships or grocery stores. Colleges could partner with their student athletes and help negotiate contracts.

Why wouldn't the NCAA want to partner with athletes and allow their likenesses to be used in video games? Why would the NCAA oppose placing an athlete's name on a basketball, football, or jersey? The money could be set aside in a fund until the student finishes his or her education. Further, it would allow schools to encourage athletes to stay in college, go to class, and get an education. These decisions must be made by the university presidents who are part of the NCAA. These individuals are extremely busy serving as both caretakers and innovators at their respective institutions. However, they must become innovators with regard to intercollegiate athletics as well. An unwillingness to act may create a divided NCAA in which the approximately sixty "big-time" athletic programs essentially decide to separate themselves from the hundreds of smaller institutions and create their own system of governance.

The changes I propose would minimize the underhanded negotiations already going on among shoe companies, sports agents, and athletes' families. These deals could be made aboveboard, and promising athletes who have an opportunity to turn pro would actually have a vested interest in not breaking the rules. In addition, these changes would encourage athletes to stay in college. I have met far too many young athletes who come from poor families and feel the pressure to turn professional long before they should, simply to help their families pay the utility bills. Many of these athletes have small children themselves and want to provide them with a decent life. The current system, as it is constructed, actually puts undue pressure on college students to *leave* school rather than stay and get an education.

If the NCAA and its universities fail to adapt to the modern world of sports business, professional organizations will do it for them. For example, the NBA's G League has bumped up the base salary to $35,000 a year, but it promises much more to the best basketball players. The problem is that the vast majority of players will earn minimal wages, never make it to the NBA, and be denied a college experience that can change their lives. In my opinion, this is a "cheap labor" scheme, and the full value of a college scholarship is worth much more to 99 percent of the players who earn NCAA Division I scholarships. However, the NCAA's current amateur student athlete narrative will not allow universities to make college athletics a more attractive alternative.

When I finished high school, I had the opportunity to sign with a major league baseball team and receive a $25,000 signing bonus. Had I taken that money and blown out my arm in the minor leagues, I would have missed out on the education and experience I needed to have a successful career over the next six decades of my life. Thankfully, I had parents who would not allow me to make such a foolish move. Many young athletes today do not have that kind of voice of wisdom in their lives.

As universities attempt to address the rewards and challenges created by successful college sports marketing, we find ourselves in the midst of the next great disruption in sports media. Streaming content through broadband Internet will eventually prove to be more of a revolution than a disruption.

Every year, millions of people in the United States are "cutting the cord" to cable and canceling satellite subscriptions in favor of "over the top" (OTT) networks such as Netflix, Hulu, Sling, and Amazon. In fifteen years, either the four major networks and ESPN will have found a way to adapt to this environment, or they will share the fate of Blockbuster: extinction. Power conferences will have to determine whether they want to collaborate with one another to keep the streaming of college sports national or focus on their own OTT networks, which will be largely regional. At the end of the day, those who control the content and have a mechanism to share it nationally or regionally will win the day, because content is king for any network.

What I have shared in this epilogue highlights one thing I have learned in my more than eighty years: the one constant in life is change. Everything changes. If we realize that, we will also see that amid all the change, the other constant is the need to develop and maintain relationships for a fulfilling life. Whether examining the past or looking to the future, the most important resource we all have, which also provides the greatest source of strength and joy, is other people. At the macrolevel, any positive change for the commonwealth of Kentucky will make people's lives better. Any improvement at UK or any other institution of higher learning will improve people's lives. Any change worth making in college athletics should help student athletes. I have witnessed all these things, but I know that we have barely begun to tap our potential.

I have had the good fortune to forge lasting relationships with amazing individuals. These people are Republicans and Democrats, blacks and whites, urban and rural, rich and poor. The lesson I have learned is that everyone has good in them, and it has been my desire to find that good and help people reach their full potential. A successful path to a prosperous future includes finding the good in people and rewarding it. A healthy culture must not tolerate dishonesty, laziness, or theft. I always told my employees at HCI to never steal a dime and always tell the truth. I have always said that when one is presented with a clear choice between right and wrong, choose the right. When an issue is gray, look at it from all perspectives. Give people the benefit of the doubt, and then give them the credit. This will promote unity and cooperation rather than division.

There is an old but true cliché: whenever something good happens in your life, there will always be people to thank. I owe a debt of gratitude to my parents, who sacrificed what little they had to give me a healthy and happy childhood. My high school coach George Conley had a profound impact on my life, as did Harry Lancaster, my baseball coach at UK. Professors like Len Press invested in me personally. I hope professors today are willing to do the same for others. My entire experience at UK provided me with the knowledge and skills I needed to have a successful professional career and what I consider a charmed life.

Governor Louie Nunn gave me an opportunity to serve the commonwealth as a cabinet head and taught me lessons in leadership along the way. Robbie Rudolph proved to be an excellent leader and a close friend during my second appointment in Frankfort. Jake Graves gave me a loan to start my business when nobody else was willing to take the risk. Lyle Wolf provided my company's first monthly retainer. Members of the National Tour Association provided a stable job for my company as it pioneered the new and perilous world of sports marketing. Walter Byers and Tom Jernstedt at the NCAA gave me a chance to market the NCAA basketball tournament while becoming my friends and mentors. Countless university presidents, athletic directors, sports information directors, and coaches opened their homes and hearts as I expanded my business. Chief among them were DeLoss Dodds, the late Dave Gavitt, and CM Newton. Conference commissioners such as Roy Kramer and the late Mike Slive at the SEC, as well as Jim Delany at the Big 10, proved to be far more than business partners. They were friends. The hundreds of employees at HCI made my dreams a reality. Any success I experienced was "our" success and the result of hardworking teams who put up with a demanding boss.

As I developed friendships across the country, I remained close to a number of dear friends back home in Kentucky. For years, I have met every month with my high school friend Jon Zachem, former state representative and Democratic political operative Terry McBrayer, and longtime general manager of Lexington's CBS affiliate Wayne Martin. We have discussed politics, sports, family life, and a variety of other topics. Retired *Lexington Herald-Leader* publisher Tim Kelly and former Democratic commissioner of public information Tommy Preston have also been friends and confidants for decades. Zachem, McBrayer, and Kelly are from the Ashland area, which will always be "home" to me. Nearly all these individuals have a different view of the political landscape than I do, but they remain close friends. I encourage young women and men today from opposing political parties to forge friendships and learn from each other as I have from these wonderful people.

I owe the greatest debt of gratitude to my family. One challenge in this modern world is that parents' primary years of building a career occur as their children are growing up. My daughter Elizabeth and my son David bore this burden as I worked to build HCI. However, I love them dearly, and seeing them happy brings me deep pleasure. My stepdaughter Tiffany has become a daughter to me as well. She is a wonderful person and continues to be a blessing to her mother and me. They all have children of their own now, and my grandkids bring me both hope and joy. Finally, my wife Pat has made every day a blessing beyond measure. I am thankful to my close friend DeWitt Hisle for introducing us. Pat and I have not had a terse word, and she has made me a better person. I could not have come close to making it without her. I thank God every day for these people. In my own life, they are the ones who have helped change the game.

Notes

Preface

1. Michael Smith, "Jim Host," *Sports Business Journal,* March 22, 2010; "What They're Saying," *Sports Business Journal,* March 22, 2010; "Jim Host's Executive Tree," *Sports Business Journal,* March 22, 2010, https://www.sportsbusinessdaily.com/Journal/Issues/2010/03/22/Champions-Of-Sports-Business.aspx.

2. Jacalyn Carfagno, "Mr. Sports Marketing," *Lexington Herald-Leader,* August 30, 1998, A16.

2. Chasing Dreams

1. Scott Merkin, "Broadcasting Legend, White Sox Exec Einhorn, 80, Mourned," *MLB News,* February 25, 2016, https://www.mlb.com/news/white-sox-executive-eddie-einhorn-dies-at-80/c-165426300.

2. Stewart Hedger, "Short Shots," *Kentucky Kernel,* May 12, 1959, 6.

5. Running for Office and Running a Business

1. Chris Poore, "Parking Plan Forced Residents Out," *Lexington Herald-Leader,* October 20, 1996, special section, 4.

6. Business in the Bluegrass and Beyond

1. D. G. FitzMaurice, "A Delayed Decision," *Lexington Herald-Leader,* June 9, 1974, C2.

7. Working in an Ever-Changing Environment

1. David Reed, "Host Bids $83,5000 for UK Football Rights," *Lexington Herald,* April 13, 1977, A7.

2. David Reed, "Host Edged out in Vote on Radio Rights to UK Sports," *Lexington Herald,* June 27, 1980, A1.

3. Mark Bradley, "Money Is the Issue as Host Loses UK Sports Radio Rights," *Lexington Leader,* June 27, 1980, A3; Rick Bailey "Kentucky Network Wins 'Gunfight at the UK Corral,'" *Lexington Leader,* June 27, 1980, B1.

4. *American Network Group, Inc. v. Kostyk,* 834 S.W.2d 296 (Tenn. Ct. App. 1991).

5. Michael Oriard, *Bowled Over: Big-Time College Football from the Sixties to the BCS Era* (Chapel Hill: University of North Carolina Press, 2014), 158.

6. Joe Nocera and Ben Strauss, *Indentured: The Inside Story of the Rebellion against the NCAA* (New York: Penguin Random House, 2016), 27.

8. The NCAA and Corporate Sponsorships

1. Joe Nocera and Ben Strauss, *Indentured: The Inside Story of the Rebellion against the NCAA* (New York: Penguin Random House, 2016), 27.

2. Walter Byers with Charles Hammer, *Unsportsmanlike Conduct: Exploiting College Athletes* (Ann Arbor: University of Michigan Press, 1995), 281.

3. Nocera and Strauss, *Indentured,* 27.

4. Bernice Kanner, "Nobody Knows the Stubble They've Seen," *New York Magazine,* May 27, 1985, 22.

5. Nocera and Strauss, *Indentured,* 28.

6. *AIAW v. NCAA,* 735 F.2d 577 (D.C. Cir. 1984).

7. "Sara Lee Giving NCAA $6 Million for Women," *News & Record,* September 20, 1990, https://www.greensboro.com/sara-lee-giving-ncaa-million-for-women/article_8f-ba2f86-621b-51a0-9eae-7b1e8988bcdc.html.

8. "1991 NCAA Woman of the Year," *NCAA News,* November 4, 1991, http://www.ncaa.org/about/resources/events/awards/1991-ncaa-woman-year.

9. Back to Kentucky and Bundled Rights

1. Jerry Tipton, "Pitino's Threat Brings Apology from TV Station," *Lexington Herald-Leader,* December 12, 1991, C1.

10. The Solid South

1. Keith Dunnavant, *The Fifty-Year Seduction: How Television Manipulated College Football, from the Birth of the Modern NCAA to the Creation of the BCS* (New York: St. Martin's Press, 2004), 223–24.

2. Dunnavant, *Fifty-Year Seduction,* 224.

3. Billy Reed, *Newton's Laws: The C. M. Newton Story* (Lexington, KY: Host Communications, 2000), 177.

4. Ashley Elkins, "Auburn Accreditation Probation Prompts Resignation Calls," *Northeast Mississippi Daily Journal,* December 11, 2003, http://www.djournal.com/news/auburn-accreditation-probation-prompts-resignation-calls/article_293c9ed9-2293-5d86-9d40-35c7eb6a997b.html.

5. Mike Carson, "Alabama Appeals Court Rejects Mike Hubbard Request for Rehear-

ing," Al.com, September 28, 2018, https://www.al.com/news/index.ssf/2018/09/alabama_appeals_court_rejects_1.html.

6. Ashley Elkins, "Ex-Coach Sherrill Sues NCAA," *Northeast Mississippi Daily Journal*, December 16, 2004, http://www.djournal.com/sports/ex-coach-sherrill-sues-ncaa/article_3a264ea0-e0a2-5f0c-a077-e92dd81e95cf.html; Parrish Alford, "Local Attorney Says Proving Defamation Could Be Difficult," *Northeast Mississippi Daily Journal*, June 12, 2017, http://www.djournal.com/sports/local-attorney-says-proving-defamation-could-be-difficult/article_0755f8f8-f935-5e2a-a16c-50ab859ff574.html; Associated Press, "Ex–Mississippi St. Coach Sherrill Settles Lawsuit," July 18, 2019, https://www.espn.com/college-football/story/_/id/27216034/ex-mississippi-st-coach-sherrill-settles-lawsuit.

7. Eric Prisbell, "Mississippi State, Croom Make History," *Washington Post*, December 2, 2003, https://www.washingtonpost.com/archive/sports/2003/12/02/mississippi-state-croom-make-history/06f5cb05-e3af-4964-aeae-09fa7c36d85a/?utm_term=.b27ea94bda50.

11. Surviving an Era of Crisis

1. Jacalyn Carfagno, "Mr. Sports Marketing," *Lexington Herald-Leader*, August 30, 1998, A16.

2. Jacalyn Carfagno, "The Growing Business of Sports Brought Host, Hicks Together," *Lexington Herald-Leader*, July 5, 1998, A1.

3. Jacalyn Carfagno, "Host Merger with Dallas Firm Is Off," *Lexington Herald-Leader*, November 26, 1998, A1.

4. Jamie Butters, "Atlanta-Based Bull Run Set to Buy Host," *Lexington Herald-Leader*, February 16, 1999, A1; Jim Jordan, "Bull Run to Put Host at Helm of New Firm," *Lexington Herald-Leader*, June 8, 1999, D1.

12. My Last Great Pitch for the NCAA

1. Ronald A. Smith, *Play-by-Play: Radio, Television, and Big-Time College Sport* (Baltimore: Johns Hopkins University Press, 2001), 190.

2. Richard Sandomir, "College Basketball; CBS Will Pay $6 Billion for Men's NCAA Tournament," *New York Times*, November 19, 1999, D5.

3. Amy Baldwin, "Host Communications Quits Bid for Next NCAA deal," *Lexington Herald-Leader*, June 27, 2000, A1.

4. Andy Bernstein and Langdon Brockinton, "ISL's Board Killed NCAA Deal after Shift in Direction," *Sports Business Journal*, November 27–December 3, 2000, 1.

5. Jennifer Lee, "Word on Who Gets CBS' NCAA Marketing Rights Expected Soon," *Sports Business Journal*, January 22–28, 2001, 20.

6. Richard Linnet, "OMD Named Media Agency for Pepsi's $575 Million Account," AdAge.com, October 15, 2001, https://adage.com/article/agency-news/omd-named-media-agency-pepsi-s-575-million-account/32966/.

7. Betsy McKay, "Coke Beats Pepsi for NCAA Rights in a Deal that Tops $500 Million," *Wall Street Journal*, June 12, 2002, https://www.wsj.com/articles/SB1023842482733184280.

8. Jennifer Lee, "Coke Won Deal after Pepsi Equaled Bid," *Sports Business Journal*, June 17, 2002, https://www.sportsbusinessdaily.com/Journal/Issues/2002/06/17/This-Weeks-Issue/Coke-Won-NCAA-Deal-After-Pepsi-Equaled-Bid.aspx.

9. McKay, "Coke Beats Pepsi for NCAA Rights."

13. A Time of Transition

1. Staff Writer, "Host Chief Leaving," *Lexington Herald-Leader,* June 21, 2003, D1.

2. Nate Ives, "The Media Business: Advertising—Addenda; 'Unbridled Spirit' Wins Kentucky Slogan Vote," *New York Times,* December 2, 2004, C2.

3. John Cheves, "State's Park Workers Told to Clean Up," *Lexington Herald-Leader,* May 21, 2004, A1.

4. Ryan Alessl, "How the State Wooed, Won Games—Tuesday's Announcement Crowned Years of Work," *Lexington Herald-Leader,* December 11, 2005, A1.

14. The KFC Yum! Center

1. Billy Reed, *Louisville's KFC Yum! Center: A Community's Dream Realized* (Louisville, KY: Butler Books, 2010). Reed's book provides an excellent timeline of the events, which helped in reconstructing the story of the KFC Yum! Center.

2. Jack Coffee, "In a World with Few 'True' Heroes, Jim Host Is Deserving of the Title," *Louisville Sports Report,* November 2010, 11–13; Reed, *KFC Yum! Center,* 98–100.

3. Reed, *KFC Yum! Center,* 108.

4. Reed, *KFC Yum! Center,* 107.

5. Reed, *KFC Yum! Center,* 113.

6. Reed, *KFC Yum! Center,* 117.

7. John R. Karman III, "Schnatter Pledges $5 Million for Arena," *Louisville Business First,* September 30, 2005, https://www.bizjournals.com/louisville/stories/2005/09/26/daily43.html.

8. Reed, *KFC Yum! Center,* 128.

9. Reed, *KFC Yum! Center,* 129.

10. Jim Host, "Coleman Helped Break Barriers," *Louisville Courier-Journal,* May 9, 2010, H1.

11. Marcus Green, "Plan to Help Minorities Find Construction Jobs," *Louisville Courier-Journal,* September 29, 2007, A1.

12. Sheldon S. Shaffer, "Arena Project Manager Chosen," *Louisville Courier-Journal,* February 27, 2007, B1.

13. Marcus Green, "Arena Bond Insurer May Be Out," *Louisville Courier-Journal,* January 26, 2008, D1.

14. Marcus Green, "Assured Guaranty Will Insure Construction Bonds for Downtown Arena," *Louisville Courier-Journal,* May 13, 2008 (online).

15. Jenni Laidman, "2010 Person of the Year: The Dealmaker," *Louisville Magazine,* December 2010.

16. Reed, *KFC Yum! Center,* 159.

17. Dan Klepal, "Old Buildings Delay Arena Work," *Louisville Courier-Journal,* March 24, 2009, B1.

18. Marcus Green, "It's Official: Arena Named KFC Yum! Center for $13.5 Million," *Louisville Courier-Journal,* April 20, 2010, A1.

19. Marty Finley, "Metro Council President Tells State Committee Fair Board Misman-

aged Yum Center," *Louisville Insider Business,* November 13, 2004, https://www.bizjournals.com/louisville/news/2014/11/13/metro-council-president-tells-state-committee-fair.html.

20. Caitlin Bowling, "KFC Yum! Center Has Generated $346.5 Million in Spending, Analysis Finds," *Louisville Business First,* June 4, 2014, https://www.bizjournals.com/louisville/news/2014/06/04/kfc-yum-center-has-generated-346-5-million-in.html.

Epilogue

1. See https://www.bizjournals.com/louisville/news/2011/08/11/louisville-lexington-mayors-discuss.html.

2. Darren Rovell, "NCAA Tops $1 Billion in Revenue during 2016–17 School Year," March 7, 2018, https://www.espn.com/college-sports/story/_/id/22678988/ncaa-tops-1-billion-revenue-first.

Index

Index